Beginning Your Day God's Way

Beginning Your Day God's Way

365 Devotions to Align Your Words, Thoughts, and Emotions to God's Will

JOYCE MEYER

First published in Great Britain by Hodder Faith in 2025
An imprint of John Murray Press

Published in the US by FaithWords
A division of Hachette Book Group, Inc.

1

Copyright © Joyce Meyer 2025

The right of Joyce Meyer to be identified as the Author of the Work has been asserted by her in accordance with the Copyright, Designs and Patents Act 1988.

Unless otherwise indicated, Scripture quotations are taken from the Holy Bible, New International Version® (Anglicised), NIV™ Copyright © 1979, 1984, 2011 by Biblica Inc. Published by Hodder & Stoughton Ltd. Used with permission. All rights reserved worldwide.

For other translations used, please see page 366–67

All rights reserved. No part of this publication may be reproduced, stored in a retrieval system, or transmitted, in any form or by any means without the prior written permission of the publisher, nor be otherwise circulated in any form of binding or cover other than that in which it is published and without a similar condition being imposed on the subsequent purchaser.

A CIP catalogue record for this title is available from the British Library

Hardback ISBN 9781399831093
ebook ISBN 9781399831109

Typeset in Adobe Garamond Pro

Printed and bound in Great Britain by Clays Ltd, Elcograf S.p.A.

John Murray Press policy is to use papers that are natural, renewable and recyclable products and made from wood grown in sustainable forests. The logging and manufacturing processes are expected to conform to the environmental regulations of the country of origin.

John Murray Press
Carmelite House
50 Victoria Embankment
London EC4Y 0DZ

www.hodderfaith.com

John Murray Press, part of Hodder & Stoughton Limited
An Hachette UK company

The authorised representative in the EEA is Hachette Ireland,
8 Castlecourt Centre, Dublin 15, D15 XTP3, Ireland (email: info@hbgi.ie)

INTRODUCTION

It's often said that what happens to you is less important than your attitude toward it. We cannot always control what happens to us—Jesus Himself said, "In this world you will have trouble" (John 16:33 NIV). Notice He said, "you will," not "you might" or "it's a possibility." While we may not be able to control what happens around us, we can control how we respond. We are in charge of the thoughts that we think, the words that we speak, and our moods and attitudes toward our circumstances. Regardless of what is going on outside of us, we are in charge of what is going on inside of us.

My insides were a mess for a long time. And for years, I blamed my bad moods, my negative attitudes, the discouraging words that came out of my mouth, and my depressing thoughts on what had happened to me. But God has shown me through His Word and His character how to press beyond the past into the good plan He has for my life (Jeremiah 29:11). It all starts on the inside.

Our minds, mouths, moods, and attitudes are closely linked; each one influences the others. The thoughts we think shape the words we speak, which then sink into our spirits, affecting our moods and attitudes. This is why it is so important to take every thought captive to make it obedient to Christ (2 Corinthians 10:5 NIV).

God has given us the mind of Christ (1 Corinthians 2:16),

the power to bless and curse (Proverbs 18:21; James 3:9), and the ability to control our minds, mouths, moods, and attitudes (2 Timothy 1:7). This power isn't limited to Bible teachers, preachers, or missionaries; it's available to everyone, including you. If you're thinking, *You don't know what I have done*, let me encourage you: God is greater than your mistakes, and He knew you would make them when He formed you in your mother's womb. The Word of God is for everyone. The same power that raised Jesus from the grave lives in you (Romans 8:11), enabling you to transform your life by renewing your mind (Romans 12:2), which reshapes your words, your moods, and your attitudes.

I believe that as you read through these devotions and take hold of the truths that God has for you, you will be amazed by the transformation you see in your life—from your health to your prayer life to your level of peace and joy, even in undesirable circumstances. God has so much more in store for you in the year ahead!

DAY 1: IT ALL STARTS IN YOUR MIND

Behold, the former things have come to pass, and new things I now declare; before they spring forth I tell you of them.

ISAIAH 42:9

Would you like to be in a good mood every day? Of course you would! Who wouldn't? I spent a lot of years being controlled by a variety of moods and believing I had no choice in how I felt. But I do have a choice! We all do. We all make choices about our thoughts and attitudes toward life.

Your mind, mouth, moods, and attitudes are all intricately connected. It starts with your thoughts, which then turn into the words you speak, shaping your emotional state and attitudes toward life. If you truly want to be in a good mood on a regular basis, it begins with deliberately focusing on good thoughts. You can start by choosing to think about things that will generate good emotions instead of bad ones.

If you desire greater emotional stability and the ability to maintain a consistently good attitude no matter what your circumstances are, then make it a goal and don't give up until you have reached it. No matter how old you are or how long you have allowed negativity to control your life, it is never too late for a fresh start. As you walk with God, you can always begin again. Your history does not have to be your destiny!

PRAYER FOR TODAY: *God, help me begin again. No more sour, negative thoughts for me! Help me choose differently. I want to think and speak things that will keep me in a good mood. Amen.*

DAY 2
YOUR MINDSET MATTERS

But my servant Caleb, because he has a different spirit and has followed me fully, I will bring into the land into which he went, and his descendants shall possess it.

NUMBERS 14:24 ESV

The story of the Israelites is a good example of what a difference our mindset can make. The Israelites had been slaves in Egypt and couldn't envision anything better for their future, so they got stuck. What was supposed to be an eleven-day journey to the Promised Land ended up being a *forty-year* journey, all because of their mindset—because their thinking was shaped by fear and doubt, not trust. But Joshua and Caleb had a different mindset, so God allowed them to enter into the Promised Land.

God wants to do great things in our lives, but we can get stuck when we focus on our past or current circumstances. Instead of getting fixated on life's challenges, we can reflect on the countless times God has guided us through them. By focusing on His promises, we can shift our mindset in the right direction and go bravely wherever He is leading us.

PRAYER FOR TODAY: *Dear God, help me set my mind on You and Your promises today. Let my thoughts be aligned with Your will. In Jesus' name I pray, amen.*

DAY 3: YOUR WORDS HAVE POWER

Death and life are in the power of the tongue, and those who love it and indulge it will eat its fruit and bear the consequences of their words.

PROVERBS 18:21 AMP

All words contain some kind of power, whether negative or positive, uplifting or downgrading. We are wise to remember that our words have the power to either help or hurt us and other people—to build up or tear down, to bring life or death. We must never underestimate the impact of our words.

When life gets messy, our moods tend to sink. When they do, we need to be careful about what we say. We may become grouchy or irritable and say things we later regret, but then it is too late. Once words are spoken, they cannot be taken back.

If you already have problems in your life, why make them worse by speaking negatively? Instead, choose faith-filled words that have the power to change your outlook and help lift you out of a difficult situation.

PRAYER FOR TODAY: *Dear God, I want to be careful about the words that I speak because I know my words have power. Help me choose positive, life-giving words. I want my words to be a source of encouragement and healing. In Jesus' name I pray, amen.*

DAY 4: SPEAK TO YOUR MOUNTAIN

Truly I tell you, if anyone says to this mountain, "Go, throw yourself into the sea," and does not doubt in their heart but believes that what they say will happen, it will be done for them.

MARK 11:23 NIV

Often, when we have a mountain-sized problem, we tend to talk about it to anyone who will listen, but what good does that do? While venting has its place, remember that God is a better sounding board than anyone else. He is the ultimate confidant and adviser.

The next time you have a problem, try speaking God's truth *to* your problems, not just *about* them. Remind those mountains of difficulty what God's Word says by proclaiming: "I am more than a conqueror" (Romans 8:37). "I can do all things through Christ" (Philippians 4:13). "No weapon formed against me shall prevail" (Isaiah 54:17).

As you declare God's Word over your situation, you will discover newfound strength and encouragement. It will help you believe that God is bigger than your problems. With Him by your side, you can handle any challenge that life may throw your way.

PRAYER FOR TODAY: *Dear God, just as Jesus declared Your Word when the devil tempted Him in the wilderness, and just as He defeated the enemy, I will too! With faith as my shield, help me overcome every challenge. Amen.*

DAY 5: A RIGHT ATTITUDE

And be constantly renewed in the spirit of your mind [having a fresh mental and spiritual attitude].

EPHESIANS 4:23

No situation in life brings out our true attitudes like trials and troubles. Trials develop patience and perseverance (James 1:3), but as I have been through trials in my life, I've found they brought a lot of other things out of me long before I got to patience. Mostly, they brought out bad attitudes that needed to be changed before God could use me.

We can actually maintain good attitudes during times of trouble if we believe the difficulty will produce blessings in our lives in the end.

I encourage you to take time to truly think about your mindset and especially consider how you react when you go through difficulties. If you notice yourself heading down a negative path, remember: you can shift your thinking before it goes too far. You can always choose a positive perspective and grace.

PRAYER FOR TODAY: *Dear Lord, I believe that a positive attitude has the power to transform a negative circumstance into a blessing! Search me, O God, and know my heart. Test me and know my anxious thoughts. Grant me the strength to change what needs to be changed. Amen.*

DAY 6
GRACE FOR THE HUMBLE-MINDED

But he gives more grace. Therefore it says, "God opposes the proud but gives grace to the humble."

JAMES 4:6 ESV

Humility isn't a very popular word. Yet, it is a recurring theme throughout the Bible. The Lord consistently guides and instructs us about the benefits of remaining humble-minded. Unfortunately, humility is often misunderstood and even wrongly perceived as a weakness. But it's the exact opposite. Embracing humility positions us to receive God's grace and to fulfill the purpose He has ordained for us.

A humble person is also a happy person who can take joy in their life and what God has called them to do, regardless of what the world thinks about it. For instance, the proud person always wants to do something they think the world will admire, something others see as "important." The truth is, we don't have to do something important to be someone important. We are important because God loves and values us. Our significance lies in His abundant love. Our worth comes from Him.

PRAYER FOR TODAY: *Lord, guide me in cultivating an attitude of humility. As I receive Your grace, help me acknowledge my true worth as one of Your cherished children. May I find contentment in Your love and purpose for my life. Amen.*

DAY 7 — TRAITS OF A HUMBLE PERSON

Live in harmony with one another; do not be haughty (snobbish, high-minded, exclusive), but readily adjust yourself to [people, things] and give yourselves to humble tasks. Never overestimate yourself or be wise in your own conceits.

ROMANS 12:16

Humility is essential in our daily life. It begins with recognizing our need for God and relying on His grace each day. When we ask Him for help, He shapes our hearts and guides us. Here are a few traits that reflect the life of a truly humble person:

1. A humble person can ask for help. They don't insist on everything being done their way.
2. A humble person is quick to forgive others, difficult to offend, and content to wait on God for vindication when they have been wronged.
3. A humble person is patient and doesn't get frustrated with the weaknesses of others.
4. A humble person is a peacemaker. They contribute to harmony in their relationships.
5. A humble person is comfortable allowing others to have center stage and doesn't feel the need to speak their mind in every situation.
6. A humble person can see their own weaknesses and readily admit them.

PRAYER FOR TODAY: *Lord, I recognize my dependency on You in every aspect of my life. Grant me Your grace to navigate each situation I encounter today and help me to develop these traits. Amen.*

DAY 8

HE IS THE WAY

We are hedged in (pressed) on every side [troubled and oppressed in every way], but not cramped or crushed; we suffer embarrassments and are perplexed and unable to find a way out, but not driven to despair.

2 CORINTHIANS 4:8

Have you ever found yourself on the brink of giving up, feeling overwhelmed by circumstances beyond your control?

Satan's strategy is to trap us in frustration and anxiety, to get us to focus on our circumstances so our thoughts are consumed with the challenges we face. However, the Bible tells us to lift our eyes to heaven. The answer to our problems lies in redirecting our focus from what's wrong to God, who remains in control, always with us, and fully capable of making the impossible possible.

When I look at 2 Corinthians 4:8 I think it's interesting that Paul says they couldn't find a way out, but he didn't say there was no way out. See, even when we can't think of a way out of our problems on our own, we can put our hope in Jesus, who has promised us that He is the Way (John 14:6). We can look to Him and trust Him with our situation.

PRAYER FOR TODAY: *God, I'm tired of trying to figure things out on my own. You are the Way, and I trust You to bring me through my circumstances. Amen.*

DAY 9

UNINVITED GUESTS

So submit to [the authority of] God. Resist the devil [stand firm against him] and he will flee from you.

JAMES 4:7 AMP

Many people let unstable moods and emotions creep into their lives like uninvited guests.

When you first feel your mood sinking, that's when you need to regain control and get hold of yourself. Resist the devil right from the onset.

A dozen opportunities for you to get offended may arise, but no matter what you feel like inside, you have a choice. Are you going to throw a fit, or are you going to go to God and ask Him to help you change your mood?

When you immediately go to Him, something will change inside your heart. Once you get into the habit of going to God first, you will start to see those moods and bad attitudes leave a little sooner. Those uninvited guests may try to come back, but you will have already decided not to let them in!

PRAYER FOR TODAY: *Dear God, help me slam the door on bad moods so that I can move forward into the things You have for me. Amen.*

DAY 10: BRIDLE YOUR TONGUE

We all stumble in many ways. Anyone who is never at fault in what they say is perfect, able to keep their whole body in check.
JAMES 3:2 NIV

According to James, the litmus test for our spiritual maturity isn't rooted in how religious we are, whether we can quote Scripture, or whether we do an abundance of good works. Instead, it hinges on the words that flow from our mouths.

James 1:26 says, "If anyone thinks himself to be religious (piously observant of the external duties of his faith) and does not bridle his tongue but deludes his own heart, this person's religious service is worthless (futile, barren)."

No matter how religious you think you are, the true test of your spiritual maturity is whether you bridle your tongue or not. *Bridle* means to restrain or control. If we don't learn to control our words, we hinder our spiritual growth and fall short of the maturity God desires for us.

PRAYER FOR TODAY: *Lord, through Your grace, I am empowered to control the words I speak. May my words be guided by Your wisdom and grace. In Jesus' name, amen.*

DAY 11

LIVE VICTORIOUSLY

Therefore I urge you, brothers and sisters, by the mercies of God, to present your bodies [dedicating all of yourselves, set apart] as a living sacrifice, holy and well-pleasing to God, which is your rational (logical, intelligent) act of worship.

ROMANS 12:1 AMP

In Romans 12, Paul is not talking about becoming believers; he's talking about living as believers. This scripture challenges us to present *all* of ourselves to God for His use: our minds, mouths, wills, emotions, eyes, ears, hands, feet...Everything.

For many years, I was active in church, and I had accepted Jesus as my Savior. I knew I'd go to heaven, but I am not sure my behaviors would have encouraged anyone else to make a commitment to Him. I was led by my emotions and circumstances and I had no victory in my daily walk.

God changed that for me. He helped me understand through His Word that He sent Jesus to die for us not only so we could go to heaven but also so we could live victoriously right here on earth.

PRAYER FOR TODAY: *God, I give it all to You—my thoughts, my words, my moods, and my attitudes. Help me to live victoriously. In Jesus' name, amen.*

DAY 12: TRANSFORMED MINDS

Do not conform to the pattern of this world, but be transformed by the renewing of your mind. Then you will be able to test and approve what God's will is—his good, pleasing and perfect will.

ROMANS 12:2 NIV

If we want to see God's perfect will proven in our lives, we need to have our minds transformed by God. We have to think differently and look at life differently. We must begin to think in agreement with God's Word and not the devil's lies.

Although God has a different plan for each one of us, one thing is the same: We are to have minds that are inwardly transformed. When our minds are transformed by the Holy Spirit, we act differently. I know that has been true for me!

Does your life need to be transformed? Start by thinking right thoughts, and then you'll see the change in yourself—and so will others around you.

PRAYER FOR TODAY: *Father God, please help me live a life that's transformed by the renewing of my mind. Help me live a life that shows Your perfect will, not only to me but also to the world. Amen.*

DAY 13: MEDITATE ON THE ANSWERS

Keep this Book of the Law always on your lips; meditate on it day and night, so that you may be careful to do everything written in it. Then you will be prosperous and successful.

JOSHUA 1:8 NIV

We all want to prosper in our labors, and God promises prosperity and success to those who meditate on His Word. To *meditate* means "to roll over and over in the mind" and "to mutter softly." I tell people that if they know how to worry, they know how to meditate.

When we worry, we meditate on our problems. But when we meditate on God's Word, we focus on the answers to our problems. He Himself truly is the answer.

I believe that by "prosperity," God means that we'll be enriched in every part of our lives. Who would not want true prosperity? We all do, and meditating on God's Word will release it into our lives.

PRAYER FOR TODAY: *God, grant me the desire to meditate on Your Word day and night and to do according to all that is written in it. In Jesus' name, amen.*

DAY 14

CONDUCT AND CONVERSATION

Blessed (happy, fortunate, to be envied) are the undefiled (the upright, truly sincere, and blameless) in the way [of the revealed will of God], who walk (order their conduct and conversation) in the law of the Lord (the whole of God's revealed will).

PSALM 119:1

What we say is important. The power of our words cannot be underestimated. Our words are direct reflections of our hearts and guide our actions. Choosing to think and speak positively lays the foundation for doing what is right.

Our declarations shape our beliefs and, in turn, influence our lives and the world around us. If I say I cannot do something, I probably won't do it. But if I say I can do something, then actually doing it becomes more likely. The more we say something, the more we believe it ourselves, because we hear and feed on our own words.

Search God's Word to see what it says about you, and then align your conversations accordingly. Do this even if you don't fully believe it yet. Declare God's Word until you believe it, then speak it in faith and watch what God will do in your life.

PRAYER FOR TODAY: *Lord God, I embrace the truth of Your Word. Help me align my words with what You say about me. In the powerful name of Jesus I pray, amen.*

DAY 15

CHEER FOR THE SOUL

When the cares of my heart are many, your consolations cheer my soul.

PSALM 94:19 ESV

God's Word has dramatically changed my life. It has taught me how to keep a right attitude in the midst of trials. It has taught me truth, and I now recognize the lies of the devil and can resist them. The same life-changing power is available to you.

I remember how frightened I was when I was diagnosed with breast cancer. I had surgery, and by God's grace, here I am, more than thirty-seven years later, cancer-free without the need for chemotherapy or radiation. Looking back, I realize how much unnecessary worry consumed me when I could have placed my trust in God.

Now when I am upset, I go to God's Word, and by reading or listening to it, I find that it calms my anxieties. In moments of distress, I know that if I turn to God's Word, I will find a soothing balm that can calm the anxiety within my soul.

Through studying His Word, we discover the profound truth that trusting in God's promises can transform troubles, trials, and even extreme difficulties into blessings.

PRAYER FOR TODAY: *God, I firmly believe that You are actively at work in my life right now. Grant me the strength to maintain a right attitude, trusting that I will witness the results in due time. In Jesus' name I pray, amen.*

DAY 16: IT'S YOUR CHOICE

This day I call the heavens and the earth as witnesses against you that I have set before you life and death, blessings and curses. Now choose life, so that you and your children may live.

DEUTERONOMY 30:19 NIV

No one is born knowing how to manage their emotions, but we all can learn to do it. Making healthy, godly decisions when we feel like doing something else is vital to enjoying a victorious life.

For years, I simply did what I felt like doing, and it got me into a lot of trouble. But God has taught me how to follow Him instead of following my emotions. I don't always succeed, but I have learned a lot about following the instructions in God's Word and will continue learning all of my life.

In Deuteronomy, God tells His people to "choose life." As we do, we learn day by day how to make life-giving decisions. And as we study and obey His Word, we find peace, joy, and stability.

PRAYER FOR TODAY: *Thank You, God, for Your Word and for the ways it teaches me to choose life. Amen.*

DAY 17
MAKE ALL OF THEM PLEASING TO GOD

May these words of my mouth and this meditation of my heart be pleasing in your sight, Lord, my Rock and my Redeemer.
PSALM 19:14 NIV

How much would your thoughts and words have to change for *all* of them to be pleasing to God? This is a sobering question, and if I ask it of myself, I have to say they would probably need to change more than I realize.

Our thoughts and words are powerful; God wants *all* our words and thoughts to be in agreement with His Word. Our conversation should be filled with gratitude toward God and people. It should be uplifting, encouraging, positive, and anchored in truth.

The Bible has much to say about both our thoughts and our words, and we should pay close attention. I think about and meditate on those scriptures regularly, and they've become essential in helping me bring my mind and speech under God's control.

PRAYER FOR TODAY: *Father, I want to please You with all my thoughts and words. I need Your help because I cannot do it alone. I lean on Your strength. In Jesus' name I pray, amen.*

DAY 18
HOPE IN GOD'S LOVE

But the eyes of the Lord are on those who fear him, on those whose hope is in his unfailing love.

PSALM 33:18 NIV

People put their hope in all kinds of things—wealth, intellect, abilities, jobs, connections, possessions, and human relationships. But godly hope is not the same as what the world calls hope. The world hopes for snow on Christmas and for their team to win the game, but true biblical hope is solid and based on confidence in God's character.

We demonstrate our hope by believing in our heart that regardless of what is happening, God loves us and is able to change things for the better.

As it says in Matthew 19:26, all things are possible with God. We also know from countless verses throughout the Bible that God loves us and is always working for our good. Choosing to believe these truths establishes a solid foundation for our hope in every situation.

PRAYER FOR TODAY: *Thank You, God, that I can rest in Your unfailing love as I hope confidently in You. In Jesus' name, amen.*

DAY 19: REMAIN STABLE

There is no one holy like the Lord; there is no one besides you; there is no Rock like our God.

1 SAMUEL 2:2 NIV

In the early years of my adult life, I was a very unhappy person. I was controlled by mood swings and wrong thinking. Although I was a Christian, my mind, emotions, and behavior were all over the place. My moods went up and down, and no one I lived with ever quite knew what to expect.

The good news is that through the power of the Holy Spirit, I learned to think right, to talk right, and to not let those moods and attitudes control me. And you can, too!

Jesus, our unshakable Rock, epitomizes stability, steadfastness, unwavering love, positivity, and constant joy. If you want to be an example to the people in your life, you can remain stable and happy by knowing who you are in Christ.

PRAYER FOR TODAY: *Lord, grant me the serenity to remain calm in times of adversity. Guide me in the journey of living, thinking, and speaking in alignment with Your Word. In Your name I pray, amen.*

DAY 20: LOOK AT THE SHIPS

Likewise, look at the ships: though they are so great and are driven by rough winds, they are steered by a very small rudder wherever the impulse of the helmsman determines. Even so the tongue is a little member, and it can boast of great things.

JAMES 3:4-5

Several years ago, I experienced a disappointing situation. I noticed that each time I talked about it, I would have a difficult time getting it off my mind for the remainder of the day. I finally realized that if I wanted to get over it, I was going to have to stop talking about it.

Just like the tiny rudder on a ship, our words have the ability to affect the entire course of our lives. They can literally make the difference in our attitudes, in our relationships, and in what kind of days we ultimately have. So, if you're not happy with the direction you're going, look at what you are talking about and make a change.

PRAYER FOR TODAY: *God, help get my mind, mouth, moods, and attitudes in agreement with Your plan for my life. In Jesus' name, amen.*

DAY 21: DESTROY THE STRONGHOLDS

Casting down arguments and every high thing that exalts itself against the knowledge of God, bringing every thought into captivity to the obedience of Christ.

2 CORINTHIANS 10:5 NKJV

The Bible talks about strongholds in our minds. These are areas of our thinking dominated by the enemy—areas where we are deceived with nagging thoughts that lead to suspicion, doubt, fear, reasoning, and theories that refute the truth of God's Word.

When these thoughts get rooted in our minds, they become strongholds that give the enemy control.

For years, I believed so many things that weren't true, and they created a mess in my life. I didn't know I had the choice to reject wrong thinking!

The good news is that the Word of God is the most powerful thing on earth. And as we read, study, learn, and live God's Word, it will literally transform us from the inside out and help us to recognize the lies we believe so we can destroy these strongholds in our thinking.

PRAYER FOR TODAY: *God, thank You for giving me the power to reject wrong thinking. Help me recognize the lies of the enemy before they become strongholds. In Jesus' name, amen.*

DAY 22

STUCK IN A RUT

The Lord our God said to us in Horeb, "You have stayed long enough at this mountain."

DEUTERONOMY 1:6 ESV

Do you ever feel like you've been going around and around the same mountain, and you've been doing it way too long? I want to say to you: Enough is enough! You've lingered in misery and bondage for too long. It's time for a change!

Some of you have been in the same place for so long, going in circles, that you've carved out a deep rut. You feel like you can't get out of it. But here's the good news: God wants to lift you out of that rut and lead you into a fresh start.

Remember this: God can't change anything if we won't change. It's useless to keep praying for God to change something if you're not going to be willing to do whatever God asks you to do. But if you are willing to be obedient and do what God says, better days are ahead!

PRAYER FOR TODAY: *God, I've been stuck in this rut long enough. I'm willing to do whatever it takes to get out of it. Help me change my attitude and speak words of faith. Help me start fresh and learn to live in victory. Amen.*

DAY 23

LETTING GO

I do not consider, brethren, that I have captured and made it my own [yet]; but one thing I do [it is my one aspiration]: forgetting what lies behind and straining forward to what lies ahead.

PHILIPPIANS 3:13

The Bible says that God called the Israelites out of Egypt to take them into the Promised Land. God brought them out to take them in, took them from something old to something new, something better.

You have to let go of old mindsets in order to take hold of a new beginning. You must let go of old attitudes in order to take hold of brighter tomorrows.

Sometimes we feel torn between the past and the future because God is trying to lead us forward, but we keep hanging on to what's behind. You almost always have to give up something in order to get something better. You almost always have to leave something to go somewhere new.

The thing about God is that He'll often call you out of something before He shows you what you're going into. He said to Abram, "Go from your country and your kindred and your father's house to the land that I will show you" (Genesis 12:1 ESV).

God was saying, "I'm not showing you yet. I want you to leave first, and trust that *I will show you.* Trust that even though you don't know where you are going, I do."

PRAYER FOR TODAY: *God, I don't know where I'm going. I don't know what's next. But You do. You have ordered my steps. You know the end from the beginning. I put my trust in You, and I set my mind on moving forward. Amen.*

DAY 24

BE HAPPY ANYWAY

Blessed (happy, fortunate, and to be envied) is the man who reverently and worshipfully fears [the Lord] at all times [regardless of circumstances], but he who hardens his heart will fall into calamity.

PROVERBS 28:14

I remember a conversation I once had with my husband, Dave, about golf. I asked him, "How would you feel if for some reason you couldn't play anymore?" His response? "I've already thought about it, and I've decided I'll be happy anyway." He is very good about setting his mind in the right direction even before he has to deal with a situation.

Instead of deciding he would be miserable if he couldn't play the game he loves, he decided he would be happy anyway. That is the mindset we can choose through the help of the Holy Spirit. We can be happy despite our circumstances. We can be happy anyway.

If the devil catches wind of you saying "I won't be happy until things change," he'll do everything in his power to keep you down. But when you declare "Even if nothing changes, I'm choosing happiness anyway," you strip the devil of his power.

Jesus has provided for us everything that we need. He went through unimaginable pain and agony to save us from our sins and secure our place in heaven. When we focus on what He's provided through our relationship with Him rather than dwelling on our circumstances, happiness becomes our constant companion.

PRAYER FOR TODAY: *God, with Your help, I can be happy at all times, regardless of my circumstances. Thank You for all that You have done and are doing in my life. In Jesus' name, amen.*

DAY 25: CHANGE BEGINS IN THE MIND

You were taught, with regard to your former way of life, to put off your old self, which is being corrupted by its deceitful desires; to be made new in the attitude of your minds; and to put on the new self, created to be like God in true righteousness and holiness.
EPHESIANS 4:22–24 NIV

A change of behavior is directly related to a change of mind. If you have a behavior that you want to change, mere effort won't get it done. The only person who can really change you is God Himself. His part is to do the work; your part is to believe and be obedient to renew your mind with His Word.

Ephesians 4:22 says, "You were taught, with regard to your former way of life, to put off your old self, which is being corrupted by its deceitful desires" (NIV). Verse 24 says, "and to put on the new self, created to be like God in true righteousness and holiness" (NIV).

So, the instruction is to stop living the way you used to, because in Christ, you are a new creation. Your old self was crucified with Him, and now you're called to live in the new life He's given you. I know you want to, but maybe you are wondering how.

The answer is in verse 23: "And be constantly renewed in the spirit of your mind [having a fresh mental and spiritual attitude]."

Renew your mind and your attitude daily. The right mindset will help you do all things through Christ, who is your strength.

PRAYER FOR TODAY: *God, thank You for giving me a fresh mental and spiritual attitude when I refresh my spirit with Your Word. Change me into the person You want me to be. Amen.*

DAY 26: WOULDA, SHOULDA, COULDA

Do not [earnestly] remember the former things; neither consider the things of old. Behold, I am doing a new thing! Now it springs forth; do you not perceive and know it and will you not give heed to it? I will even make a way in the wilderness and rivers in the desert.

ISAIAH 43:18–19

In today's verse, God says, "I am doing a new thing!" Right now, He is trying to do a new thing in your life. Cooperate with Him by saying "Something good is going to happen for me today. God is doing a new thing in my life."

Hebrews 11:15 says, "If they had been thinking of that land from which they had gone out, they would have had opportunity to return" (ESV). In other words, if our minds are fixated on the past, we'll find ourselves constantly drawn back to it.

I don't know about you, but I don't want to revisit all my failures and all my mistakes and all the things I woulda, shoulda, coulda done. Don't waste any more of your time thinking about all the things you wish you would've done or the things you wish you wouldn't have done. Just start now doing the right thing.

PRAYER FOR TODAY: *God, thank You for doing a new thing in my life. The old is gone; the new is come. You are for me and not against me. The past is in the past. Your plans for my life are good. Amen.*

DAY 27: EYES OF FAITH

And his delight shall be in the fear of the Lord. He shall not judge by what his eyes see, or decide disputes by what his ears hear.
ISAIAH 11:3 ESV

No matter what Jesus died to give us and already has stored up for us, if we can't see with eyes of faith, we're never going to possess the promises of God. We'll just sit in church and hear about them and be frustrated because we don't understand why we're not getting our breakthroughs.

People who can't see beyond where they are right now—who believe their current situation is permanent—are not viewing their future through eyes of faith.

The Bible says that Jesus did not judge by the sight of His eyes nor by the hearing of His ears (Isaiah 11:3). He didn't make decisions based on what He saw and heard. He acted according to the will of the Father, rooted in God's truth and promises.

You need to change your thinking before anything else is going to change. You need to see with eyes of faith—believing God's promises even before they are visible. You may not see them in your circumstances, but with eyes of faith you can see them in your heart, and they will begin to take shape in your life.

PRAYER FOR TODAY: *God, thank You for giving me eyes of faith to see the promises that You have for me. I am standing on Your promises and expecting good things. Amen.*

DAY 28: THE BIBLE SAYS

Now to Him Who, by (in consequence of) the [action of His] power that is at work within us, is able to [carry out His purpose and] do superabundantly, far over and above all that we [dare] ask or think [infinitely beyond our highest prayers, desires, thoughts, hopes, or dreams].
EPHESIANS 3:20

The Bible is our ultimate guide to discerning right from wrong thinking.

For example, the next time you think *It's too late for me*, tell that thought to get out of your mind. You won't find that thought anywhere in the Bible. The Bible says that the vision comes at the "appointed time" and "If it seems slow, wait for it" (Habakkuk 2:3 ESV).

Have you ever thought *I'm no good; I'll never do anything right; I'm a mess!*? Well, guess what? That's not in the Bible, either. In fact, the Bible says you are precious, special, and created in God's image, and He's got a good plan for your life.

Is the enemy whispering that you'll never have enough or always be lacking? That's a lie. The Bible says God promises to supply all your needs through Christ Jesus (Philippians 4:19). Don't repeat the enemy's lies—speak God's truth instead: "My God is able to do exceedingly, abundantly above all I could ask or imagine. He will provide what I need—and more—so I can generously bless others."

Start aligning your thoughts and words with His truth, and watch as His promises begin to unfold in your life!

PRAYER FOR TODAY: *God, thank You for pointing me to the truth found in Your Word. I hold on to the promise that at the right time, I will reap a harvest of good things. Amen.*

DAY 29
GOD REWARDS A GOOD ATTITUDE

But, on the contrary, as the Scripture says, What eye has not seen and ear has not heard and has not entered into the heart of man, [all that] God has prepared (made and keeps ready) for those who love Him [who hold Him in affectionate reverence, promptly obeying Him and gratefully recognizing the benefits He has bestowed].
1 CORINTHIANS 2:9

After his brother died, Abram raised his nephew Lot. They both became so prosperous that there wasn't enough grass for all of their cattle. Abram knew the dangers of strife, so he told Lot to choose whatever part of the valley he wanted, and he would take what was left: "If you go to the left, I'll go to the right; if you go to the right, I'll go to the left" (Genesis 13:9 NIV).

So Lot took the best, most lush part of the Jordan Valley, and Abram had what was left. Now, pay attention to Abram's attitude in this situation because there's a lesson in it for us today. He didn't get upset or resentful because Lot took the prime land. Instead, he remained steadfast in his trust in God. He knew that as long as he behaved according to God's will and maintained a positive attitude no matter what he lost, God would always provide abundantly. And that's exactly what happened.

God said to him, "How far can you see? Look north, south, east, and west. It's all yours. It's for you, and your children, and your children's children, forever" (Genesis 13:14–17, paraphrased).

PRAYER FOR TODAY: *God, help me keep a good attitude, especially when it feels like I've lost something I thought I deserved. Remind me that whatever is taken from me, You will always replace it with something greater. Amen.*

DAY 30
AND KEEP IT SET

And set your minds and keep them set on what is above (the higher things), not on the things that are on the earth.

COLOSSIANS 3:2

What goes on in your mind affects you more than you can imagine. Your thoughts have the power to propel you toward your dreams or to keep you stuck in a place you don't want to be.

We often talk about what *not* to do or say or think, but I think we should put a greater emphasis on what *to do* and say and think. Colossians 3:2 says to set your mind and keep it set on right things. If our minds are full of right things, then when the devil comes along with his lies, there's no room for the wrong things. In other words, if we are thinking right thoughts, there won't be room for wrong thoughts.

When we focus so much on trying to get rid of the bad, we just end up in a wrestling match with the devil, and we never get around to doing what's right. So, set your mind where you want to go, not where you've been or where you are right now. Have a vision for your life. Have a vision for your children. Have a vision for your home. Have a vision for your career or ministry. And keep your thoughts set on that.

PRAYER FOR TODAY: *God, I will set my mind on right thoughts. Help me keep them set! I believe You have a good and perfect plan for my life, my home, and my future. Amen.*

DAY 31: JOY IS YOUR RESPONSIBILITY

So for the present you are also in sorrow (in distress and depressed); but I will see you again and [then] your hearts will rejoice, and no one can take from you your joy (gladness, delight).

JOHN 16:22

You are responsible for your own joy. Yes, you!

Responsibility means responding with the ability that God has placed in you, or responding to an opportunity that is put in front of you. I wonder how many opportunities we miss in life because we don't want to respond, it's an inconvenient time, or we want someone else to do the hard work for us.

I'll never forget the moment when the Lord spoke to my heart and said, "Stop putting the responsibility for your joy on Dave." In the early years of our marriage, I wasn't the happiest camper. And let me tell you, an unhappy person can't stand being around happy people. Dave was like a ray of sunshine, and I tried everything to dim his light and ruin his day. But he wouldn't let me. It was maddening, but it also caused me to change.

Through Dave's example, the Holy Spirit taught me that we are each responsible for our own joy. It wasn't Dave's job to make me happy; it was only his responsibility to keep his own peace and joy. Likewise, I had the power to be happy if I wanted to be happy, and no one had the power to steal my joy once I got my mind right.

PRAYER FOR TODAY: *God, I know that my joy is my responsibility. When others have negative attitudes, help me stay positive. When my attitude isn't where it needs to be, remind me that I hold the reins of my mind, mouth, mood, and attitude! Amen.*

DAY 32
AN ATTITUDE OF EXCELLENCE

His divine power has granted to us all things that pertain to life and godliness, through the knowledge of him who called us to his own glory and excellence.

2 PETER 1:3 ESV

God's Word has so much to say about our everyday lives. It teaches us how to conduct ourselves—at the grocery store, in traffic, at home, and at work. In all these areas, God desires that we have an attitude of excellence.

Living with an attitude of excellence means being authentic and honest. It means not taking home paper clips or other supplies from the office or scrolling through social media while you are on the clock. It means believing the best of the person who cuts you off in traffic and taking that extra step to return your grocery cart where it belongs.

You might think these things are inconsequential, but God cares about our attitudes in the little things and the big ones. When you do something you know is wrong, even if you pretend it's okay, even if everyone else is doing it, it still leaves a heaviness on the inside of you.

There's no greater satisfaction than lying down at night knowing that even though we may not have been perfect, we did our best to honor God throughout the day. That feeling of peace and contentment can't be matched by anything else.

PRAYER FOR TODAY: *God, I will do my best every day to have an attitude of excellence. Show me where I need to grow in this area, and bring encouragers into my life to help me continue to choose the better way. Amen.*

DAY 33: THE OTHER SIDE

He who calls you is faithful; he will surely do it.
1 THESSALONIANS 5:24 ESV

In Mark 4, Jesus says to His disciples, "Let us go over to the other side [of the lake]" (v. 35). Jesus and His disciples then climbed into the boat and pushed off from the shore.

No sooner did they get to the middle of the lake than a great windstorm arose. The waves were crashing into the boat, and fear was beginning to flood the disciples' hearts. And Jesus? Jesus was at the stern of the boat, taking a nap.

Does it ever seem like when you need God the most, He's having a nap?

The disciples woke Jesus up and said, "Master, do You not care that we are perishing?" (v. 38). Jesus rebuked them, saying, "Why are you so timid and fearful? How is it that you have no faith (no firmly relying trust)?" (v. 40). In other words, check your attitudes. Jesus had said they were going to the other side, and even though they ran into a storm on their journey, His word came true. Two verses later, in Mark 5:1, the Bible says, "They came to the other side of the sea."

When God says, "Let us go over to the other side," no storm in the middle can stop you from reaching your destination if you trust the Lord, hold on and don't give up!

PRAYER FOR TODAY: *God, help me hold on to Your promises. If You said it, I believe it. I won't give up in the middle; that is when I will cling to my faith and trust that it will happen in Your way and timing. Amen.*

DAY 34: CHOOSE HAPPY, HOPE-FILLED THOUGHTS

For to set the mind on the flesh is death, but to set the mind on the Spirit is life and peace.

ROMANS 8:6 ESV

Although we do not always have the power to change every unpleasant circumstance in our lives, we do have the power to change our outlook. We can look out at life from our inmost being with faith-filled thoughts and attitudes, or we can allow the events of life to shape our thoughts and attitudes. This is a decision that only we can make—no one can make it for us!

Sadly, we can waste most of life believing the misconception that joy and enjoyment come from our circumstances. But the truth is that they come from our attitude toward each circumstance—not the circumstances themselves. Obviously, nobody enjoys troubling or painful circumstances, but when we approach them with hope and faith, we can witness God's hand at work, turning all things for our good (Romans 8:28).

Enjoying life begins with the thoughts you choose to think. Yes, it is that simple! No matter what is going on in your life today, if you choose happy, hope-filled thoughts, you'll find yourself feeling happier. Our thoughts are intricately connected to our feelings, so if we want to feel better, we've got to start thinking better.

PRAYER FOR TODAY: *God, help me choose to look at my circumstances with a positive, hope-filled attitude. Even though not all of my circumstances are good, I know that You can work them out for good, and because of that I am happy! Amen.*

DAY 35: INTERRUPT THE DEVIL

Pray at all times (on every occasion, in every season) in the Spirit, with all [manner of] prayer and entreaty. To that end keep alert and watch with strong purpose and perseverance, interceding in behalf of all the saints (God's consecrated people).

EPHESIANS 6:18

If we leave our minds empty and idle, the devil will gladly step in and fill them with all sorts of destructive thoughts.

I remember one day the devil started attacking me with negative thoughts when I was working on a book about the mind. He was very sneaky about it. They were vague, discouraging notions in my ear, saying that I didn't have the creativity I needed to write that day, and I should just put it off until tomorrow. No big deal, right? But if I had given in, tomorrow might have arrived with those same whispers again, perhaps even louder, and before long, I could have abandoned the book altogether.

Instead, the Holy Spirit caused me to recognize what was going on, so I stopped and prayed, asking God to protect my mind from negative, energy-draining thoughts. The Bible teaches us to cover everything with prayer (Ephesians 6:18), so that's exactly what I did. You and I have the power to interrupt the devil's plans through prayer. With God's help, I refocused my mind and penned that book, and God claimed the victory!

PRAYER FOR TODAY: *God, when the enemy comes to me with seeds of negativity, give me the courage and strength to send them away. Cause me to pay attention to what I am thinking so that I can choose to think good, positive, and godly thoughts every day. Amen.*

DAY 36: MORE THAN CONQUERORS

Yet amid all these things we are more than conquerors and gain a surpassing victory through Him Who loved us.

ROMANS 8:37

There is no doubt that thinking positive is much easier when life is not difficult, but it is self-defeating to think that you can't be positive in every circumstance. Be careful not to just focus on your problems, but remember to also focus on and be thankful for your blessings.

It is very important for each of us to learn how to have the victory in our minds in the midst of our problems. God's Word reassures us that we are not just conquerors but more than conquerors even during life's toughest moments (Romans 8:37).

When life gets tough, I often turn to Romans 8:35–39 to remind myself of God's unwavering love. I try to remember that, at times, I may appear as a sheep being led to slaughter, but in the midst of these things, I am more than a conqueror.

To me, this simply means that we can always be assured of eventual victory. We may go through very difficult things, but following the principles God has set for us in His Word will bring us through safely every time. It is very helpful during difficult times to remember that they won't last forever. That is what helps me keep my joy in adversity.

PRAYER FOR TODAY: *God, I know that You love me and that I am more than a conqueror. I need you in my current situation. I believe victory is coming! I will trust You all the way to the finish. Amen.*

DAY 37: LIFE-ENERGIZING THOUGHTS

Yet they seek me daily and delight to know my ways, as if they were a nation that did righteousness and did not forsake the judgment of their God; they ask of me righteous judgments; they delight to draw near to God.

ISAIAH 58:2 ESV

The way to put off our old life and put on the new, enjoyable life that God offers is by renewing our mind and attitude daily (Ephesians 4:22–24). We need to choose positive, godly thoughts on purpose every day, so that it becomes a habit and we don't have to work quite as hard at it. The devil will still try to put evil thoughts in our minds, so we need to resist him daily.

Daily sounds daunting though, doesn't it? Don't you wish Scripture said, "Do this once and enjoy victory the rest of your life"? However, it doesn't say that, and if we truly want to live life to the fullest and enjoy each moment of it, we need to form habits of thinking life-energizing thoughts instead of life-draining ones. One simple way to practice this is to think about what you *do* have instead of what you *don't* have and be grateful for every blessing, no matter how tiny it may seem.

Instead of wishing you had a bigger house, be thankful you have indoor plumbing. Instead of wishing your kids were in a different season of life, be thankful they are healthy. Instead of resenting the price of gasoline, thank God you have a car to put gas in. Look around you right now. There is so much to be thankful for!

PRAYER FOR TODAY: *God, help me replace every negative thought with a life-energizing one. Open my eyes, my mouth, and my heart to the blessings I do have. I want to be thankful and say so! Amen.*

DAY 38
BAD MOODS AND BAD ATTITUDES

He who dwells in the secret place of the Most High shall remain stable and fixed under the shadow of the Almighty [Whose power no foe can withstand].

PSALM 91:1

One of the things that I appreciate about my husband, Dave, is that he is extremely stable. I never have to wonder what kind of a mood he will be in when he wakes up. This has been important to me because I grew up in a home that was exactly the opposite. Bad moods were ever-present. I'm sorry to say that I learned and then continued the same behavior that I despised.

Dave has shared that he remembers driving home from work at night and thinking, *I wonder what kind of mood Joyce will be in tonight.* Women often control the emotional atmosphere of the home, and I was good at making ours unpleasant.

Like most people, I wasn't fully aware of how bad my attitude was. I did know that I was unhappy, and that finally opened my eyes and I realized that something was wrong. God graciously opened my eyes to the truth: It was difficult for people to be in a relationship with me, and I'd wasted too much of my life being in bad moods.

Being open to the truth is the starting point for all personal breakthroughs. If you are ready to be happy, allow God to help you deal with what's going on in your mind.

PRAYER FOR TODAY: *God, I know that you are the secret to my happiness in life. Give me the strength to hear the truth from You so that I can begin to change. I want to enjoy my life! Amen.*

DAY 39: THINK LIKE GOD THINKS

"For who has understood the mind of the Lord so as to instruct him?" But we have the mind of Christ.

1 CORINTHIANS 2:16 ESV

If you want to have what God wants you to have, learn to think like God thinks.

Pay particular attention to the thoughts going through your mind, because they will energize the rest of what you do. You can jump-start your day by thinking good things on purpose as one of your first acts of the day. Thinking and speaking good thoughts is a powerful combination.

You may meditate on and confess things from God's Word like: *This is the day God has made, and I am going to enjoy it. I can handle whatever comes my way today through Christ, who is my strength. Today, I am energetic and creative. I have favor with God and people everywhere I go. Everything I lay my hand to prospers and succeeds. I enjoy being a blessing to others.*

Setting your mind in an uplifting direction cannot have anything other than a good effect on you and your entire day. This doesn't mean that unpleasant situations won't arise, but the beauty lies in your ability to choose your thoughts, words, and attitude toward life. Your attitude is within your control, and no one can impose a negative one upon you unless you permit it.

PRAYER FOR TODAY: *God, guide me to think in alignment with Your thoughts and Your ways. I am grateful for Your ongoing work in my life. My focus is set on heavenly things, and I embrace positive thoughts. Amen.*

DAY 40

CAST THEM AGAIN

Casting down imaginations, and every high thing that exalteth itself against the knowledge of God, and bringing into captivity every thought to the obedience of Christ.

2 CORINTHIANS 10:5 KJV

The Bible teaches us to cast down wrong thoughts, but there are days when I feel like I spend the entire day casting them down because they keep coming back. You will experience days like this, and I urge you not to give up! The enemy will try to convince you that you'll never overcome, but remember, the devil is a liar. Everything he says contradicts God's Word, and he may even twist Scripture to deceive you.

When Jesus was enduring His testing and temptation in the wilderness, the devil said to Him, "If You are the Son of God, throw Yourself down; for it is written, He will give His angels charge over you, and they will bear you up on their hands, lest you strike your foot against a stone" (Matthew 4:6). Satan misused Scripture by quoting it out of context to try to lure Him. Jesus immediately responded by quoting Scripture correctly: "On the other hand, it is written also, You shall not tempt, test thoroughly, or try exceedingly the Lord your God" (v. 7).

No one can win the battle in their mind unless they know God's Word. The Word of God is truth, and we can believe that above all else.

PRAYER FOR TODAY: *God, I receive the help You have for me today. I will win this battle in my mind. I am getting stronger every day. Help me recognize negative thoughts as attacks from the enemy so I can refuse to entertain them. Amen.*

DAY 41: BUILT FOR THE BATTLE

No temptation has overtaken you that is not common to man. God is faithful, and he will not let you be tempted beyond your ability, but with the temptation he will also provide the way of escape, that you may be able to endure it.

1 CORINTHIANS 10:13 ESV

God has equipped and anointed us to do hard things. He allows us to go through difficulties to bring glory to Him. He shows Himself strong through us. He told Paul that His strength is made perfect in our weakness (2 Corinthians 12:9). We may think we can't make it through difficulties, but those thoughts are inaccurate according to God's Word. God has promised to never burden us beyond what we can bear.

During life's difficulties, the thoughts that are usually persistent are *I can't do this; it is just too much; it is too hard.* Watch out for that type of thinking, and when you recognize it, remember that it is a lie and replace it with a confession based on God's Word that goes something like this: *I can do what I need to do because God is with me. This season will soon be over; better days are coming.*

Perhaps you need to see yourself in a new way. If you find yourself easily discouraged or tempted to give up, know that you're not alone in your struggles. As a matter of fact, your battles belong to the Lord, and He will fight for you as you continue to trust Him.

PRAYER FOR TODAY: *God, thank You that I can do all things because You are my strength. Because my hope is in You, I will remain peaceful even when things aren't going my way. Amen.*

DAY 42
HOW TO THINK ABOUT YOURSELF

But you are a chosen people, a royal priesthood, a holy nation, God's special possession, that you may declare the praises of him who called you out of darkness into his wonderful light.

1 PETER 2:9 NIV

The devil loves to highlight our flaws and shortcomings, bombarding us with thoughts of all the things we can't seem to do right. For that reason, we need to be well-versed in God's thoughts toward us and meditate on them often. God has very good thoughts toward you, and it is important that you learn to think about yourself in the same way that He does.

People in general tend to think about all their faults more than they do their strengths, but it is much better to consider both. While it's important to acknowledge our flaws, focusing solely on them can lead to discouragement and even depression. We must also recognize our strengths and the good within us.

Challenges will come, but they don't define who you are in Christ. You are equipped with strength and grace to overcome. Don't dwell on flaws or failures—focus on God's truth and the good He's doing in you. Remember, we overcome lies and discouragement not by trying harder, but by filling our minds with what is good and true (Romans 12:21; Philippians 4:8).

PRAYER FOR TODAY: *God, thank You for the talents, gifts, and abilities that You have given me. I intend to use them for Your glory. Even in my weaknesses, I ask for Your strength to trust You in all things. Amen.*

DAY 43: CHOOSE YOUR ATTITUDE

A happy heart is good medicine and a joyful mind causes healing, but a broken spirit dries up the bones.

PROVERBS 17:22 AMP

The thoughts we allow into our minds and the attitudes we choose to have determine whether we have misery or joy.

Choosing to live with a good, godly, positive, loving attitude is something that each of us can do. We should not bounce back and forth between good and bad, godly and ungodly, positive and negative, and love and hate. As God's Word says, "Choose life" (Deuteronomy 30:19 ESV). Choose what breathes life into you and those around you.

It is foolish to have bad attitudes about something we have to do anyway. As long as we are going to do it, why not do it with a good attitude so we can find some joy in doing it?

Good thoughts always precede a good attitude, and we cannot have one without the other. A good attitude makes life better even if it is difficult. People may wonder how you could possibly be happy with the troubles you have, but your secret is simply maintaining a good attitude—an attitude that says things will be made right in the end and that is hopeful when others are giving up.

PRAYER FOR TODAY: *God, thank You for giving me the free will to choose my attitude. Help me choose good, godly, positive thoughts and a joy-filled, hopeful attitude regardless of my circumstances. Amen.*

DAY 44
SELF-PITY IS A TRAP

Blessed (happy, to be envied, and spiritually prosperous—with life-joy and satisfaction in God's favor and salvation, regardless of their outward conditions) are the poor in spirit (the humble, who rate themselves insignificant), for theirs is the kingdom of heaven!

MATTHEW 5:3

Because I have a lot of experience with self-pity and how destructive it can be, it is one of the attitudes I definitely avoid, and I encourage others to do the same. Self-pity is actually a form of idolatry because we are turning inward and idolizing ourselves, letting ourselves be consumed with thoughts of perceived injustices and disadvantages, and leaving no room for peace of mind.

If we truly look at what others have, there are plenty who have much less than we do. When we allow our minds to rotate around and around all the things we don't like about our lives, we have no peace of mind.

Your life may not be perfect, but feeling sorry for yourself will never change that. Use your energy for something useful instead of something useless. Self-pity is a trap. It is like being in a prison in solitary confinement. All our thoughts are consumed by how bad off we are. When we live in the darkness of self-pity, we fail to see how truly blessed we are in many ways.

But there's a way out: focusing on the blessings God has given us. Instead of wallowing in what we lack, we can choose to reflect on all that we have and all the ways we're blessed. Think on those things.

PRAYER FOR TODAY: *God, equip me to keep my mind on all of the blessings You have given me. When I am mistreated, when I am disadvantaged, when life doesn't feel fair, that's when I need Your help the most to remember all that I have to be thankful for. Amen.*

DAY 45: ENJOY THE WAIT

Wait and hope for and expect the Lord; be brave and of good courage and let your heart be stout and enduring. Yes, wait for and hope for and expect the Lord.

PSALM 27:14

Impatient attitudes bring a lot of stress into our lives, and the simple truth is that we all have to wait on things we want, so we might as well learn to wait patiently.

One of the keys to cultivating patience is staying present in the moment. Don't become so fixated on the destination that you miss out on the beauty of the journey. In our fast-paced society, where everything moves at lightning speed, it's easy to fall into the trap of constant hurrying. However, it is not good for us, and it can cause us to have short fuses when things don't go our way. When we're in a hurry, it doesn't take much imposition or inconvenience to make us blow up!

It is often said that practice makes perfect, so let's practice having patient attitudes with situations, people, and ourselves. Most of all, let's be patient with God when we are waiting on Him to do something we have asked Him to do. God has a perfect timing for all things, and He will not be rushed. So, settle in, trust in His timing, and find joy in the waiting.

PRAYER FOR TODAY: *God, help me be a more patient person so I can make it through difficulties with joy and a good attitude. I pray that Your best plans for my life will come at just the right time, and they will be worth the wait! Amen.*

DAY 46: GOD'S PROMISE TO YOU

And [so that you can know and understand] what is the immeasurable and unlimited and surpassing greatness of His power in and for us who believe, as demonstrated in the working of His mighty strength.

EPHESIANS 1:19

If you're feeling incapable or overwhelmed today, I have good news: God has promised to give us His power and authority. But we have to believe it! If we think we're incapable, we'll live up to that belief. But if we believe we can handle challenges with God's help, we'll find strength we never knew we had.

Think weak and be weak...think strong and be strong! We are strong in Christ, not in ourselves. When you need to do something, look to Jesus and know that in Him you are able.

Here is God's promise to you: "Behold! I have given you authority and power to trample upon serpents and scorpions, and [physical and mental strength and ability] over all the power that the enemy [possesses]; and nothing shall in any way harm you" (Luke 10:19).

Let us commit ourselves to think like God thinks so we can live the joy-filled lives He purchased for us.

PRAYER FOR TODAY: *God, thank You for promising to give me authority and power and not leaving me to rely on my own strength. I can do all things in Your strength, and I always want to remember that! Help me believe what Your Word says. Amen.*

DAY 47
YES, YOU CAN!

And let us not grow weary of doing good, for in due season we will reap, if we do not give up.

GALATIANS 6:9 ESV

I wonder how many blessings and provisions we miss in life because we simply have the wrong attitudes. How often is God merely waiting to see how we respond to difficulties before He moves to help us?

It can be easy to slip into a "This is too hard—I can't do it" attitude, deciding that something is too hard before you have even tried and or even giving up if it doesn't come easily. Even if we try and fail a few times, we must remember what God's Word tells us: not to grow weary in doing what is right, for in due time, we will reap a harvest if we don't give up (Galatians 6:9).

The battle is often fought and lost in our minds before we even begin. Maintaining an "I can" and, more importantly, "God can" attitude is the key to living by faith as we believe for God's blessings and provision. Instead of looking at how hard something seems, replace those thoughts with recognizing the amazing opportunity God has put in front of you.

Instead of living in fear with an "I can't" attitude, live by faith in God and be assured that He is well able to see you through.

PRAYER FOR TODAY: *God, I believe that with You by my side, I've got this! Your power is sufficient. Nothing is too hard for You. I pray that I will not miss another opportunity because of a wrong attitude. Amen.*

DAY 48: STEP OUT AND FIND OUT

Many plans are in a man's mind, but it is the Lord's purpose for him that will stand.

PROVERBS 19:21

Many years ago, I tried to be my pastor's secretary. I was told the position just wasn't right for me, and I was let go. I felt devastated, but little did I know, that disappointment was a divine redirection. Had I clung to that role, I wouldn't be where I am today. When things don't work out the way you planned, you don't have to get discouraged and depressed; instead, you can believe that God has something better for you and get excited to see what it is.

One of the ways we can find God's perfect will for us is to step out and find out what works and what does not. If something doesn't work out, don't give up or let your disappointment stop you from pressing on. Simply scratch it off the list and move forward to the next opportunity. If we do the things God has truly assigned us to do, He always gives us the grace to do them peacefully and joyfully.

Sometimes I look at finding God's perfect will as trying to find the perfect new outfit. I go shopping and try on different things. I see how they fit and how they look on me. I see if they are comfortable or not, and eventually I find the perfect thing that is just right for me.

You can look at the dreams you have for your life with a similar mindset. Keep dreaming and having goals until you find the perfect fit for you!

PRAYER FOR TODAY: *God, I want to serve You with my life. Help me let go of my own plans and expectations so that I can do Your will and live in the joy it brings. Amen.*

DAY 49
BOOK OF REMEMBRANCE

For the Lord God is a sun and shield; the Lord bestows favor and honor. No good thing does he withhold from those who walk uprightly.

PSALM 84:11 ESV

I keep a book of remembrance of amazing little things that God has done for me, because I never want to forget His goodness. Some people might chalk those things up to coincidence, but I know it is the mercy and favor of God.

Here's an example: I was trying to get theater tickets for a couple of shows that were going to be in town. My assistant was helping me try to secure those tickets. She called the minute they went on sale, but the only tickets left were in the back row at the very top of the building.

You have to know my assistant, though. She has a real gift because she's so nice to people that they end up wanting to give her favor. Soon after she hung up the phone, the lady from the box office called back. Her boss had agreed to sell me two box seats to one show and then tickets to the other show I wanted to attend, and those tickets weren't even on sale yet! That is the favor of God.

It is important that we remember and think about all of the things, big and small, that God has done for us. It's hard to feel sorry for yourself when you pay attention to how often God goes out of His way to let you know He is watching over you!

PRAYER FOR TODAY: *God, watch over me today. I never want to overlook all of the good things You do for me. Help me pay attention to the details. When I am having a hard day, cause me to think about all of the times You have shown me Your favor. Amen.*

DAY 50
WHERE IS YOUR MIND IN TIMES OF SUFFERING?

[After all] what kind of glory [is there in it] if, when you do wrong and are punished for it, you take it patiently? But if you bear patiently with suffering [which results] when you do right and that is undeserved, it is acceptable and pleasing to God.

1 PETER 2:20

Today's verse says it takes a mature person to keep a good attitude while going through suffering, especially when you don't understand it, when it isn't deserved, when it goes on longer than you like. But you can do it if you keep your mind on Christ.

First Peter 2:19 says, "For this is a gracious thing, when, mindful of God, one endures sorrows while suffering unjustly" (ESV).

Gracious means it is a good thing. *Endures* means that you aren't running away from it; you are facing your sorrows head on and don't intend to give up. So, the scripture is saying that it is a good thing to think about God while you are enduring, because it will help you keep a good attitude when life is unfairly sorrowful. Suffering itself doesn't glorify God, but keeping a godly attitude during it does, and that's possible if you are mindful of God.

First Peter 2:21 says, "For to this you have been called, because Christ also suffered for you, leaving you an example, so that you might follow in his steps" (ESV). Jesus understands! He is our example in everything, even in what kind of attitude to have while we are suffering.

PRAYER FOR TODAY: *God, I love You and I trust You just as much in the valleys as I do on the mountaintops. I am called to follow in Jesus' footsteps; therefore, when I suffer, I will do so with a godly attitude because I know this pleases you. Amen.*

DAY 51: CRUCIFY THE FLESH

Those who belong to Christ Jesus have nailed the passions and desires of their sinful nature to his cross and crucified them there.
GALATIANS 5:24 NLT

Decades ago, I worked at a church where I taught a weekly women's ministry. There was a woman in the church who felt like God wanted her to teach the meeting instead of me. She started telling lies about me and doing everything she could to get me out of there. By God's direction, I did eventually end up leaving that position, and I started doing what I'm doing now.

A couple years after this happened, God put it on my heart to give that woman a favorite piece of jewelry. I wanted to tell God I would give it away, but please let me give it to anyone but her! That's not how God works, though. We are called to crucify the flesh and obey Him in doing *exactly* what He asks of us.

So, I gave her the jewelry, and every time I saw her wear it, I suffered. It wasn't fair! It's in moments of obedience that we most reflect the heart of God.

Knowing that we are doing the will of God can make even the hardest things enjoyable. Have the attitude that you can do all things through Christ, and then look forward with joy to what He'll ask you to do next.

PRAYER FOR TODAY: *God, if following You was easy, everyone would do it. Today, I ask for Your strength. I will choose to walk in obedience to You even when it's hard. Help me! I know that when I am weak, You are strong. Amen.*

DAY 52
IF YOU THINK YOU CAN'T, YOU WON'T

I have strength for all things in Christ Who empowers me [I am ready for anything and equal to anything through Him Who infuses inner strength into me; I am self-sufficient in Christ's sufficiency].
PHILIPPIANS 4:13

Right thinking can enable you, and wrong thinking can disable you. It's amazing what you won't do if you think you can't.

My mom knew about the abuse that was happening to me as a child, but fear and doubt crippled her from doing anything about it. She said she couldn't face the scandal. It took her three long decades after I left home to confront the truth and apologize for her inaction. Her wrong mindset and her belief that she couldn't handle the consequences tragically impacted not just my life but the lives of many. Things could have turned out differently if she had thought *With God's help, I can do this.*

Because of God's goodness, things have turned out well for me. I stuck with God and fought through a lot. But I had a brother, who was nine years younger than me, who turned to drugs and alcohol instead, and ultimately ended his own life. Oh, how I wish he would have known then what I'm sharing with you now—that our thoughts and beliefs shape our actions. Wrong thinking can disable us, but right thinking, rooted in God's truth, can empower us beyond measure.

PRAYER FOR TODAY: *God, help me have right thinking. Help me remember that I don't have to do things in my own strength. You are here for me to strengthen me and uphold me with Your righteous right hand. Amen.*

DAY 53: HE OPENED NOT HIS MOUTH

He was oppressed, and he was afflicted, yet he opened not his mouth; like a lamb that is led to the slaughter, and like a sheep that before its shearers is silent, so he opened not his mouth.

ISAIAH 53:7 ESV

Isaiah 53:7 says Jesus "was oppressed, and he was afflicted" (ESV). He suffered for our sins. He took our punishment, and His heavenly Father sent Him to do it. We forget sometimes how God, out of His love for us, allowed His own Son to suffer, and then we complain when something is hard or inconvenient, which is foolish on our part.

The scripture continues, "yet he opened not his mouth" (ESV). Despite everything that Jesus went through, He did not complain. He didn't blame God; He didn't question God. At the very end, when His suffering was at its worst, He did cry out, "My God, my God, why have you forsaken me?" (Mark 15:34 ESV). He had to experience everything that we would ever experience, so in the end, He felt completely abandoned and forsaken.

We don't even know what suffering means compared to what Jesus went through for us. He took our sin upon Himself, and because of that, we're free! Hallelujah!

So, what do we have to complain about? If Jesus didn't complain, if He "opened not his mouth" even when He was being beaten and oppressed, then we should follow His lead.

PRAYER FOR TODAY: *God, I am so grateful for what Jesus did for me. Help me never take for granted the freedom He died for me to experience. I will focus on my gratitude and keep my complaints to myself. Amen.*

DAY 54: APPRECIATE WHAT YOU DO HAVE

His master replied, "Well done, good and faithful servant! You have been faithful with a few things; I will put you in charge of many things. Come and share your master's happiness!"

MATTHEW 25:21 NIV

I will never forget the first time I went to India. We visited a leper colony. I remember a man afflicted with leprosy who was so excited to show me his home. When he took me to it, it was a hole dug out of the side of a dirt mound. He had dug enough dirt out of the mound to make room for a hammock to sleep in. Over in the corner, there was a bowl and a cup. That was his home—his whole entire home. And he was so excited about it! He was so proud to show it to me. I think sometimes the less you have, the more you appreciate what you do have.

If we're honest, none of us like being uncomfortable, and it's easy to focus on what we don't have. But we don't want to love our stuff so much that if we lose a little bit of our comfort, we focus on our lack and start complaining.

I do fall into that trap sometimes, and I have to remember the lessons we are learning here in this book. There is a constant battle going on in our minds, and the words we let come out of our mouths affect our moods and attitudes. So, what we choose to think and say is very important.

PRAYER FOR TODAY: *God, help me be faithful with all that You have given me, whether that be little or much. I will be grateful for all that I have, and I will keep an open hand and an open heart so that my joy doesn't depend on comfort or things. Amen.*

DAY 55: THE GOD OF ALL COMFORT

Blessed be the God and Father of our Lord Jesus Christ, the Father of mercies and God of all comfort, who comforts us in all our affliction, so that we may be able to comfort those who are in any affliction, with the comfort with which we ourselves are comforted by God.
2 CORINTHIANS 1:3-4 ESV

The Bible says that we have a High Priest who understands what we are going through. Jesus, our High Priest, has compassion and understands because the Bible says He has suffered all of the same things.

Just as Jesus understands what you are going through, your trials can help you understand what others are going through. You can decide to have the attitude that God will get you through it and He will use you to minister to others.

If you come to me and say, "Joyce, I'm a smoker. I've smoked for thirty years, and I'm just really having a hard time giving it up!" I can tell you, "I get it!" because I had a hard time giving up cigarettes. It was forty years ago, but I still remember how hard it was. If you come to me and say, "Joyce, I just got a cancer report," I can tell you, "I understand because I had breast cancer. But that was over thirty-seven years ago, and I'm still here!"

I can't explain why you go through what you go through, but I do know that if you keep trusting God, your trials can give you compassion for others in similar situations, and you will come out on the other side with a victory.

PRAYER FOR TODAY: *God, I don't understand why I have to go through what I'm going through right now, but I trust You, and I believe that it is going to make me a stronger person. I will see the victory in Your perfect time. Amen.*

DAY 56

FIGHT FOR IT

Lean on, trust in, and be confident in the Lord with all your heart and mind and do not rely on your own insight or understanding.

PROVERBS 3:5

Our minds have a lot to do with how fast we make it through tough seasons and to the other side of God's promises.

After God brought the Israelites out of Egypt, they wanted to possess the Promised Land. Did you know that *to possess* actually means "to dispossess the current occupants"? They wanted the land of milk and honey, but God knew that they were going to have to fight to take possession of it, and they weren't strong enough yet. They weren't mature enough yet. They didn't trust Him enough yet.

The same is true in our lives. God has incredible promises in store for us. We hear about them in church, week after week. But I'll be honest: I used to grow weary of hearing about promises without seeing their fulfillment in my life. It took me years to realize that the reason I wasn't seeing fruit was because my mindset wasn't mature enough to receive it.

Just as it took the Israelites forty years to shed their negative mindsets before claiming the Promised Land, it took years of God's work within me to align my beliefs with His truth and trust Him wholeheartedly. No matter how long it takes, don't give up!

PRAYER FOR TODAY: *God, help me trust You with my mind. Help me dispossess every negative attitude and mindset, clearing the path for Your promises to take root in my life. Where I see barrenness, I trust You to cultivate growth. Amen.*

DAY 57: JUST A LITTLE WHILE

And after you have suffered a little while, the God of all grace [Who imparts all blessing and favor], Who has called you to His [own] eternal glory in Christ Jesus, will Himself complete and make you what you ought to be, establish and ground you securely, and strengthen, and settle you.

1 PETER 5:10

If you keep the attitude of "This suffering is just a little while," you can more easily resist the devil and the temptation to complain.

Everything we go through in life is just a little while when compared to eternity. When I focus on that, it's easier for me to live in the present and not dwell on the what-ifs or say, "I'll be happy when..."

None of us is ever going to be completely happy until we get to heaven. The Bible says there will be no more crying or tears when we get there. I'm in my eighties now, and I'm really starting to look forward to heaven. That's not a death wish; that's just keeping my eye on the prize, the day I get to meet Jesus. I love my husband and my kids, but nothing on earth will compare to seeing Jesus face-to-face!

That is why I'm not stopping here in this life. I want as many people as possible to experience that same thing, to get their own day of glory when they can run into the arms of Jesus!

PRAYER FOR TODAY: *God, I need you today. I know what I'm going through won't last forever. Help me endure it for a little while longer. Help me have the strength and energy to serve You all the days of my life. Amen.*

DAY 58: DO THE RIGHT THING

So, since Christ suffered in the flesh for us, for you, arm yourselves with the same thought and purpose [patiently to suffer rather than fail to please God]. For whoever has suffered in the flesh [having the mind of Christ] is done with [intentional] sin [has stopped pleasing himself and the world, and pleases God].

1 PETER 4:1

Today's scripture tells us to have the same kind of thinking that Jesus had. Jesus thought nothing was more important than following His Father's will for His life, even though He knew that obeying God wouldn't always feel good to the flesh.

There were countless times when people didn't treat Jesus right, but instead of retaliating, He forgave them. There were times when He could have defended Himself, but instead He didn't say a word. He always trusted God to vindicate Him, and He always did the right thing at all times.

If we are going to think like Jesus thinks, we have to stay focused on those things for ourselves, to keep doing the right thing even if the right thing isn't happening to us, to keep doing the right thing even if no one else is, to keep doing the right thing even if no one else is watching, to keep doing the right thing even if it hurts, and to always trust God in every situation.

When you think like Christ, He gives you the strength to suffer patiently and do the right thing, even when it's hard.

PRAYER FOR TODAY: *God, You know all things. I want Your will more than I want my way. Help me keep my mind focused on Your plans for my life. I've got one job, and I want to do it well. Amen.*

DAY 59
FOCUS MEANS SAYING NO

Delight yourself in the Lord, and he will give you the desires of your heart.

PSALM 37:4 ESV

Focus requires understanding that you can't have too many top priorities. When we do too many things at once, we end up doing nothing well.

If you have a goal you truly want to accomplish, you need to focus your thoughts, energies, and time on it. It is useless to *wish* you could do something; if you truly desire to do something, you must rely on God, focus, and *do* it! Always give thanks to God for any success you have.

In order to focus, you will have to say no to many other things—including some things you want to say yes to. Always remember that God promises to give us the desires of our heart if we will delight ourselves in Him (Psalm 37:4). Even if you have to let go of something you would like to have or do, God is able to replace it with something better than you could imagine.

The world is filled with dissatisfied, unfulfilled people, and I suspect it is due to them either not having a relationship with God or not giving themselves to what they were meant to do. God has given each of us gifts and abilities, and it fills us with joy when we nourish and develop these gifts. They enable us to do His will.

So, I encourage you to find out what God's will is for you, and focus on it with everything you have.

PRAYER FOR TODAY: *God, give me the power to focus on the present moment and the things You have called me to do in this world. Help me maintain that focus! And give me the strength to say no to the things that aren't mine to do or to have. Amen.*

DAY 60
SET YOUR MIND ON THE RIGHT DIRECTION

For those who are according to the flesh and are controlled by its unholy desires set their minds on and pursue those things which gratify the flesh, but those who are according to the Spirit and are controlled by the desires of the Spirit set their minds on and seek those things which gratify the [Holy] Spirit.

ROMANS 8:5

Paul wrote to the Romans and told them to set their minds on and seek those things that gratify the Spirit (Romans 8:5). We must first set our minds on the right direction before we can go in the right direction. Focus requires that we set our minds and keep them set on what is important to us at any given time. Distractions are abundant. The devil uses them to keep us from bearing good fruit and being fulfilled, but with God's help and some determination, we can focus.

Try to get to your main priorities while your mind is fresh and not filled with too many other things. We each have only a certain amount of energy for any given day, and if we divide it among too many things, we end up giving a weak effort to everything instead of a focused and creative effort to the main things.

Don't be discouraged if you frequently find that you have allowed your priorities to get out of line—just refocus and get back on track. Be determined to finish the things you start and give yourself to what you truly want to do.

PRAYER FOR TODAY: *God, help me set my mind and keep it set on the right direction. When I get distracted, remind me of Your grace so I can simply refocus and get back on track quickly. Thank You for Your amazing grace! Amen.*

DAY 61: EXPOSURE TO THE LIGHT

For once you were darkness, but now you are light in the Lord; walk as children of Light [lead the lives of those native-born to the Light].
EPHESIANS 5:8

My exercise coach is a very enjoyable, positive, encouraging person, and I always look forward to seeing him. His attitude makes the entire experience of working out pleasant. Even though the exercises themselves are usually difficult, he makes me feel like I am amazingly strong through his positive comments to me.

Like my coach does for me, one of the best ways we can minister to people is going out in the world and being positive, joyful influences on them. But in order to have a positive effect on people, we need to be positive people ourselves!

If you realize your mind is constantly filled with negative thoughts, an easy way to start changing your mind is to avoid spending excessive time with other negative people and to spend generous amounts of time with positive, hopeful people. The best way to get rid of darkness is to expose it to the light. Dave was a light to me when I was stuck in a rut of negativity, and his joy eventually made me hungry for a change in my own behavior.

Don't accept the lie that you can't be happy because you have too many problems. If anyone can be happy, you can be happy, because God's promises are for anyone who will believe them and receive them by faith.

PRAYER FOR TODAY: *God, I believe that I am to be happy! I have much to be thankful for. I ask you to bring positive people into my life to encourage me. Allow me to be a light to those still stuck in darkness. Amen.*

DAY 62
CALL BACK A WANDERING MIND

Keep your foot [give your mind to what you are doing] when you go [as Jacob to sacred Bethel] to the house of God. For to draw near to hear and obey is better than to give the sacrifice of fools [carelessly, irreverently] too ignorant to know that they are doing evil.

ECCLESIASTES 5:1

The writer of Ecclesiastes said we are to give our minds to what we are doing (Ecclesiastes 5:1). I don't know about you, but my mind has a tendency to wander, so I have to keep calling it back to what is at hand.

I think we often get sidetracked because we want to be involved in everything that is going on. We don't want to miss anything! But we simply cannot do everything. We must choose what God has asked us to focus on, because the more we allow our minds to run wild, the wilder they will become. However, they can be trained to focus with some diligent effort.

You will never control your thoughts if you don't believe that you can. At any moment, you can stop thinking about something you don't want to think about and start thinking about something you want to think about. I tell people, "If you don't want to think about something, then think about something else!"

Discipline is our friend, not our enemy. Learn to discipline your mind and practice focusing. It may take time and effort, but once you gain a measure of success, you will find life much easier and more fulfilling.

PRAYER FOR TODAY: *God, I know that You have given me the power to think about what I want to think about. Call to my attention when my mind is wandering so that I can bring it back to what's important. Amen.*

DAY 63

POSITIVE SELF-TALK

Even as [in His love] He chose us [actually picked us out for Himself as His own] in Christ before the foundation of the world, that we should be holy (consecrated and set apart for Him) and blameless in His sight, even above reproach, before Him in love.

EPHESIANS 1:4

It is God's will for you to love yourself in a healthy, balanced way. If you dislike and disrespect yourself, your self-talk will be negative and devastating to your spiritual growth and progress in spiritual maturity. We shouldn't be in love with ourselves or be the center of our universe, but we must maintain a healthy self-image. This is only possible by personally knowing the love of God, as well as His grace, forgiveness, mercy, and long-suffering kindness.

Are you kind to yourself? Do you say nice things about you to yourself, or are you more inclined to meditate on all of your faults? If we want to walk with God, we need to learn to think like God thinks. What does God think of you? He thinks you are awesome and that you have great possibilities. He is not blind to our faults, but He looks at them in light of our entire lives and not as just one event in which we didn't behave well. If you love God, that is the most important thing to Him, and love covers a multitude of sins (1 Peter 4:8). Don't focus on your faults—because God doesn't, either. I can assure you that there is more right with you than there is wrong, but perhaps you have never taken the time to see it.

PRAYER FOR TODAY: *God, thank You for Your endless grace and mercy! Help me have that same grace and mercy for myself so I can love the person You have created me to be, the person that I am in the process of becoming through Christ. Amen.*

DAY 64
RIGHT THINKING PREPARES US FOR RIGHT ACTION

God made him who had no sin to be sin for us, so that in him we might become the righteousness of God.

2 CORINTHIANS 5:21 NIV

We can prepare ourselves for right action by practicing right thinking. I recommend spending a few minutes every day in thought about how merciful God is to you, and then plan to be merciful to others.

Here are some things that God says about you in His Word:

- You are a new creature in Christ (2 Corinthians 5:17).
- Jesus has made you the righteousness of God in Him (2 Corinthians 5:21).
- You have the mind of Christ (1 Corinthians 2:16).
- God has accepted you, and He will never reject you (John 6:37).
- You are forgiven and your sins forgotten (Hebrews 10:17).
- God created you, and everything He created is good (Genesis 1:31).

God views us as being right with Him through Jesus Christ. It is His will for us to think good things about ourselves. This, in turn, helps us treat others better also.

PRAYER FOR TODAY: *God, I am so grateful for Your mercy and love! Help me pour out that mercy and love on others. Because You created me, the good in me is bigger than my faults. Thank you for giving me right-standing through Your Son, Jesus Christ. Amen.*

DAY 65

DON'T "WAIT AND SEE"

Those who trust in themselves are fools, but those who walk in wisdom are kept safe.

PROVERBS 28:26 NIV

When you wake up each morning, do you wait to see how you feel before you decide what you will do? If so, you won't end up doing much of what you should do.

If I waited until I woke up in the morning to decide if I was going to go to the gym to exercise, there would be many times I would decide I didn't feel like it. But because I determine ahead of time that I will get up and go and I don't even ask myself how I feel about it, I always go when I say I will go.

God gave us free will so that we can decide ahead of time to do what we know we should do, regardless of how we think or feel in the moment.

Emotions are part of being human, but we don't have to let them set the tone for our days. We don't have to let our feelings lead us toward unhealthy and unwise decisions. We can choose to think right thoughts. We can choose to make a plan and stick to it, regardless of how we feel. We can determine to enjoy each day no matter what comes our way. The best way to defeat the devil is to remain stable at all times, and that requires right thinking.

PRAYER FOR TODAY: *God, I want to follow You and Your plan for my life. Help me to acknowledge my feelings but to not use them as a guide for my day. I ask for Your strength and wisdom to determine ahead of time how to spend my time so I can enjoy my day no matter what surprises come my way! Amen.*

DAY 66
YOU ARE LOVED AND ACCEPTED

But God shows and clearly proves His [own] love for us by the fact that while we were still sinners, Christ (the Messiah, the Anointed One) died for us.

ROMANS 5:8

God wants us to feel loved and accepted. This is why His Word includes so many scriptures that remind us of His unconditional love for us. According to Romans 5:8, while we were still sinners and before we cared anything about God, He sent His Son to die for us, to pay the price for our sins, and to make a way for us to live in close fellowship with Him. Later, in Romans 8:35–39, we are told that nothing—*nothing*—can separate us from the love of God.

I challenge you to believe that God loves and accepts you completely, that He thinks highly of you, and that you are rightly related to Him through Christ. Think a positive thought about yourself today or speak a positive word about yourself based on how God feels about you. I'm not talking about being prideful, but I am encouraging you to be bold enough to believe you really are who God says you are.

David says to God in Psalm 139:14, "I am fearfully and wonderfully made" (ESV). It may be difficult to believe such positive words about yourself, but I hope and pray that you will believe them for yourself, because they are true!

PRAYER FOR TODAY: *God, thank You for loving me. Show me how to accept and live in Your unconditional love and to see myself the way You see me. Amen.*

DAY 67
TALKING ABOUT OUR FEELINGS

The one who has knowledge uses words with restraint, and whoever has understanding is even-tempered.

PROVERBS 17:27 NIV

People tend to talk a lot about how they feel. Some talk about their feelings more than almost anything else. They may feel good or bad, happy or sad, excited or discouraged, fearful or bold, stressed or at ease, loved or unloved, angry or peaceful—sometimes all in the same day!

Do you have a tendency to share how you feel with anyone who will listen? I've noticed that we often say much more about our negative feelings than our positive ones. If I wake up feeling energetic and excited about the day, I rarely announce it. But if I feel tired and discouraged, I want to tell everyone. It has taken me years to learn that talking about how I feel increases the intensity and duration of those feelings, so it seems to me that we should talk about our positive feelings and not dwell on our negative feelings.

We can always tell God how we feel and ask for His help and strength—He's our Father and Friend in every situation. But talking about and rehashing negative feelings with others only increases the power those feelings have over us. If negative feelings persist, asking for prayer or seeking advice can be helpful, but I want to stress that talking about it just to talk about it is not productive. Even if you say, "I feel tired," you can follow it with "but I believe God will energize me." When you talk about how you feel, use your words to speak positively.

PRAYER FOR TODAY: *God, I don't want my negative feelings to last any longer than they have to, so help me talk sparingly about them and focus instead on my positive feelings so that they will fuel my day. Amen.*

DAY 68

THOUGHTFUL THINKING

The thoughts of the [steadily] diligent tend only to plenteousness, but everyone who is impatient and hasty hastens only to want.
PROVERBS 21:5

Have you ever done or said something that caused you to say something like "I'm sorry; I just wasn't thinking"?

We've all done things without thinking about the consequences, and those things almost always bring pain and destruction to others or ourselves. We might make commitments without serious consideration that cause us to fail someone else or make purchases without consulting our budgets. Maybe we say something without thinking that hurts someone and even ruins their day. We might practice mindless eating, causing damage to our health. Such thoughtless acts aren't necessarily good or evil; they are just thought*less* instead of thought*ful*!

Our lives would be so much better if we formed habits of thinking before speaking or taking action. Proverbs says, "Wise people think before they act" (13:16 NLT) and "the mind of the wise instructs his mouth" (16:23). I imagine it will take a lifetime of continued discipline to ever accomplish this completely, but we can start moving in the right direction today. Slow down and ask God for His wisdom each day so that we can be thoughtful thinkers.

PRAYER FOR TODAY: *God, I'm confident Your plan for me is to be a thoughtful thinker. Thank You for giving me the free will to choose my thoughts. Help me to exercise that will and to think about what I am thinking about before I say or do something! Amen.*

DAY 69

GRACE FOR TODAY

Give us this day our daily bread.

MATTHEW 6:11

I have noticed that when I look at my calendar to see what I have scheduled for the month, I have to battle against feeling pressured and irritated. That's because when I look at all I have to do in one huge lump, it seems impossible! Instead, I should be trusting God to give me His strength and ability to do the thing He has called me to do one day at a time.

If you give yourself over to worry and reasoning, your thoughts may sound like this: *How am I going to do everything I have to do? My life is impossible! This is more than I can handle.* Instead of worrying about the future, you could think things like *God loves me, and He will take care of everything in my future. He will give me the strength and ability to do each thing I need to do as it comes up.*

When we trust Him, God gives us grace daily to do the things we need to do, but He doesn't give us grace to put in the bank, so to speak. When we worry about things that haven't taken place yet, we are on our own. God gives us grace only for today so we can fully live and enjoy today while trusting Him completely for the future.

PRAYER FOR TODAY: *God, I need Your grace for every area of my life. Help me trust You to not worry about tomorrow so that I can enjoy today. Amen.*

DAY 70
WORRYING, WANDERING, AND WONDERING

You keep him in perfect peace whose mind is stayed on you, because he trusts in you.

ISAIAH 26:3 ESV

When we worry, it's often because we've let our minds wander around from the past to the present to the future. When we wonder about what is going to happen to us or feel guilt or shame about the past, we lose our peace. God intends for us to keep our minds on the present.

I don't mean to say that we never take time to learn from the past or to make plans for the future. But when we do, it should be something we do purposely and with God's help.

The prophet Isaiah said that God would keep us in perfect peace when our minds are fixed on Him: "You will guard him and keep him in perfect and constant peace whose mind [both its inclination and its character] is stayed on You, because he commits himself to You, leans on You, and hopes confidently in You (Isaiah 26:3).

Do you want to be peaceful, guarded by God, and satisfied? Then begin with the thoughts that you choose to think. Don't let your mind wander off to worry. Trust God and choose your thoughts today according to His promises for you.

PRAYER FOR TODAY: *God, when I begin to worry, wander, or wonder, help me bring my thoughts back to You and the perfect plan You have for my life. I ask for the perfect peace that comes from fixing my mind on You. Amen.*

DAY 71
BE THOUGHTFUL ABOUT YOUR DAY

Therefore encourage and comfort one another and build up one another, just as you are doing.

1 THESSALONIANS 5:11 AMP

Our thoughts affect the way we relate to people and the world around us, so it's helpful to take time to think through your day before you begin it.

I like to start my day writing, while my mind is fresh and creative. During that time, I need quiet so that I can focus and so I don't get involved in other things.

My afternoons usually involve meetings or appointments. When I go out, I plan to be friendly with and compliment the people I come in contact with. It is wise to be thoughtful, because everyone we meet is probably fighting some kind of battle.

After my business is complete, I spend time with Dave, and I ask him about his day. We might go to dinner. If we go with other people, I want to be thoughtful and interested in what they are doing in their lives. When I am with people, I plan to make them feel important, and one of the ways I can do that is to show genuine interest in them.

Being thoughtful about the scheduled parts of my day helps me behave in a way that pleases God. Things will happen that I am not planning, but I intend to respond calmly to those things. Being thoughtful about people and events will help you enjoy your day.

PRAYER FOR TODAY: *God, I don't know everything this day will hold, but You do. Help me be thoughtful about how I behave and react. Open my eyes to other people and their needs so I can lift their spirits and be a blessing to those I encounter. Amen.*

DAY 72

GOOD IDEAS

May the Lord make your love increase and overflow for each other and for everyone else, just as ours does for you.
1 THESSALONIANS 3:12 NIV

I believe God gives all of us good ideas of ways we can bless others, but it's up to us to hang on to those thoughts long enough to take action. For example, I think God puts people on our minds frequently when He wants us to call them or write them a note of encouragement because He knows they need it even if we don't. But how often do we get busy doing other things and never get around to making the call or writing the letter?

When good things come into your mind, keep them and ask God if you need to take action on them. When bad things come into your mind, reject them as soon as you recognize them, because they are not going to help you or anyone else.

When you have a thought about being a blessing to someone else that is immediately followed by a bad thought discouraging you from doing it, that's the devil trying to stop you.

Have you ever had the Holy Spirit nudge you to buy someone else's meal at a restaurant or in the drive-thru, but you pushed the thought down, thinking that you would look silly? That is the devil trying to stop you from being a blessing!

Let's be committed to taking hold of the good ideas that God gives us to be a blessing to others.

PRAYER FOR TODAY: *God, fill my mind with good ideas on how to be a blessing to others, and give me the fortitude to follow through. If any thoughts come up to try to discourage me from being a blessing, help me cast them down immediately. Amen.*

DAY 73
SEE WHAT GOD SEES

I have told you these things, so that in Me you may have [perfect] peace and confidence. In the world you have tribulation and trials and distress and frustration; but be of good cheer [take courage; be confident, certain, undaunted]! For I have overcome the world. [I have deprived it of power to harm you and have conquered it for you.]

JOHN 16:33

When circumstances are bad, focusing on them and saying negative things about already negative situations doesn't increase our personal joy or anyone else's.

Jesus teaches us by word and example to be positive about the problems of life. Jesus said that in the world we would have tribulation but we should cheer up because He has overcome the world (John 16:33).

When the disciples were in a severe storm and Jesus was asleep in the boat, they became very frightened and were focused only on the storm. But Jesus rebuked them for their lack of faith, and He asked them why they were upset since He was with them (Mark 4:36–40). Jesus wanted them to see Him as greater than the storm.

When we see problems, the Lord sees possibilities. When we see messes, He sees miracles. When we see endings, He sees new beginnings.

Our attitudes can make our problems harder to deal with or easier—it is up to us.

PRAYER FOR TODAY: *God, give me eyes to see how You see. Help me see possibilities instead of problems, miracles instead of messes, new beginnings instead of endings. Amen.*

DAY 74: THE MIND IS A BATTLEFIELD

For the weapons of our warfare are not physical [weapons of flesh and blood], but they are mighty before God.

2 CORINTHIANS 10:4

The devil is alive and active on earth, and we need to be aware of him so we can learn how to deal with him aggressively. The basic truth is that the devil is a liar, and he uses our minds as battlefields to do warfare with us. He is the source of dark and harmful thoughts.

Scripture says in 2 Corinthians 10:3–5 that though we live in the world, we don't fight with human weapons, and the enemies we capture are wrong thoughts put there in our minds by the devil.

We see from these verses that we are definitely in a spiritual war with the devil, who tries to control our thoughts. Thoughts cannot be seen, but we do see the results of them. Since we can't see them, it's easy to forget just how powerful they are. We tend to ignore what we cannot see, and yet God's Word teaches as much, or more, about the unseen spiritual realm as it does the seen natural realm.

The good news is that God has given us power and authority to deal with the devil, but it is up to us to take ownership of our thoughts and recognize where they are coming from so that we can either accept or reject them.

PRAYER FOR TODAY: *God, You have given me the power and authority to take captive wrong thoughts and to replace them with right thoughts. Today, help me choose to exercise that power and cast down anything that the devil puts in my head. Amen.*

DAY 75

BITTER OR BETTER

As for you, you thought evil against me, but God meant it for good, to bring about that many people should be kept alive, as they are this day.

GENESIS 50:20

Since our perspectives involve our thought processes, we would be wise to realize that they also affect our moods. If I am in a bad mood, I may need a perspective adjustment. Perhaps I am looking too much at what I don't have and not enough at what I do have. Or I may be looking at what people don't do for me instead of what they do for me. Our perspective on anything, especially events and people we don't like, have long-range effects. How we view events that took place as far back as our childhoods may still be negatively affecting us. If you were abused in any way, trust God to work good out of it instead of feeling angry and bitter or holding on to unforgiveness.

When I learned to think of the abuse in my childhood as something that was unfortunate but could be used by God for good, the pain began to lessen, and I began to heal emotionally.

If you are dealing with a broken heart or a wounded soul, try asking God to help you make a connection between your perspective and your current feelings. If you are willing to change the way you view the situation, you will begin to make progress toward wholeness instead of remaining broken. Life breaks all of us in one way or another, and it is up to us whether we remain broken and bitter or we let God use it to make us better and more like Him.

PRAYER FOR TODAY: *God, I cannot do anything about the past, but I can choose to not let it affect my future any longer. Change my perspective, heal my soul, and rid me of my bad moods! Amen.*

DAY 76

COUNT IT ALL JOY

Consider it a sheer gift, friends, when tests and challenges come at you from all sides. You know that under pressure, your faith-life is forced into the open and shows its true colors. So don't try to get out of anything prematurely. Let it do its work so you become mature and well-developed, not deficient in any way.

JAMES 1:2–4 MSG

James 1:2 says, "*Count it all joy*, my brothers, when you meet trials of various kinds" (ESV, emphasis mine). Notice that James doesn't say "*feel* joyful" when trials come. He says to "count it all joy." What does that mean exactly? That means you can set your mind in the right direction and believe that everything is going to work out for your good, no matter how much you dislike it in the moment.

God is good, and He promises that He will work everything out for our good—*if* we keep good attitudes and continue trusting God.

I don't believe that God does bad things to us. But I do believe that sometimes He doesn't get us out of bad situations as fast as we would like because He's a loving parent who wants us to learn something—and I mean *really* learn it—so He doesn't have to keep teaching it to us again and again. God doesn't cause our problems, but He will use them to our benefit.

God wants us to get to the point where we trust Him no matter what and keep our joy regardless of our circumstances. Joy gives us strength, and the devil always wants to take it away from us.

PRAYER FOR TODAY: *God, thank You for working all things together for my good. Help me trust You in this temporary trial and not lose my joy over it. Amen.*

DAY 77
DON'T TAKE GOD'S BLESSINGS FOR GRANTED

Enter into His gates with thanksgiving and a thank offering and into His courts with praise! Be thankful and say so to Him, bless and affectionately praise His name!

PSALM 100:4

If there's anything we all need as human beings, it's to learn to stay thankful and not start taking God's blessings for granted.

Take work, for example. Maybe you prayed and prayed for a job, and God answered. Let's say you got a job working for Joyce Meyer Ministries. But then you find out that not only do you have to work, but you have to work hard, you have to show up on time, and you can't waste time playing computer games or being on social media all day. In fact, we have a higher standard of accountability, excellence, and integrity than many other workplaces out in the world.

Now, this thing you counted such a blessing a little while ago presents some challenges for you, and maybe you start to complain about it. But it's the thing you prayed for! It's an answered prayer! That's what I mean by staying thankful and not taking God's blessings for granted. God is more interested in our spiritual growth than in our comfort and convenience.

The truth is, there is plenty we could choose to complain about, but as Christians we can choose to have a different, eternal perspective. The life we have here on earth is very short compared to eternity, so we can choose to enjoy the journey and make a positive impact before we get to our eternal home in heaven.

PRAYER FOR TODAY: *God, I don't want to complain about the things I prayed for. Help me to be forever grateful for all of the blessings in my life and especially to never forget to thank You for those things that are an answer to prayer. Amen.*

DAY 78
IT'S NOT MY FAULT... OR IS IT?

So then each of us will give an account of himself to God.
ROMANS 14:12 ESV

Like lots of other people, I used to suffer from what I call the "it's not my fault" mindset. I blamed other people for my bad behavior because of the abuse I suffered when I was growing up. Eventually, I realized that even though I wasn't responsible for what happened to me, I was responsible for my behavior after I became a Christian.

We see this over and over again in the Bible. Adam ate the fruit in the garden, but when God asked him about it, Adam said, "The woman *you* gave me, she gave me the fruit, and I ate it" (Genesis 3:12, paraphrased). *Eve gave me the fruit, and You gave me Eve, so it's not my fault!*

Eve had the same wrong mindset. She blamed the serpent for tempting her instead of owning up to her own free will to choose (Genesis 3:13). Temptation will always be part of life, but we should grow to the level of maturity where we can be tempted and not give in to the flesh.

The Bible says that every person will stand before God and give an account of their life. God will never ask you to give an account for somebody else, and He will never ask somebody else to give an account for you. We each have to take responsibility for our own life and ask God to help us make the right choices.

PRAYER FOR TODAY: *God, I am responsible for my own behavior, but I can't do it all on my own. I'm asking for Your help with every decision, every action, and every word that I speak. When I fall short, help me repent and call on Your strength to help me make better choices. Amen.*

DAY 79: IF YOU CAN'T HELP YOURSELF, HELP SOMEONE ELSE

So if the Son liberates you [makes you free men], then you are really and unquestionably free.

JOHN 8:36

Something that has always amazed me is that when we're in seasons where we can't seem to help ourselves, that's when God anoints (enables) us to help somebody else. That's because helping somebody else while we're hurting can eventually bring our own breakthroughs.

Even though we know this in our minds, it is still hard! Getting out of that "what about me?" mindset is hard. But it is worth it! As long as we are feeling sorry for ourselves, we will never get past the hurt. You will start to feel better only when you get your mind off your situation and do something for someone else.

I remember, in the early years of our marriage, Dave infuriated me because he refused to feel sorry for me. I would be storming around, cleaning the house loudly, and instead of giving in to my bad behavior, Dave would ask me to make him tea if I was on my way to the kitchen. Ha! He showed me that the only way I was going to feel better was by turning over whatever was going on with me to God.

We may think we have every reason to feel sorry for ourselves, but God says that's not true because He is willing to set us free. And that starts by helping someone else or working on a project that will get your mind off of your problem.

PRAYER FOR TODAY: *God, I'm tired of feeling sorry for myself. Use me to help someone else today. While I am helping others, I will trust You for my breakthrough. Amen.*

DAY 80: GOD'S BLESSINGS ARE FREE

If the Lord delights in us, then He will bring us into this land and give it to us, a land flowing with milk and honey.

NUMBERS 14:8

Sometimes people don't receive God's blessings because they think they don't deserve them. This belief isn't entirely wrong—we don't deserve them! But Jesus died so that we could receive His grace as a free gift. You can't earn a gift. People who try to earn God's grace are constantly in works of the flesh and wear themselves out because it's impossible to do enough in our own strength to earn what He has freely given.

This attitude came into play when Moses sent the twelve spies into the Promised Land (Numbers 13–14). Ten of those spies had a poor self-image. They saw the land flowing with milk and honey, but they saw themselves as small and incapable of taking what was rightfully theirs. But two of the spies, Joshua and Caleb, knew it was possible simply because God had promised it to them. It was His free gift to His chosen people. They didn't deserve it, they hadn't earned it, and they couldn't take it on their own—but it was theirs because He said it was.

God doesn't choose us and bless us because we're wonderful or perfect or lovable. But you can have a wonderful, amazing life, not because you're good, but because God is good and He delights in you.

PRAYER FOR TODAY: *God, I don't deserve all of the amazing blessings You have given me, and I am so thankful You give them anyway. When I feel incapable or unworthy, help me remember that You are good and strong on my behalf. Amen.*

DAY 81
AN ATTITUDE GOD LOVES

But the Scriptures [picture all mankind as sinners] shut up and imprisoned by sin, so that [the inheritance, blessing] which was promised through faith in Jesus Christ (the Messiah) might be given (released, delivered, and committed) to [all] those who believe [who adhere to and trust in and rely on Him].

GALATIANS 3:22

Genesis tells the story of twin boys, Jacob and Esau. Esau was the firstborn, so he was entitled to a double portion of the inheritance. But one day, Jacob took advantage of his brother at a time when he was hungry and convinced Esau to give him his birthright for a bowl of stew. After that, Jacob fled in fear of Esau's wrath.

Years later, Jacob decided to go home and face what he had done. Scripture says that he sent his family across the stream and spent the night alone. Sometimes you have to be willing to walk away from everything you have and seek God wholeheartedly.

Jacob wrestled all night with the angel of the Lord. That night, Jacob's hip was put out of joint, and he forever walked with a limp after that. When morning came, the angel said, "Let me go!" He was done wrestling. But Jacob said, "I will not let you go unless you bless me" (Genesis 32:26 ESV).

God honors those who seek Him with persistence and faith. This is an attitude that says, *I am going to press on based on the Word, not based on my performance.* Jacob had this attitude and he ended up blessed.

PRAYER FOR TODAY: *God, I believe what Your Word says, therefore I will receive in faith all that You have promised me. Remind me of Your promises today so I can boldly accept Your blessings. Amen.*

DAY 82 — SOW AND SEE

So shall My word be that goes forth from My mouth; it shall not return to Me void, but it shall accomplish what I please, and it shall prosper in the thing for which I sent it.

ISAIAH 55:11 NKJV

I think it's relatively easy for people to believe that God's Word is powerful. However, we often forget that we are God's representatives here on earth, and we can speak His Word just as He would—boldly, with authority, and believing it has power to change lives and circumstances.

Isaiah 55:10–11 shares a powerful principle about God's Word:

> For as the rain and snow come down from the heavens, and return not there again, but water the earth and make it bring forth and sprout, that it may give seed to the sower and bread to the eater, so shall My word be that goes forth out of My mouth: it shall not return to Me void [without producing any effect, useless], but it shall accomplish that which I please and purpose, and it shall prosper in the thing for which I sent it.

Isaiah teaches us that the Word of God will not return void. In other words, it accomplishes what it was sent to do! Proclaim the truth of God's Word today and walk in the boldness only God can give.

PRAYER FOR TODAY: *God, I believe that Your Word is powerful. It truly changes hearts and lives. Help me use the boldness and authority You've given me to proclaim Your Word. Amen.*

DAY 83: SAY WHAT GOD SAYS

A man's [moral] self shall be filled with the fruit of his mouth; and with the consequence of his words he must be satisfied [whether good or evil].

PROVERBS 18:20

Confession means "to say the same thing as." It's so important for us to say what God says: to speak His Word, not what our feelings, other people, or our circumstances are telling us.

When I first began learning these principles, I was terribly negative. I was a Christian and I loved God, but I didn't know I could do anything about my circumstances. God began teaching me that I should not think and say negative things, because a negative person cannot be happy. As I took action to stop speaking negatively, I became happier.

After a while, however, I felt like my circumstances really weren't that different. I asked the Lord about it, and He spoke to my heart and said, "You have stopped talking negative, but you are not saying anything positive."

So, I started making a list of the things that were rightfully mine according to the Word of God. I confessed the truth of His Word out loud twice a day. My faith increased, and I started seeing positive changes! Change does not always come quickly, but little by little it will come if we don't lose heart.

PRAYER FOR TODAY: *God, I have the right to declare Your Word over my life, and I want to choose to do that in all circumstances. When a negative thought comes, give me the courage to intentionally replace it with a truth from Your Word. Amen.*

DAY 84: CONSISTENT CONFESSION

Do two walk together except they make an appointment and have agreed?

AMOS 3:3

Consistent confession is so important! When you hear *confession*, you might think of confession of sin (which is also important!), but I'm talking about confessing the Word of God in every situation. I encourage you to become God's mouthpiece and confess the Word of God out loud *throughout the day* as the Holy Spirit prompts you.

Can we confess things that we can't find a chapter and verse for? Yes, I believe we can, if we are reasonably sure that we're declaring God's will for our lives and not just what we want.

While the Bible may not specifically mention our exact situations, it does contain wisdom and direction for every area of our lives—health, finances, work, family, relationships, and so on. That is one reason why it's so valuable to read, study, and know what God's Word says.

I have kept a list of confessions that I have made over the years, and it absolutely amazes me how many of the things that I wrote and confessed have come to pass—things that seemed impossible at the time! And so much of it has to do with getting in agreement with God and consistently confessing His will over my life. We cannot walk with God concerning His plan for our lives unless we are willing to agree with Him—in our hearts and with our words. Start saying the same thing God says in His Word, and get ready to see exciting changes.

PRAYER FOR TODAY: *God, I believe in the importance of speaking Your Word. Thank You for caring about the situation I am in and for giving me Your Word for wisdom and direction. Help me to seek Your will and to consistently confess it over my life. Amen.*

DAY 85: PERSPECTIVE AND POWER

For God did not give us a spirit of timidity (of cowardice, of craven and cringing and fawning fear), but [He has given us a spirit] of power and of love and of calm and well-balanced mind and discipline and self-control.

2 TIMOTHY 1:7

The apostle Paul suffered greatly during his years of ministry. He was beaten and imprisoned for no crime other than believing in Jesus Christ and encouraging others to do the same. Look at what he writes in 2 Corinthians 4:

> We are hedged in (pressed) on every side [troubled and oppressed in every way], *but not cramped or crushed*; we suffer embarrassments and are perplexed and unable to find a way out, *but not driven to despair*. We are pursued (persecuted and hard driven), *but not deserted* [to stand alone]; we are struck down to the ground, *but never struck out and destroyed*.
>
> 2 Corinthians 4:8–9 (emphasis mine)

It doesn't sound like Paul's circumstances could have been much worse, and yet we see a glimmer of hope and refusal to cave in to a negative mindset.

We should not deny our circumstances, but neither should we give them permission to control our attitudes and behavior. God has given each of us the ability to live above our circumstances if we choose to have a positive perspective.

PRAYER FOR TODAY: *God, thank You for giving me the power to cling to hope regardless of my circumstances. I am determined to keep a positive attitude no matter what comes my way. Amen.*

DAY 86: TWO TYPES OF FAITH

Therefore we do not become discouraged (utterly spiritless, exhausted, and wearied out through fear). Though our outer man is [progressively] decaying and wasting away, yet our inner self is being [progressively] renewed day after day.

2 CORINTHIANS 4:16

I often say that I have had two types of faith in my life, and I believe we need both of them. One is the type of faith that asks for and receives an immediate pleasurable answer. God delivers quickly and miraculously, and we get very excited. The second type of faith is one that doesn't receive the answer it had hoped for but continues to believe anyway that God is good and is working in ways that cannot yet be seen. Although not as emotionally exciting, it is my personal opinion that the second type of faith is the greater faith.

We don't get to choose which way God will work. At times, He delivers us from something difficult, and at other times, He gives us grace to endure it with good attitudes. What God does or does not allow us to go through is His decision, and His alone, because He knows and understands things we don't.

When we are going through something, it may make no sense at all. Yet later on, we can look back and clearly understand that God's choice was better for us than what we would have chosen. There is also the possibility that we will never understand. But even then, the heart of faith bows in worship, knowing that trust requires understanding that we may always have some unanswered questions while still believing that God's ways are perfect.

PRAYER FOR TODAY: *God, I trust You. Help me trust You always—when my prayers are immediately answered and even when You determine I need to wait. Amen.*

DAY 87: THE BENEFITS OF WORDS

With the tongue we praise our Lord and Father, and with it we curse human beings, who have been made in God's likeness.
JAMES 3:9 NIV

God has given us the ability to bless, encourage, praise, sing, and worship with our words.

But our mouths can get us into trouble. For years, I struggled with not controlling my words, creating havoc in my life and the lives of those around me. If you struggle in this area as well, be encouraged, for there is freedom. This is what the Bible has to say about our mouths:

> But the human tongue can be tamed by no man. It is a restless (undisciplined, irreconcilable) evil, full of deadly poison. With it we bless the Lord and Father, and with it we curse men who were made in God's likeness!
> James 3:8–9

Our words can do severe damage to our relationships, our careers, and our circumstances in life. But with the help of the Holy Spirit, they can also do great good.

Relationships can be restored through words. Careers can accelerate when we choose positive and encouraging words. The world around us can benefit from the words we speak and the ones God helps us not to speak. You've only got one mouth, so be sure to use it to do great good!

PRAYER FOR TODAY: *God, I am accountable for the words that I speak, but I cannot control my tongue on my own. I need Your help! Give me wisdom in using my words for great good. Amen.*

DAY 88: SOUL RESTORATION

Therefore if any person is [ingrafted] in Christ (the Messiah) he is a new creation (a new creature altogether); the old [previous moral and spiritual condition] has passed away. Behold, the fresh and new has come!
2 CORINTHIANS 5:17

God is in the business of restoration! And as believers in Jesus Christ, we are in the process of restoration. Scripture even describes the "new you" that is being created (2 Corinthians 5:17).

I remember when I desperately needed to recover from the sexual and verbal abuse from my past. I had thought that when I was old enough to leave home, I would leave the pain behind, but the problem was in my soul—my mind, will, and emotions. I needed healing and restoration so I wouldn't continue to be poisoned by things that had happened to me all those years when I was growing up.

I came to this realization after a woman came to speak at our church and shared her testimony of how she had been abused and God had healed her. My husband, Dave, bought her book for me, and when I started to read it, it was so painful that I threw it across the room and refused to pick it up.

But then I clearly heard the Holy Spirit speak to my heart: "It's time, Joyce." God had a much better life for me than what I had known up to that point, and He wanted to restore my soul so I could experience it—and He wants to do the same for you! I had to face it to get past it, and although it was painful, it was worth it.

PRAYER FOR TODAY: *God, I believe You are saying "It's time." Give me the strength and power to walk in the fullness of life that You have for me. Thank You for walking through this process of restoration with me and making me new. Amen.*

DAY 89: DOUBLE FOR YOUR TROUBLE

Instead of your [former] shame you shall have a twofold recompense; instead of dishonor and reproach [your people] shall rejoice in their portion. Therefore in their land they shall possess double [what they had forfeited]; everlasting joy shall be theirs.

ISAIAH 61:7

Isaiah 61:7 says, "Instead of your shame you will receive a double portion" (NIV). God can completely restore us—no matter what we've done or been through. And He wants to bring us to places that are better than where we would have been if we had never gone through the messes in our lives. He wants to give us double for our trouble!

Notice the phrase "instead of your shame." I had a shame-based nature for many years because of the abuse I experienced from my father. It made me feel like something must be wrong with me for him to do the things he did to me.

But the first thing Jesus gives us through our relationships with Him is righteousness, or "right standing with God" (2 Corinthians 5:21). The enemy wants us to think about everything we think is wrong with us. But when we do this, it just gives our problems more strength over us.

We need to learn how to "walk by the Spirit," because then we will "not gratify the desires of the flesh" (Galatians 5:16 ESV). This is what it means to be transformed into the image of Christ. And while it's not always easy, we can do it with God's help, and I guarantee it will be worth it in the end.

PRAYER FOR TODAY: *God, You know what I have been through. We have been through it together. While I would be happy with complete restoration, You are a God Who goes above and beyond all I can imagine, so I trust that You will not only restore me, but give me double for my trouble. Amen.*

DAY 90

FULLY RESTORED

Restore to me the joy of Your salvation and uphold me with a willing spirit.

PSALM 51:12

When a person restores an old piece of furniture, the first thing they do is strip off the old layers of paint or varnish. When we start a restoration process with God, we all have things that need to be stripped away in our lives.

Maybe it's old attitudes and mindsets that don't line up with the way God thinks and acts, or maybe unhealthy relationships are holding you back. Whatever it is, you can pray, "Lord, strip me of everything that is hindering my walk with You."

Then there's the "sanding" process. Is there anyone in your life whose personality irritates you? They're like divine sandpaper that God uses to get the rough edges off of us; and after the sanding, there is "sealing." For us, that means we're sealed with the Holy Spirit, "marked, branded as God's own, secured" (Ephesians 4:30).

After all this, the furniture must be dusted and polished from time to time. God is always polishing my life in some area! When the Holy Spirit convicts us of sin, He's polishing us and making us more like Christ.

Wherever you are in life, God is ready and able to restore you. And when He does, He won't simply repair what was broken; He will make you stronger, and better than before.

PRAYER FOR TODAY: *God, do what You need to do in my life to fully restore me. Strip me, sand me, seal me, and keep me polished so that I can have a life that is better than what I could imagine. Amen.*

DAY 91
SPIRIT, SOUL, BODY

May the God of peace Himself sanctify you through and through [separate you from profane things, make you pure and wholly consecrated to God]; and may your spirit and soul and body be preserved sound and complete [and found] blameless at the coming of our Lord Jesus Christ (the Messiah).

1 THESSALONIANS 5:23

God loves you, and He is interested in every single part of your life—not just the spiritual part. Just look at what 1 Thessalonians 5:23 says about this: "Now may the God of peace himself sanctify you completely, and may your whole spirit and soul and body be kept blameless at the coming of our Lord Jesus Christ" (ESV).

This verse clearly says that we can be sanctified completely, "wholly consecrated to God." God created us as tri-part beings: We are spirits, we have souls, and we live in bodies. Your spirit is the part of you that receives revelation from God, and your conscience functions through it. Your soul is made up of your mind, will, and emotions, and your body is the house you live in.

God wants every part of our lives to be healthy and whole. This is important, because if even one of those areas is unhealthy, we won't be able to fully enjoy the life Jesus came to give us. Not only does God want you to be spiritually sound—born again through a personal relationship with Jesus—but He also wants a life for you that's free from depression, anger, unforgiveness, and so on. He wants you to have peace and joy in your soul!

PRAYER FOR TODAY: *God, thank You for caring about every part of my life. I commit to You my soul, my spirit, and my body. Thank You for working in me to make me whole. Amen.*

DAY 92: HAVE AND ENJOY LIFE

For the Son of Man came to seek and to save that which was lost.
LUKE 19:10

John 10:10 is one of my favorite scriptures because it shows us the kind of lives God intends for us to have. It says that Jesus "came that they may have and enjoy life, and have it in abundance (to the full, till it overflows)."

I talk about this a lot because I used to be a miserable Christian who looked like I had it all together on the outside but was a big mess on the inside. And I've met a lot of other Christians who love God, but they don't love their lives.

The truth is, we don't have to settle for miserable lives, just hoping we can hold on until Jesus comes back to get us. Luke 19:10 says "the Son of Man came to seek and to save that which was lost." Notice it doesn't say "who" was lost but "that which was lost." Jesus wants to restore every part of our lives—spirits, souls, and bodies.

If your spirit is not right with God, the rest of you will never be fully right or be whole. And to be spiritually healthy, the first thing you need to do is receive Christ as your Savior. When you do, your spirit is made new, and God comes to dwell within you—making you His home.

PRAYER FOR TODAY: *God, come and live in my spirit! Since I am Your home, I want it to be a happy home, filled with joy in every area of my life. Help my thoughts to be happy, my mind to be joyful, my mood to be good, and my attitude to be positive! Amen.*

DAY 93
IT TAKES TIME

No one born (begotten) of God [deliberately, knowingly, and habitually] practices sin, for God's nature abides in him [His principle of life, the divine sperm, remains permanently within him]; and he cannot practice sinning because he is born (begotten) of God.
1 JOHN 3:9

When we surrender our lives to Christ—acknowledging Him as Lord, confessing our sins, and accepting His sacrifice (the blood He shed) as the payment needed to cleanse us from sin—the life of God is deposited in our spirits. We get new natures and new hearts, and we don't have the desire for ungodly or sinful things anymore because it's not in our God-given natures.

Developing the new Christlike nature that's planted in us like a seed takes time. It's like a pregnant woman: In the beginning, she's not showing right away. It takes months for the baby to grow so that you see the changes in the mother.

In a similar way, it takes time for us to grow spiritually until the life of God shows in our behavior. We must spend time with God in prayer, receiving His love, loving Him in return, worshipping Him, watering the seed of His life inside us by reading and confessing the Word, and letting the light of His love shine on us.

If we diligently seek God, eventually people will see God's characteristics in us—His love, joy, peace, and righteousness, and everything else He is.

PRAYER FOR TODAY: *God, thank You for the seed of new life planted within me. Help me water it with Your Word so that others can see You in me! Amen.*

DAY 94: TWO-EDGED SWORD

For the word of God is alive and active. Sharper than any double-edged sword, it penetrates even to dividing soul and spirit, joints and marrow; it judges the thoughts and attitudes of the heart.
HEBREWS 4:12 NIV

Feelings are fickle. They can be up one day and down the next. So when we're making decisions, we can't rely on our feelings to always steer us in the right direction. One of the greatest things we can ever do is ask ourselves: *What does God's Word say to do?*

It's easy to make decisions based on what we want, think, and feel, but we need to follow something much wiser and much more dependable: the Word of God.

Hebrews 4:12 says that God's Word is "sharper than any two-edged sword" and is involved in "judging the very thoughts and intentions of the heart" (AMP). In other words, God's Word gives us wisdom to know right from wrong and keep our thoughts and attitudes in control.

When we feel strongly about something, we can easily deceive ourselves into believing it's God's will. Consult the Word of God, or take a step back and allow your emotions to subside and ask the Lord about it. Be patient and wait until you feel peace about your decision.

PRAYER FOR TODAY: *God, I want Your will for my life. When it comes to making decisions, help me seek Your will in Your Word and trust the answers I find there. Give me Your wisdom for every situation! Amen.*

DAY 95
WISDOM SAYS WAIT

Wait for and expect the Lord and keep and heed His way, and He will exalt you to inherit the land; [in the end] when the wicked are cut off, you shall see it.

PSALM 37:34

During my research on emotions, I came across part of a dictionary definition I really like. It says emotions cause us "to excite and to move out." This is so true! We get excited, and we want to act on that excitement *right now*.

Satan likes to play on our emotions. He wants us to follow through with our impulses when we get excited and do things we will later regret.

Wisdom, on the other hand, is doing now what you will be happy with later on. Wisdom says to wait a little while until our emotions settle down, then check to see if we really believe it's the right thing to do. This is a good principle to remember: Wisdom says "Wait," while emotions say "Hurry!"

We need to be able to step back and view our situations from God's perspective. That way we can make decisions based on what we know and what God says rather than what we feel.

When faced with any difficult decision, wait until you have a clear answer before taking a step. Emotions are wonderful, but they must not be allowed to take precedence over wisdom and knowledge from God. Remember, with God's help, we can control our emotions instead of letting them control us.

PRAYER FOR TODAY: *God, I want to make decisions that I will be happy with in the long run and that line up with Your will for my life. When my emotions say "Hurry," help me wait. Amen.*

DAY 96

FOLLOW PEACE

Let the peace of Christ rule in your hearts, since as members of one body you were called to peace. And be thankful.

COLOSSIANS 3:15 NIV

God speaks to us through His Word (Psalm 119:105; 2 Timothy 3:16–17), He speaks to our hearts through His Holy Spirit directing us and helping us to supernaturally "know" the right thing to do (John 14:26; 16:13), He speaks through wisdom and common sense (Proverbs 4:6–7), and He will even speak to us through other people. But regardless of how God speaks, He will always lead us by His peace.

Colossians 3:15 says, "And let the peace (soul harmony which comes) from Christ rule (act as umpire continually) in your hearts."

Part of the umpire's job in a baseball game is to decide what is safe and what is out. So this verse is saying that we should allow the peace and harmony in our hearts to act like an umpire, making decisions and settling all questions in our minds. Peace is God's way of telling us what things are safe for us and what things we should leave out.

If you don't have peace about something, that is a clear indication that God doesn't want you to do it. But when you have peace, you should proceed.

PRAYER FOR TODAY: *God, I ask for the Holy Spirit to be my spiritual umpire. When I receive Your peace in response, help me act accordingly. And when I don't sense your peace, help me follow where You lead. Amen.*

DAY 97: BE WILLING TO FORGIVE

Be gentle and forbearing with one another and, if one has a difference (a grievance or complaint) against another, readily pardoning each other; even as the Lord has [freely] forgiven you, so must you also [forgive].

COLOSSIANS 3:13

One of the greatest gifts God has given us is the ability to forgive. In fact, learning to forgive quickly and generously is the will of God, and forgiving brings us great peace. Even if your enemy doesn't deserve your forgiveness, you deserve peace.

Forgiveness spoils the enemy's plan to destroy our relationships. It disarms the sting of bitterness, invites the peace of God, and brings healing power to our souls.

Ask yourself: *How do I respond when someone hurts my feelings? Do I allow my emotions to rob me of my joy? Am I angry with anyone right now?*

It's easy to do and say whatever we feel like without seeking the Holy Spirit's guidance. However, when we cooperate with God to do what His Word says, even when our emotions make us want to do the opposite, we invite blessings into our lives.

When we choose to forgive someone and pray for them, it helps us perhaps even more than it helps them. It's difficult to stay mad at someone if you are actively praying for them. If we choose to forgive and show kindness, it's only a matter of time before our feelings will catch up.

PRAYER FOR TODAY: *God, Your Word says there is power in forgiveness. I do not want anger and resentment to rob me of my joy. Help me to forgive quickly and generously. Amen.*

DAY 98
FORGIVENESS IS A CHOICE TO TRUST GOD

Bless those who curse you, pray for those who mistreat you.
LUKE 6:28 NIV

Whenever I teach on forgiveness, I can imagine what is going through people's minds. *Joyce, you're asking me to forgive? You have no idea what I have been through!*

Trust me, I do understand. Your hurt, your pain, and your desire to see others pay for what they've done makes forgiveness seem like a difficult choice. But here's the truth: It is harder in the long run not to forgive. I often say that staying angry is like drinking poison and hoping that your enemy will be harmed: The person you're really hurting is yourself!

If someone is abusing you, then you may need to put some distance between you and them, but you can still forgive them from your heart and pray for them. The Bible says we need to let God be our vindicator. Forgiveness is simply a choice you make to trust God to be the judge instead of yourself. When you give God control over the situation, it opens the door for the love, power, favor, and peace of God to flow in your life.

First Peter 3:9 says, "Do not repay evil with evil or insult with insult. On the contrary, repay evil with blessing" (NIV). God has given us His grace to be good to people—even to people who aren't being good to us. He has given us the power to be obedient to Him, pray for our enemies, and not be mad at people who have hurt us. We just have to choose forgiveness!

PRAYER FOR TODAY: *God, You know how I feel right now. It's not easy to forgive, so help me trust You and give me the strength to forgive the person who has hurt me and even bless them. Amen.*

DAY 99: FEELINGS ARE UNRELIABLE

That You may give him power to keep himself calm in the days of adversity, until the [inevitable] pit of corruption is dug for the wicked.

PSALM 94:13

I've discovered that feelings are a lot like unreliable people: We can't depend on them to be what we want or need them to be all the time. Not only that, but they also aren't necessarily interested in what's best for us. And they usually want to have their way.

Feelings get us excited about going shopping when we really don't have any money to spend. They entice us to eat cheesecake when we're trying to avoid extra calories, and they lead us to stay up late working or watching TV when we need to get up early the next day. Then after the damage is done, we have to deal with the consequences.

Our feelings are fickle—they change like the wind. Yet it's amazing how much we let them have their way in our lives. But as believers in Christ, we have something much better and more dependable to follow than our feelings—and that's the Word of God.

I want to encourage you to consistently take time to focus on what the Bible says. It will empower you to control your emotions and do what God says is best for you. The more we discipline ourselves to say no to our feelings and yes to the wisdom of God, the easier it becomes to win the spiritual tug-of-war.

PRAYER FOR TODAY: *God, I want to be content in every situation I face. You have given me the power to keep calm in times of trouble. Help me tap into that power and trust You more than my feelings. Amen.*

DAY 100: SET YOUR MIND TO DO WHAT'S RIGHT

Since, then, you have been raised with Christ, set your hearts on things above, where Christ is, seated at the right hand of God.
COLOSSIANS 3:1 NIV

The first step toward managing our emotions is found in Colossians 3:2. It says, "Set your mind and keep focused habitually on the things above [the heavenly things], not on things that are on the earth [which have only temporal value]" (AMP).

There are many things in this world that could easily affect our minds and emotions—and we need to learn how to rise above them all. When negative thoughts are building up and trying to take control of your emotions, take a few minutes to set your mind on God and His Word and on something positive.

Have a chat with yourself that goes something like this: *My family may not be everything I'd like them to be, but I am thankful I have a family. My house is not as tidy as I would like it to be, but I'm grateful I still have a nice place to live. I don't see how I'm going to get through this painful situation, but Jesus is with me, and He will help me overcome it!*

Sometimes we want to ask God to instantly change our circumstances when we're struggling. But the truth is, God can develop our character during times of waiting. He may be giving us the opportunity to set our minds on Him.

PRAYER FOR TODAY: *God, I may not be exactly where I want to be or have exactly what I want to have, but I am learning to be content in my circumstances. Help me shift my focus and my attitude to the things I do have. I know that comes by setting my mind on You. Amen.*

DAY 101
MAKE IT BETTER

This is the day that the Lord has made; let us rejoice and be glad in it.

PSALM 118:24 ESV

Did you know we can make life's challenges better or worse by the way we talk about them? In fact, our words can affect our moods, attitudes, decisions, and even our relationships.

I used to be pessimistic, judgmental, and simply no fun to be around! But even worse, I was cursing my life and my relationships through the negative things I said, but I didn't know it.

Look with me at Proverbs 18:20–21. God has used these verses to help change my life: "A man's [moral] self shall be filled with the fruit of his mouth; and with the consequence of his words he must be satisfied [whether good or evil]. Death and life are in the power of the tongue, and they who indulge in it shall eat the fruit of it [for death or life]."

When we confess God's Word, it stirs our faith—it helps release God's will into our lives and makes a way for things to get better. However, when we speak negatively, we open the door for Satan to bring bad things into our lives and our relationships. When you get a revelation of that truth, you'll begin to see how important it is to choose your words carefully.

PRAYER FOR TODAY: *God, help me today to declare Your Word over my feelings and circumstances. I trust You to turn something difficult into something better through my obedience. Amen.*

DAY 102
SPEAK THE TRUTH IN LOVE

Rather, speaking the truth in love, we are to grow up in every way into him who is the head, into Christ.

EPHESIANS 4:15 ESV

I can still remember many years ago when I would go out to lunch after church on Sundays. Although I was with a group of people who supposedly loved their church and the pastor, we inevitably spent a good deal of time talking about everything we didn't like.

Now, chances are the pastor and other church staff never heard anything we said. However, walking in love requires us to cover other people's faults and treat them the way we would want to be treated (1 Peter 4:8; Luke 6:31).

I want to tell you something that will bring you a lot of peace and also save your relationships: Sharing your critical opinions about other people is always a mistake. We need to speak about one another in love, instead of uncovering their weaknesses and pointing out their flaws.

Yes, there will be times when you need to sit down with your spouse, family member, or friend and discuss something negative they have said or done in order to maintain the health of your relationship. However, this should always be done in love. The intention should never be to hurt or criticize them.

Be sparing with your correction and generous in compliments and encouragement.

PRAYER FOR TODAY: *God, how I speak about other people is important. Help me to always speak about others in love. I'm not perfect, yet You love me anyway. Help me choose to see others the way You see them, with eyes of love. Amen.*

DAY 103 — BELIEVE THE BEST

Love bears up under anything and everything that comes, is ever ready to believe the best of every person, its hopes are fadeless under all circumstances, and it endures everything [without weakening].

1 CORINTHIANS 13:7

Years ago, when the Lord began dealing with me about being judgmental, He spoke to my heart and said, "Joyce, you are looking at everybody else through a magnifying glass, but you look at yourself through rose-colored glasses."

Wow—that got my attention! It was easy for me to pick other people apart and talk about their faults and wrong motives. But I was a big mess myself, and I couldn't see it.

With the help of the Holy Spirit, we can choose to begin speaking good things about others when we are tempted to judge. When my husband, Dave, and I are tempted to speak negatively about someone, we intentionally try to believe the best instead of assuming the worst. Often, we don't have all the facts and have no idea what it's like to walk in someone else's shoes. If we knew what they've been through, we probably wouldn't judge so harshly.

Try it for yourself. The next time you're tempted to judge someone, stop for a moment and choose to believe the best. Find something good about them and focus on that.

PRAYER FOR TODAY: *God, I choose to believe the best and only speak positive words about others. Remind me that I don't know what others are going through and that encouragement always goes a long way. When I am tempted to judge, help me stop and choose to believe the best. Amen.*

DAY 104: GOD'S GRACE CAN HELP

But the human tongue can be tamed by no man. It is a restless (undisciplined, irreconcilable) evil, full of deadly poison.

JAMES 3:8

Maybe the most important lesson I can teach you is to rely on God's grace and strength to help you change your habits and the way you speak.

The book of James tells us that no man can tame the tongue—not by himself. That's why we need the help of the Holy Spirit to control what we say.

Yes, we have our part—God will not do it all for us. We must learn to discipline our own mouths and take responsibility for what comes out of them. However, if we try to do it all on our own, apart from God's grace, we will simply end up frustrated.

If you want to see positive changes in the way you think and speak, I encourage you to regularly spend time reading and studying God's Word and talking to Him in prayer. Even if it's only for five or ten minutes at first and you grow from there, take some time each day to renew your mind with what the Lord says about you. Begin your day by asking for His help.

You won't change every habit overnight, but with God's help, little by little, you can begin to change the way you speak and begin declaring words of life over yourself and others.

PRAYER FOR TODAY: *God, please put a guard on my mouth and keep me from saying things I shouldn't. Help me today to say things that will bless others and build them up. Amen.*

DAY 105
HOW TO GET OVER DISAPPOINTMENT

In the multitude of words sin is not lacking, but he who restrains his lips is wise.

PROVERBS 10:19 NKJV

Anytime our expectations go unmet, we can be tempted to talk about it, which just fuels bad moods. For instance, I remember a disappointing situation with someone I considered to be a close friend. I noticed that each time I talked about it, I would have a difficult time getting it off my mind, and it would affect me for the rest of the day. I finally realized that if I wanted to get over it, I was going to have to stop mentally and verbally going over it again and again.

People kept asking me about the situation out of genuine concern, but I ultimately realized that I had to answer "It is better for me if I just don't talk about it."

Words can literally make the difference in our attitudes, our relationships, and what kind of days we ultimately have. That's because the words that come out of our mouths go into our ears then drop down into our souls, where they give us either joy or sadness, peace or anxiety, hope or discouragement.

When we truly understand the power of our words and realize we can choose what we think and speak, our lives can be transformed.

PRAYER FOR TODAY: *God, I give my feelings to You today. When I've been hurt or disappointed, help me stop focusing on it and talking about it so I can get past it. Amen.*

DAY 106
OUR THOUGHTS IMPACT OTHERS

Be devoted to one another with [authentic] brotherly affection [as members of one family], give preference to one another in honor.
ROMANS 12:10 AMP

Many years ago, I was with one of my daughters, who was a teenager at the time. Her hair didn't look very good that day, in my opinion, and she had some blemishes on her face that she had tried too hard to hide with makeup. As we spent the day together, I must admit that each time I looked at her, I thought, *You sure don't look good today.* As the day went by, I noticed that she appeared to be getting depressed. I asked her what was wrong, and she said, "I just feel really ugly today!" It took God only a millisecond to tell me it was my fault. Ouch! But He was right, as He always is, and it was a lesson on the power of thoughts that I will never forget.

I am not saying that people can read our minds, but I do think that our thoughts, good or bad, have an impact on those around us. They certainly show on our faces, in our body language, and in our behavior toward people.

Be careful of the thoughts you think about people because your thoughts shape your attitude and behavior. Over time, what's in your heart tends to come out in your words, tone, and actions, and others are affected by it even if they can't pinpoint why.

PRAYER FOR TODAY: *God, help me to take captive any evil or negative thoughts about others and to replace them with right thoughts. I want others to feel good around me, and that starts with the thoughts I think about them. Amen.*

DAY 107
WHAT DIRECTION ARE YOU GOING?

If we set bits in the horses' mouths to make them obey us, we can turn their whole bodies about.

JAMES 3:3

James 3:3–6 says that just like the bit in a horse's mouth or the tiny rudder on a ship, our words have the ability to affect the entire course of our lives. So, if you're not happy with the direction you're going, it's important to pay attention to what you are talking about.

Are you praying for your children to change? Then be determined to declare good things. Say, "My son might be going through some challenges right now, but I know God has a great plan for his future, and He will work all of this out for our good in the end" (Jeremiah 29:11; Romans 8:28).

Do you need a breakthrough in your finances? Then focus on what God says about the situation. Say things like, "God always meets all of my needs, and I have more than enough!" (Philippians 4:19; Psalm 37:25).

The Bible says that God's Word is alive, active, and full of power (Hebrews 4:12). And when you begin to speak His Word from your mouth, you are cooperating with Him to bring about His good plan for your life.

Are there things you would like to see change? Would you like to experience greater levels of the Lord's grace and strength in your life? You can, by speaking in agreement with God's Word.

PRAYER FOR TODAY: *God, I trust that You are bringing good things my way. While I'm waiting for my breakthrough, help me trust and believe Your promises and Your Word and show me areas where I need to change my words. Amen.*

DAY 108: AT ALL TIMES

I will bless the Lord at all times; His praise shall continually be in my mouth.

PSALM 34:1

In Psalm 34:1, David says that he will "bless the Lord at all times." He does not say, "I will bless the Lord when everything is going my way," or "I will bless the Lord when this big problem gets solved." He was determined to speak words of praise and exaltation to God *all* the time, in *every* situation.

We learn from today's scripture that David did not allow his circumstances or his emotions to affect his worship. In fact, throughout the Bible, we read stories of people who chose to praise God in difficult situations. God always brought them through those hard times and gave them victory. This is a powerful lesson, and one you can begin to apply to your life today.

If things in your life are not going as well as you would like—perhaps you are facing a stressful situation or dealing with fear, disappointment, or confusion—you may not feel like praising God. But you can choose to praise and thank Him. He is much bigger than any circumstance, and you can praise Him for who He is, for what He has done in the past, for never forsaking you, and for working all things for your good, whether you can see it right now or not.

PRAYER FOR TODAY: *God, I praise You today. I ask You to equip me to speak Your Word in all circumstances, even when I don't feel like it. You are worthy of praise regardless of my feelings and attitude. Amen.*

DAY 109
GET TO KNOW PEOPLE

Be honest in your judgment and do not decide at a glance (superficially and by appearances); but judge fairly and righteously.
JOHN 7:24

Have you ever met someone you immediately disliked? I'm sure we all have. But how could we honestly dislike someone we barely know or perhaps don't know at all?

I believe it's because we have let an attitude, or a mindset, affect our feelings and opinions without ever examining where the thought came from or why we have it.

There are lots of reasons why we might not like someone, but none of them are valid reasons to judge them. Perhaps they have a personality type that we don't enjoy, or they may have a personality that reminds us of someone who has hurt us in the past. An insecure woman could meet a very beautiful woman and feel a dislike for her simply because she feels threatened by her good looks. It took me a few years to realize that I rejected people who reminded me of my father. He was gruff, negative, and generally unfriendly, so I preferred people who had none of those traits, even though I was that way myself.

It is important that we get to the root of these problems, because God's Word teaches us not to judge at a glance or superficially. And if we take time to get to know people a little more intimately, we may even like them more.

It is wise to always treat others the same way we want them to treat us.

PRAYER FOR TODAY: *God, I want to see people the way You see them. Give me Your eyes and Your heart. Let me give people a chance, and not judge superficially. Amen.*

DAY 110: THE WAY GOD SEES PEOPLE

But the Lord said to Samuel, Look not on his appearance or at the height of his stature, for I have rejected him. For the Lord sees not as man sees; for man looks on the outward appearance, but the Lord looks on the heart.

1 SAMUEL 16:7

It is very important to see people the way God sees them. First Samuel 16:7 says: "For the Lord sees not as man sees; for man looks on the outward appearance, but the Lord looks on the heart." God spoke these words to Samuel when he was on his way to anoint the next king—not the oldest, strongest, tallest son of Jesse, but a shepherd boy, the youngest of all his brothers, and, at first glance, the least likely candidate for king.

If we are willing, we can learn to think about people the way God thinks about them. When we do, we'll recognize each person as a valuable possibility instead of a potential problem. This comes with spiritual maturity—it is a by-product of walking in the Spirit rather than walking in the flesh. It is often a sacrifice, because we may not want to take the time to know them more deeply.

We cannot be best friends with everyone we meet, but we can at least be kind and stop evaluating people at a glance. There will always be people we can relate to better than others, but that should not be an excuse for having an exclusive attitude.

PRAYER FOR TODAY: *God, I confess that I have had an exclusive attitude and that I have judged at a glance, but I don't want to do it any longer. I want to be kind and generous and to have eyes to see people the way You see them. Amen.*

DAY 111

WAIT WELL

Why are you cast down, O my inner self? And why should you moan over me and be disquieted within me? Hope in God and wait expectantly for Him, for I shall yet praise Him, my Help and my God.

PSALM 42:5

God gives us dreams for our lives, but there's often a time of waiting and preparation before we step into them. These in-between times are opportunities to grow stronger in our faith and in our relationship with the Lord.

For instance, the Lord first spoke to my heart about Joyce Meyer Ministries in the 1970s. I believed He was telling me that I would one day have a large ministry and teach the Word of God all over the world. However, I had a lot of maturing to do. I had a gift to teach His Word, but I didn't have the spiritual maturity to go with it yet. This big vision God had given me was going to be a process that took years.

I'll admit, during this in-between time, I battled fear and doubt. The enemy wanted to convince me that I had never heard from God in the first place, or I had done something so wrong that it changed my destiny. In reality, this season was simply a training ground. God wanted me to learn how to trust Him, despite what my circumstances looked like. He wanted me to learn how to wait well and put my faith in His ways and timing.

If you're in an in-between season, I encourage you to trust God and wait well, and watch how He moves.

PRAYER FOR TODAY: *God, the in-between season is hard! Help me to wait well and to keep my mind focused on Your promises for my life. When Your vision for my life comes to fruition, I want to be able to look back and say that I waited well. Amen.*

DAY 112: HIS PLAN AND HIS TIMING

For my thoughts are not your thoughts, neither are your ways my ways, declares the Lord.

ISAIAH 55:8 ESV

My personality is what is called type A. That means I like to be in control, and I like to take action and accomplish things.

When I began teaching a Bible study in my home, there were years when I was ministering to only fifteen or twenty people. I knew it was God's plan for me at the time, but I also wanted to see my dreams come to pass—I wanted to teach thousands.

I remember one day in particular when I was really struggling with how slow God seemed to be moving. I lay on the floor, held on to the leg of the desk, and begged God to help me yield to His plan and His timing.

If I had decided to try to make my dreams happen on my own, simply because I was impatient, and then succeeded, I would not have been in God's will. I would never have been able to help the number of people I do now.

Has the Lord spoken something to your heart, and it seems like it will never come to pass? Whatever it is, don't give up! Continue doing everything He shows you to do, and remember, if He gave you a dream for your life, He will make it happen at the right time if you keep your trust in Him.

PRAYER FOR TODAY: *God, forgive me for the times I find it hard to trust You. I know that You know what is best for me, but sometimes it is hard for my mind and my emotions to get on the same page. Help me seek Your will for my life more than anything else. Amen.*

DAY 113: THE FRUIT OF PATIENCE

But the fruit of the [Holy] Spirit [the work which His presence within accomplishes] is love, joy (gladness), peace, patience (an even temper, forbearance), kindness, goodness (benevolence), faithfulness.

GALATIANS 5:22

Waiting and patience go hand in hand, but patience is not simply waiting; it is how we act while we are waiting.

Galatians 5:22 says that patience is a fruit of the Holy Spirit. When we begin a relationship with Jesus Christ, the Holy Spirit comes to live inside of us and God plants a seed of everything He is inside of us. However, for that seed to grow, it must be watered, developed, and cultivated.

God uses our times of waiting to help cultivate the fruit of patience in our lives. If we never have to wait for anything—if we never go through difficult circumstances or need to trust God—then we wouldn't need patience at all. But waiting is not optional for any of us. So, we may as well decide to keep a good attitude and enjoy our lives while we're waiting for God's will and timing.

Being sad, discouraged, bitter, or frustrated won't make things happen any faster; in fact, our attitudes can even prevent us from receiving the very thing we want! However, when we can be happy and joyful while we wait, it's a sign that we are trusting God, growing spiritually, and developing patience.

PRAYER FOR TODAY: *God, thank You for the seed of patience You planted within me. The potential is there, and I know that it is in the waiting seasons when it will grow. Teach me how to enjoy my life while my patience develops. Amen.*

DAY 114: OUR PART AND GOD'S PART

For we are fellow workmen (joint promoters, laborers together) with and for God; you are God's garden and vineyard and field under cultivation, [you are] God's building.

1 CORINTHIANS 3:9

When we're waiting for God to answer our prayers and bring the changes we desire, it's tempting to want to "help" God. However, during the waiting period, it's important to do our part while trusting God to do His part.

When I started Joyce Meyer Ministries, the Lord gave me direction, and I was faithful to do what He said. I worked hard and taught at conferences where He opened the door, and my husband, Dave, and I were careful to spend plenty of time seeking God and keeping Him first in our lives. But I wanted the ministry to grow faster.

In the early days, I sent out flyers advertising my teaching ministry to all of the churches and pastors in my city. There was just one problem—God never asked me to do that. As a result, I didn't receive any response, and I just frustrated myself. When we waste our energy trying to make things happen that only God can make happen, frustration is always the result!

What's our part? Our part is to spend time with God through prayer and in His Word, and then take whatever steps He shows us to take. In the meantime, God will be working behind the scenes on your behalf, and He will answer your prayers in His perfect timing.

PRAYER FOR TODAY: *God, I don't want to waste any more energy trying to do what only You can do. Show me what You want me to do and strengthen me to do it. Help me to do my part and to trust You to do Yours. Amen.*

DAY 115: THE PARABLE OF THE FARMER

He sleeps and rises night and day, and the seed sprouts and grows; he knows not how.

MARK 4:27 ESV

Are you praying for a breakthrough, and it seems like nothing is happening? Jesus gave us a parable about a farmer to illustrate what we should do in this exact situation:

> This is what the kingdom of God is like. A man scatters seed on the ground. Night and day, whether he sleeps or gets up, the seed sprouts and grows, though he does not know how. All by itself the soil produces grain—first the stalk, then the head, then the full kernel in the head. As soon as the grain is ripe, he puts the sickle to it, because the harvest has come.
>
> Mark 4:26–29 NIV

The farmer doesn't know exactly how or when the harvest is going to happen. He just keeps doing what he can to enrich his soil and cultivate his crops, but he leaves the rest in the hands of the Creator. He knows that only God can bring the harvest at the perfect time.

Whatever you are waiting for, be like the farmer. Cultivate your relationship with God and do everything He has put in your heart to do. Then trust Him to bring your "harvest" at the perfect time.

PRAYER FOR TODAY: *God, I want to grow closer to You in this season. Help me to pray, to believe, and to wait with a good attitude. I trust You, and I know that the harvest will be beautiful when it comes. Amen.*

DAY 116: ENJOY THE JOURNEY

The thief comes only in order to steal and kill and destroy. I came that they may have and enjoy life, and have it in abundance (to the full, till it overflows).

JOHN 10:10

I'll never forget the time when I was praying for God to help me reach more people. The Lord spoke to my heart and said, "Joyce, if I asked you to minister to only fifty people for the rest of your life, would you do it just because you love Me?"

In hindsight, I believe one of the reasons this ministry remained small for so long was because God wanted to teach me how to be happy with Him regardless of how big the ministry was. On the day that He asked me, I was grateful that I had finally reached a point where I could answer "Yes." If that was what the Lord truly wanted me to do, then I could do it with joy because I love and trust Him.

Learning to enjoy my life while I wait is truly one of the greatest lessons God has ever taught me. I think most people are like I was. We're convinced we will be happy *when* God finally answers our prayers, *when* we get that promotion, *when* our spouse begins acting nicer, or *when* the "problem" goes away. However, when we choose to remain stable in our emotions regardless of our circumstances, God will help us enjoy where we are on the way to where we are going.

PRAYER FOR TODAY: *God, help me get to the place where I can be content regardless of my circumstances. Too often my emotions are tied to what is going on in my life, Teach me that I can enjoy my life while it is still a work in progress. Amen.*

DAY 117: DON'T SETTLE FOR MEDIOCRE

So Abraham left the land of the Chaldeans and lived in Haran until his father died. Then God brought him here to the land where you now live.

ACTS 7:4 NLT

The book of Genesis shares the story of Abraham's father, Terah, who gathered his family, packed up everything, and set out for his ultimate destination: Canaan.

However, Genesis 11:31 tells us that "they went forth together to go from Ur of the Chaldees into the land of Canaan; but when they came to Haran, they settled there."

So often, people set out to do one thing in life but settle somewhere else along the way because they get tired or find it's convenient. Are there areas in your life where you have "settled" instead of pressing on to the finish line?

The Lord has called us to excellence; however, we often settle for being mediocre. The word *mediocre* means "average, status quo, moderate-to-low in quality." And that's where so many people live; they haven't completely failed, but they're also not where they really want to be!

Sometimes we get used to the place where we are and almost forget there's something better. Life gets busy, complicated, or even comfortable, and we lose sight of the dreams and goals we used to have. That's when we need to stir up our faith and become determined to follow every single part of God's plan for our lives.

PRAYER FOR TODAY: *God, I believe You have called me to great things, to more than what I am currently experiencing. Remind me of the dreams I've lost sight of, and help me on the road to success. Amen.*

DAY 118

WHAT IF?

Do your best to present yourself to God as one approved, a worker who has no need to be ashamed, rightly handling the word of truth.
2 TIMOTHY 2:15 ESV

Let's take a few moments to ask ourselves, "What if?"

What if you decided to give God your all and seek Him with your whole heart? What if you demanded the best from yourself instead of settling for "just average"?

What if you stopped making excuses for why you can't accomplish your dreams and goals? What if you changed the way you speak and refused to say anything negative? What if you started confronting problems instead of running away from them?

Can you imagine where you would be this time next year if you followed through on even just one or two of these things?

The Bible is full of scriptures that encourage us to do our best. 2 Timothy 2:15 says, "Study and be eager and do your utmost to present yourself to God approved (tested by trial), a workman who has no cause to be ashamed." I love the phrase "do your utmost." Imagine for a second what could happen if you decided to give your utmost in your marriage, at your job, or in other areas of your life. I believe the outcome would be amazingly wonderful.

PRAYER FOR TODAY: *God, it is hard for me to picture my life anywhere but where it is right now. Give me a creative mind to imagine all the possibilities and the courage to believe they will happen when I give my utmost to the things You are calling me to do. Amen.*

DAY 119
IT'S FOR YOU

"For I know the plans I have for you," declares the Lord, "plans to prosper you and not to harm you, plans to give you hope and a future."

JEREMIAH 29:11 NIV (EMPHASIS MINE)

Regardless of what's happened in the past or what obstacles seem to be in our way, God has a big, full life in store for each one of us. However, it's up to us to get the best out of life by making the most of our time, talents, relationships, and opportunities.

This applies to every area of our lives. Maybe you have begun studying the Word of God, and you've set a goal to really know your Bible and develop a vibrant relationship with the Lord. If that's the case, don't settle for reading a chapter a day just to check it off your list—stay determined to make it a priority and reap the benefits of truly knowing God.

Or maybe you have a goal to lose twenty pounds. If so, decide now that you're not going to give up when it gets difficult. Even if you have a bad day and gain weight, be determined to bounce back the next day.

A great life isn't just for someone else—it's for you, too. Yes, it's going to require effort and determination, and in many cases it may require you to push past fear so you can enjoy greater freedom and success. Most of all, it will require a lot of help from God. But I promise you this: It is always worth it.

PRAYER FOR TODAY: *God, help me believe that a great life isn't just for other people; it's for me, too. I've made a lot of mistakes, but by Your grace You still want to use me for Your glory. Help me give my best in every area of my life, even if I have to do it afraid. Amen.*

DAY 120

NEW EVERY MORNING

The steadfast love of the Lord never ceases; his mercies never come to an end; they are new every morning; great is your faithfulness.
LAMENTATIONS 3:22–23 ESV

How do you handle life's disappointments—when things don't work out the way you had hoped? Do you fall apart? Or do you trust God's Word in Lamentations 3:23 and believe His mercies are new every morning?

There was a time when I would let today's disappointments ruin tomorrow. I would raise my voice at Dave, say things I regretted, and then spend days feeling guilty and condemning myself because of my behavior. Or other times, I missed opportunities and was sure I ruined God's plan for my life.

Little by little, God has helped me change my attitude about these disappointments. Instead of focusing on what has been lost, God helped me to focus on the good things He can do in the future.

We live our lives one day at a time. God gives us new opportunities every morning to start fresh! It's a chance to begin again—to try again, hope again, and to watch Him do something we never expected.

You see, God is about restoration and change—He is always doing a new thing and working behind the scenes in our lives to bring about new beginnings. Where we see failure, God sees potential for something new.

PRAYER FOR TODAY: *God, it's not easy when life doesn't go according to my plan, but I'm learning to trust You and Your plan for my life. Help me to leave the past in the past and to focus on the good You want to do in me and through me today. Amen.*

DAY 121

WORTH THE WAIT

For still the vision awaits its appointed time; it hastens to the end—it will not lie. If it seems slow, wait for it; it will surely come; it will not delay.

HABAKKUK 2:3 ESV

I've noticed people often give up right before God is about to bring their breakthrough. If they could have stayed determined a little longer, they would have seen the fulfillment of God's promises come to pass. This time is often when it is the most difficult, but this is when we need to really press in and stay determined to not give up!

Think about a woman who is ready to give birth. She has carried the baby for nine months and made it to full term. But now, right before the baby is born, she has important work to do: She has to *push*!

Similarly, we each "birth" the promises, dreams, and visions that God gives us. If it seems impossible, like it is never going to happen, then chances are you are right on the edge of your breakthrough. The Lord is saying the same thing to many of you today that the doctor says to the pregnant woman in labor: "*Push!* Don't give up! Keep going, because you're almost there!"

Whatever you're believing God for today, and no matter how long you've waited, the greatest advice I can give you is to never give up. If you continue to wait on God and keep your trust in Him, you will see His will come to pass in your life. And it will have been worth the wait.

PRAYER FOR TODAY: *God, the last thing I want to do is give up right before my breakthrough. Help me push through this hardest part. I can't give up now. Give me Your strength to get to the finish line of Your will for me. Amen.*

DAY 122
GOD'S PLAN B

And we know that in all things God works for the good of those who love him, who have been called according to his purpose.
ROMANS 8:28 NIV

Regardless of what happened yesterday, last week, or last year, God has a great plan for your life—a plan for you to succeed and experience the peace and joy that Jesus died to give you.

This means that when plan A falls apart, you don't have to be afraid. God has you in the palm of His hands, and He's already been working on plan B. In fact, God knew your plan A wasn't going to work out and had a better plan B in the works from the beginning! Instead of staring at the past, He wants you to look through the eyes of faith and get excited about the future.

I've discovered that God's plan B is often better than my plan A could have ever been. Even when someone else or an unforeseen circumstance affects our lives, God promises to take the negative things that happen and use them for our good (Romans 8:28).

Maybe you feel like you missed an opportunity or messed up what could have been a good relationship, or maybe you feel like you made a mistake and there's no chance that things will turn around. That's simply not the case. Jeremiah 29:11 tells us that God already has His plans for you all laid out—and they are plans for you to prosper in this life.

PRAYER FOR TODAY: *God, give me eyes to see that You are able to bring good out of my life. You planned my future before You formed me in my mother's womb. I want to honor You by receiving the future You have for me. Amen.*

DAY 123: RESTORE MORE

I will repay you for the years the locusts have eaten—the great locust and the young locust, the other locusts and the locust swarm—my great army that I sent among you.

JOEL 2:25 NIV

When you're following God, no one can ever truly take anything away from you. If you will trust Him, He can take a bad situation and turn it around for good.

For instance, as a young adult, I was convinced that being abused as a child had ruined me forever. I felt like I would always have a second-rate life.

But all things are possible with God! Where we see dead ends, He sees new beginnings. He wants to take the pain of our past and not only heal it but also restore to us more than we would have had in the first place! God has worked miracles out of my abuse, and I've been able to help a lot of people who have also been abused.

When we're in the middle of a bad day or disappointing moment, it's so tempting to give in to thoughts like *It's over* or *It's too late*. But it isn't too late! It's never too late to have a fresh start when you have life in Christ. Tomorrow is a new day! It's a new opportunity to finish that project, mend that relationship, or get back to your exercise routine.

Where have you been seeing a dead end in your life? I encourage you to look at each day as a new beginning, a chance to start again. If you'll let God, He will restore to you more than what was taken.

PRAYER FOR TODAY: *God, thank You for giving me a fresh start each day. Despite the hard things I've been through in life, I want to follow You into a new beginning. Teach me to see each day as new opportunity to walk with You. Amen.*

DAY 124: IT HAD TO BE GOD

Jesus said to him, "[You say to Me,] 'If You can?' All things are possible for the one who believes and trusts [in Me]!"

MARK 9:23 AMP

The older we get, the faster time seems to pass. Before we know it, the ambitions, hopes, and dreams of our youth fade into the background of life and are forgotten until one day we reflect and wonder, *Should I have done things differently? Did I choose the right path? Is it too late to be what I wanted to be?*

I want to encourage you that no matter how old you are or what you've been through, God has a good plan for your life. He wants to fill your heart with a sense of destiny and purpose that will satisfy your soul.

Every one of us should have goals, dreams, and visions for our lives. Maybe your vision is to own your own home, restore a relationship, go to college, or run a 5K.

Many times, God speaks to our hearts and gives us a vision of something He wants to do in our future that seems impossible. But that's the way so many of our dreams and visions start—because God wants us to have faith and rely on Him. Then, when our dreams and visions come to pass, we know it had to be God.

PRAYER FOR TODAY: *God, remind me of the dreams of my youth, the visions that You planted in my heart. I want everything You have for me in this life, especially those things that I can't do on my own. Amen.*

DAY 125
THE SILENT YEARS

Because of faith also Sarah herself received physical power to conceive a child, even when she was long past the age for it, because she considered [God] Who had given her the promise to be reliable and trustworthy and true to His word.

HEBREWS 11:11

There will be seasons of your life when it seems like God isn't doing anything at all, and you don't see any visible progress. I often call these times "the silent years." During this time—however long it lasts—the greatest thing you can do is keep a good attitude and refuse to give up on what God has placed in your heart. He is working even though you don't see it.

During these seasons, your faith will be tested and stretched to its limits. I can tell you from experience that you may be tempted to question your ability to succeed, the decisions you made, and your reasons for pursuing your vision. There will be a temptation to think and say negative things about your situation.

When this happens, it's important to cling to God's Word and decide that you're going to agree with what He says about your future. It's time to hold on to that vision God has placed in your heart.

Remember, your thoughts and words are powerful because they can breathe life and hope into your situation. To continue moving forward, it's important to maintain a good attitude and stay in God's Word so your faith remains strong and you are able to see things God's way instead of your own.

PRAYER FOR TODAY: *God, help me speak only positive, lifegiving words that line up with Your Word. I know that one day I will see the fulfillment of my dreams, and on that day I will be so glad I didn't give up! Amen.*

DAY 126

WRITE IT DOWN

And the Lord answered me and said, Write the vision and engrave it so plainly upon tablets that everyone who passes may [be able to] read [it easily and quickly] as he hastens by.

HABAKKUK 2:2

The Bible tells us to write down our vision so we can see it plainly. This helps to remind ourselves often of what God has spoken to our hearts. It stirs us up and keeps us moving in the right direction. Whatever your vision, it's important to keep moving toward it. God is always on the move, and we need to continually move forward with Him.

I encourage you to record your victories, challenges, and thoughts along the journey toward your vision. When you go through difficult seasons, it's so encouraging to look back and see how God has helped, guided, and strengthened you along the way.

It has been wonderful to have a record of what God has brought me through. When I look at my old journals, I see how God brought me through times when I didn't think I could make it. Those journals not only encourage me, but they also are a testimony of my progress.

Maybe God has just given you a new vision for your life. Or maybe there is something you've been praying and believing for over the course of many years and have faithfully kept going. Wherever you are, be patient with yourself! If you are committed to the process and never give up, your vision will come to pass.

PRAYER FOR TODAY: *God, thank You for all the things You have brought me through. When I'm having a tough day, bring those things to my mind so I can be encouraged to keep going. Amen.*

DAY 127: CHARACTER BUILDING

And endurance (fortitude) develops maturity of character (approved faith and tried integrity). And character [of this sort] produces [the habit of] joyful and confident hope of eternal salvation.

ROMANS 5:4

The journey toward our goals is just as important as the destination itself. The journey builds our patience, faith, endurance, and self-discipline. It prepares us for the destination.

Romans says that we can rejoice in trials because they bear the fruit of godly character (5:3–4). If the destination you are working toward still seems a long way off, think of it as character building. Maintaining a good attitude and keeping your trust in God while you wait is training you to be able to handle all the blessings and the challenges that come your way.

God has equipped us to achieve the dreams He's put inside us. He wants to prepare us by building godly character in us so that we are able to handle future challenges with grace and future victories with humility. If we don't have strong godly character, we will set ourselves up for failure, and we won't be able to sustain our vision once it comes to pass.

In his second letter to the Corinthians, Paul concludes by charging them to "grow to maturity" (2 Corinthians 13:11 NLT). The Amplified Bible says it like this: "Be made complete [be what you should be]." The journey is where we become what we should be, where we are made complete.

PRAYER FOR TODAY: *God, thank You for all of the opportunities You have given me to grow. Give me a positive attitude as I learn to rejoice even when challenges come. Help me remember that it is through these trials that I will become what I should be—what You created me to be. Amen.*

DAY 128: IT'S NEVER TOO LATE

But even now I know that whatever you ask from God, God will give you.

JOHN 11:22 ESV

God is always doing a new thing. He is constantly working behind the scenes in our lives to bring about new beginnings. Where we see failure, God sees potential for something new. The minute we stumble, God is already planning our comeback. With God, it's never too late.

In Isaiah 43:19, God says, "Behold, I am doing a new thing! Now it springs forth; do you not perceive and know it and will you not give heed to it? I will even make a way in the wilderness and rivers in the desert."

Instead of having a "give up" attitude, why not try again and again and again if need be? God has your fresh start planned, but you must cooperate with Him by stepping out in faith and believing it's not too late. Proverbs 24:16 says that "a righteous man falls seven times and rises again." One of the greatest things you can have is an attitude that says, *I will never give up!*

Whatever it may be, God wants you to know that it's never too late to begin again and have a great life. He is on your side, and if need be, He can even make a way in the wilderness and rivers in the desert.

PRAYER FOR TODAY: *God, remove the phrase* it's too late for that *from my vocabulary! If You can make rivers in the desert, then I can trust You to make a way for me where there seems no way. Amen.*

DAY 129: STAY DETERMINED

For as many as are the promises of God, in Christ they are [all answered] "Yes." So through Him we say our "Amen" to the glory of God.

2 CORINTHIANS 1:20 AMP

One of the greatest things we can do to cooperate with God's plan for our lives is stay determined. When you feel disheartened, when others doubt or criticize you, or when your dreams seem impossible, that's when you need to keep moving forward!

Years ago, when I started talking about the call of God on my life, some of my "friends" decided I must be mistaken. They said, "Joyce, we really don't think you have the right personality to do this kind of ministry."

But I believed God had spoken to my heart, and I had a gift and a passion to teach His Word. So I kept praying and believing. I kept operating in my gifts and believing that, at the right time, God would open all the necessary doors to the worldwide ministry that He had planted in my heart. As a result, I lost some friends and was eventually asked to leave my church. Even some of my family members turned their backs on me.

Yes, it was difficult in the moment, but if I had given up when I felt that rejection, I would have missed out on my calling and so many incredible opportunities to help people. I urge you to keep going so you don't miss out on the good things God has planned for you.

PRAYER FOR TODAY: *God, it's hard to keep moving forward when it feels like no one is on my side. Help me keep my mind off the discouragement of others so that I can focus on Your promises, which are "Yes" and "Amen." Amen.*

DAY 130: A CHEERFUL HEART

All the days of the desponding and afflicted are made evil [by anxious thoughts and forebodings], but he who has a glad heart has a continual feast [regardless of circumstances].

PROVERBS 15:15

It's not uncommon for past experiences, especially traumatic ones, to shape our perspectives and expectations. For example, because I was abused as a child, I developed a vague fear that something bad was always about to happen.

We will all face difficult times in life, and when we do, it's easy to dread the future and have anxious thoughts and forebodings. But as we spend time in the Word, growing in our faith and our knowledge of God and His great love for us, we can learn to agree with God and His Word when trouble comes.

We can activate our faith by saying, "God is love. God will take care of me and protect me. God will give me the grace and strength to do what I need to do. God works all things together for good."

Proverbs 15:15 says that our days are "made evil [by anxious thoughts and forebodings], but he who has a glad heart has a continual feast [regardless of circumstances]." Yes, we can have a cheerful heart regardless of our circumstances. Life may not feel good right now, but you can keep the attitude that good things are coming, that God has a good plan for Your life, and the joy of the Lord is your strength.

PRAYER FOR TODAY: *God, how great would it be if my moods weren't up and down with my circumstances! I want to be steady and happy, but I can't do it alone. Help me to have a cheerful heart regardless of whether it's an up day or a down day and to grow in agreement with You. Amen.*

DAY 131

FULL OF HOPE

Such hope [in God's promises] never disappoints us, because God's love has been abundantly poured out within our hearts through the Holy Spirit who was given to us.

ROMANS 5:5 AMP

When we are going through difficult seasons in life, it's so important to hold on to hope. Hope has to do with what we believe. It has to do with our faith and expecting God to do good things in our lives. Hope says, "Things may not be going well at this moment, but I know God has great things in store!"

I encourage you to take control of your thoughts and words first thing every morning. When you wake up, don't settle for thoughts like *Well, I guess I'll try to make it through another day.* Instead, anticipate good things from God. Think and declare things like "God, with Your help, I am going to have a good attitude and a great day today." Then, expect your breakthrough and new beginning.

It's important to realize that we can't live by how we feel if we want to have a positive, hope-filled life. When negative feelings come, they will die if we don't give in to them and feed them.

So don't allow yourself to get caught in the trap of waiting to feel hopeful, but instead, decide to be full of hope. When you make a conscious decision to think positive, faith-filled thoughts throughout the day, your feelings will eventually catch up with your decision.

PRAYER FOR TODAY: *God, help me to be hopeful every day and to think positive thoughts that align with Your Word. With Your help, today could be a day of breakthrough! Amen.*

DAY 132: AGAIN, AGAIN, AGAIN

May the God of hope fill you with all joy and peace as you trust in him, so that you may overflow with hope by the power of the Holy Spirit.

ROMANS 15:13 NIV

Every single one of us goes through difficult times. It can be a tragedy, sickness, death of a loved one, financial hardship, or even the disappointment of a setback or unfulfilled dream. And during these times, we need to be determined to never give up.

It's very easy to want to give up when things get hard. Sometimes people get stuck where they are and don't know how to get out, so they think giving up is the only answer.

Maybe that's where you are today. Maybe you're grieving the loss of a loved one, and moving forward without them seems impossible. Or maybe you've disappointed yourself; you feel like you've failed at something and can't imagine starting over.

I know what you're going through is very difficult. That's why you need the power of the Holy Spirit to help you. He will give you the grace and strength to get up and move forward. He will lead you one step at a time into the good life God has planned for you. Your part is to take those steps and never give up.

Tragedy or failure does not mean there are no more options. When all else fails, you can start again, try again, and dream again. If you can hold on and trust God through it all, He can restore you more fully than you ever imagined.

PRAYER FOR TODAY: *God, I want my life to overflow with hope. Empower me by Your Spirit to move forward. Help me to begin again, try again, and dream again. I'm holding on and trusting You! Amen.*

DAY 133: WHAT TO DO WHEN YOU DON'T KNOW WHAT TO DO

But the Comforter, which is the Holy Ghost, whom the Father will send in my name, he shall teach you all things, and bring all things to your remembrance, whatsoever I have said unto you.
JOHN 14:26 KJV

Are you in a painful season right now? The most important thing you can do is trust God. When something isn't going the way we'd like, we can trust that God has a plan that's better than ours and that He will ultimately work the situation out for good (Romans 8:28). If you are stuck in a place of pain, remember these five practical suggestions:

- Never give up! Fight the temptation to think there's no way out. Jesus is the Way (Galatians 6:9; John 14:6).
- Do what's right even when it's hard. Do something good for others (Psalm 37:3).
- Don't withdraw, sulk, or isolate yourself. God can use others to encourage you (Proverbs 27:17).
- Don't stop believing. Don't give up hope that God can improve your situation (Psalm 27:13)!

There will always be obstacles to overcome in life. But with God, there will also be second chances and new beginnings. So if you're hurting and don't know what to do, don't give up hope! God is with you to comfort you and give you a fresh start.

PRAYER FOR TODAY: *God, I need Your guidance when I feel stuck and don't know what to do. Give me faith to believe in better days, and bring someone into my life to encourage me. Amen.*

DAY 134: POSITIVE EXPECTATION

He has delivered us from such a deadly peril, and he will deliver us again. On him we have set our hope that he will continue to deliver us.

2 CORINTHIANS 1:10 NIV

One definition of *hope* is "a favorable and confident expectation."

Many times we take passive attitudes, deciding we'll just wait and see if something will change. But God wants us to expect *on purpose* and actively anticipate good things. So what are you expecting?

The enemy wants to convince you that things will never change. But God wants you to know that He loves you and you can trust Him to make a miracle out of your mess.

There is a story in the Bible about a father who asks Jesus to heal his son. The father said, "If you can do anything, take pity on us and help us," to which Jesus replied, "'If you can'?... Everything is possible for one who believes" (Mark 9:22–23 NIV).

Hope says: "Things may have been this way for a long time, but God is the God of the impossible, and things can change." Do you believe it?

The father responded to Jesus: "I believe; help my unbelief!" (Mark 9:24 ESV). Ask God to help you believe and expect that something good is going to happen for you.

PRAYER FOR TODAY: *God, thank You for the reminder that You are bigger than my problems. I am sorry for the times that I get discouraged and give in to negative thoughts. Grow my expectations to believe that, at the right time, You will turn things around. Amen.*

DAY 135: SHAKE IT OFF

Blessed is the man who remains steadfast under trial, for when he has stood the test he will receive the crown of life, which God has promised to those who love him.

JAMES 1:12 ESV

There is a story about a donkey that illustrates how we should respond to challenging circumstances. The story begins when a donkey falls into a pit. Upon seeing what happened, his owner examined the pit, the problem, and the possibilities. He saw that the pit was deep and the donkey was old. So he decided his best option was to bury the donkey.

As he began to shovel dirt into the pit, the donkey cried out, obviously terrified of his situation. Later, the donkey went quiet. The owner assumed he'd probably died, buried under all that dirt. But the donkey had not died.

When the owner looked down in the pit, he saw that every time dirt fell on his back, the donkey would shake it off and step on it, packing it down under his hooves. This continued for hours until, finally, the donkey had packed the dirt enough to step out of that pit!

Life will throw dirt on us. You may be tempted at times to lie down and let it bury you, but there is another option: You can follow the lead of the Holy Spirit. He will show you how to shake off the dirt and step up.

PRAYER FOR TODAY: *God, thank You for the gift of the Holy Spirit, who is there to lead and guide me. Teach me to be attentive to His leading, so I can shake off the dirt that life throws on me from time to time. This thing that the devil tried to use to bury me will turn into my chance to step up. Amen.*

DAY 136

THE BRINK OF BREAKTHROUGH

Keep on asking and it will be given you; keep on seeking and you will find; keep on knocking [reverently] and [the door] will be opened to you.

MATTHEW 7:7

In the early days of my ministry, God used one scripture in particular to encourage me not to quit, and it continues to speak to me today:

> Let us not become weary in doing good, for at the proper time we will reap a harvest if we do not give up.
>
> Galatians 6:9 NIV

Satan wants us to quit and give up. The Bible says he is the "father of lies" (John 8:44). He continually lies to us and says, "That's never going to happen! Do you really believe that God spoke to you? You think someone like *you* could do something like *that*?"

It's often in those moments that we're on the brink of a breakthrough. Keeping faith and pressing on can lead us to the realization of God's promises. It's a reminder to persevere even when things seem most challenging.

Wherever you are today, know that God loves you, He sees you, and He is with you. God is not only the author of new beginnings, He's also the author of great finishes.

PRAYER FOR TODAY: *God, I don't want to lose heart, but sometimes it feels impossible to keep going. I know that the devil is a liar. Teach me to drown out the devil's voice in my head and replace it with all the thoughts You think toward me: thoughts for new beginnings and great finishes. Amen.*

DAY 137

SOMETHING GOOD

Finally, brothers and sisters, whatever is true, whatever is noble, whatever is right, whatever is pure, whatever is lovely, whatever is admirable—if anything is excellent or praiseworthy—think about such things.

PHILIPPIANS 4:8 NIV

When was the last time you said to yourself, "Something good is going to happen to me"? If you're like most people, it's been a long time. I believe our natural inclination is to focus on the negative. It's easy to concentrate on everything that does or could go wrong. It doesn't take much effort to meditate on how things may not work out the way we want.

The media is also filled with primarily negative news. It's been proven that negative news attracts attention. The more shocking, the more threatening, and the more fear-filled it is, the more potential it has to affect us and the quicker the message spreads.

The bottom line is, if we're going to focus on the good, it has to be a choice!

I've heard that God says "Fear not" 365 times in the Bible. He doesn't want us to be afraid, anxious, or worried a single day of our lives. He wants us to trust that He's in control, He loves us, and He's greater than our greatest fears. He wants us to say, "Something good is going to happen to me!" He wants us to choose faith, hope, and good thoughts, and to always believe the best.

PRAYER FOR TODAY: *God, I believe You are up to something good. Your Word says that You have a good plan for my life, so give me faith to trust that something good is going to happen to me. The temptation to be negative is there, but with Your help I can choose to focus on the good. Amen.*

DAY 138: HOW TO DEFEAT FEAR

So do not fear, for I am with you; do not be dismayed, for I am your God. I will strengthen you and help you; I will uphold you with my righteous right hand.

ISAIAH 41:10 NIV

You can't defeat fear by being logical and rational—if you rely on your own strength, it will fail you. The way you deal with fear is by trusting God's promises and receiving His love.

Every time you have a fearful thought, purposely stop and say to yourself, "God hasn't forsaken me—He's with me, and He's in control of my life. I have nothing to fear because God loves me." Stop immersing yourself in worst-case scenarios and start immersing yourself in things that cause you to expect the best. It may not be easy at first, but you can retrain your mind to begin expecting great things.

God wants us to believe every single thing His Word says. He wants us to believe that He loves us, He has a great plan for our future, and He's working on our behalf (Romans 8:38–39; Jeremiah 29:11; Romans 8:28).

God wants you to actively believe and expect that good things are going to happen to you because He has a good plan for you. When you choose to believe what God says, it fills your life with joy, peace, and hope and enables you to defeat fear.

PRAYER FOR TODAY: *God, stir up my imagination with best-case scenarios. I want to believe the best, knowing that You will do better things in my life than I can imagine. Thank You for giving me the power to defeat fear by believing in Your Word. Amen.*

DAY 139

FAITH AND PATIENCE

We do not want you to become lazy, but to imitate those who through faith and patience inherit what has been promised.
HEBREWS 6:12 NIV

Today's scripture tells us we inherit God's promises "through faith and patience" (NIV). Hebrews 12:1 says, "Let us run with patient endurance and steady and active persistence the appointed course of the race that is set before us."

Patience is a big part of faith. Most things won't happen overnight, and faith requires us to wait for God's appointed time without giving up or wavering. Patience is an attitude that says, "I'm going to stay calm and believe God is going to do exactly what He said He's going to do."

When we see God's promises in His Word or He speaks something specific to our hearts, our part is to believe and then do every little thing God shows us.

Sometimes we can get so weary from waiting that it's hard to imagine waiting one more second. But that's when we need to hold on; that's when we need to keep waiting on God and trusting Him with a sweet and simple faith.

Never give up on seeing God's Word come to pass in your life. If the Lord has spoken something to your heart or given you a vision for the future, hang on to it and refuse to quit, regardless of how long it takes. God may not be early, but He will never be late.

PRAYER FOR TODAY: *God, I am holding on to Your promises for my life. Show me how to trust You and remind me that You are using this time to prepare me for the things You have in store for me. Help me keep a good attitude while I wait! Amen.*

DAY 140: LOWER THE NETS AGAIN

For he and all who were with him were astonished at the catch of fish which they had taken.

LUKE 5:9 NKJV

Luke 5:1–11 contains a great lesson about faith. Jesus tells Peter, "Put out into the deep [water], and lower your nets for a haul" (v. 4). Peter responds: "Master, we toiled all night [exhaustingly] and caught nothing [in our nets]" (v. 5). Peter was exhausted. He'd been out all night and not seen any results. The last thing he wanted to do was go out with the possibility of trying and failing again.

Despite his exhaustion, Peter says to Jesus, "But on the ground of Your word, I will lower the nets [again]" (v. 5). When we are tired, we can be tempted to give up. When we haven't gotten our breakthrough, we can be tempted to give in. When the Lord has given us a vision for our lives but it seems like nothing has happened after so much time has passed, we can feel like we've missed our chance.

That's when Jesus says, "I know you are tired, but try again." And like Peter, we have to dig deep, stand on His Word, and act in faith. Scripture says Peter went out and lowered the nets again, "And when they had done this, they caught a great number of fish" (v. 6).

Like He spoke to Peter, the Lord is asking you to keep going, keep believing, keep trusting, and keep taking steps of faith. In due time, you will be astonished by what God does!

PRAYER FOR TODAY: *God, I am tired of waiting. I am tired of trying and not seeing any results. But I want to do Your will, so if You say so, if You tell me to try again and again and again, I will do it. Help me be determined to never give up. Amen.*

DAY 141: THE BATTLE IS SPIRITUAL

For we are not fighting against flesh-and-blood enemies, but against evil rulers and authorities of the unseen world, against mighty powers in this dark world, and against evil spirits in the heavenly places.

EPHESIANS 6:12 NLT

The toughest enemy to fight is the one we don't know about. That's why Ephesians 6:12 is such an important scripture to understand. It says "we do not wrestle against flesh and blood, but...against the spiritual forces of evil" (ESV).

Our enemies aren't our circumstances, other people, or even ourselves. Behind all of the things that are happening on the surface, there is also a very real *spiritual* battle taking place.

The Bible says that Satan's sole purpose is to "steal and kill and destroy" (John 10:10 ESV). And one of the primary ways he does this is through deception. He lies to us and brings all kinds of negative thoughts to our minds, hoping we will receive them as truth.

John 8:44 teaches us that Satan is a liar and the father of lies. The enemy attempts over and over to get us to believe things that aren't true. Even though they are lies, he knows that if we believe they are true, they become a reality for us and negatively affect us in so many ways.

We are in a spiritual battle, and we must fight with a spiritual weapon: God's Word. God's Word is the only thing powerful enough to renew our thinking and protect us from the negative thoughts of the enemy.

PRAYER FOR TODAY: *God, keep my thoughts focused on the truth found in Your Word. Give me the desire to read and study Your Word so that when I need it, I can use it to fight against the enemy. I want a mind totally renewed by Your Word. Amen.*

DAY 142

BEWARE SATAN'S STRONGHOLDS

For the weapons of our warfare are not of the flesh but have divine power to destroy strongholds... and take captive every thought to obey Christ.

2 CORINTHIANS 10:4-5 ESV

A stronghold is an area where the enemy entrenches himself and takes control. *Stronghold* is often used to refer to soldiers fighting battles, but the Bible uses it to refer to strongholds in our minds. These are areas of our thinking dominated by the enemy—areas where we are deceived.

Satan comes against us by bombarding our minds with nagging thoughts that lead to suspicion, doubt, fear, reasoning, and theories that refute the truth of God's Word. When these thoughts take root in our minds, they become strongholds that give the enemy control.

So many of God's children are struggling because they are believing lies, such as "I'm really not that important—no one would even miss me if I wasn't around." "I'll never be successful. My family's always been poor, and that's just the way life is." "This is too hard! I don't think I can do this anymore. I should just give up." "My past is such a mess—no one is ever going to love me."

But we can take heart in the Word of God! It has the power to destroy the enemy's strongholds and lead us to a better life.

PRAYER FOR TODAY: *God, I'm struggling with my thoughts. It's so hard not to believe Satan's lies, but I want to do better. I want to think better. Give me greater understanding of Your Word and what it says about me. Amen.*

DAY 143

A NEW MINDSET

The Spirit of the Lord is on me, because he has anointed me to proclaim good news to the poor. He has sent me to proclaim freedom for the prisoners and recovery of sight for the blind, to set the oppressed free.

LUKE 4:18 NIV

Because I came from a background of abuse, I did not know how to have faith for a positive future. My childhood was filled with fear and torment, and my personality was a mess. As a young adult trying to follow the Christian lifestyle, I knew where I had come from, but I did not know where I was going. I felt that my future would always be marred by my past.

I thought, *How could anyone who has the kind of past I do ever really be all right? It's impossible!*

However, Jesus said that He came to heal those who are brokenhearted, wounded, and bruised—those broken down by calamity.

You may have had a miserable past. You may even be in negative circumstances right now or facing situations that are so bad that it seems you have no real reason to hope. But regardless of where you've been or where you are in life right now, please know that your past or your present does not determine your future!

Make a decision to have a new, positive mindset. No matter what has happened in your life, you can choose to believe that "with God all things are possible" (Mark 10:27 NKJV).

PRAYER FOR TODAY: *God, I believe Your Word, which says that all things are possible with You. When I'm facing a situation that makes that hard to believe, I need You to help me remember. I know You can take all of the negative things that have happened to me and turn them into something good. Amen.*

DAY 144
PITIFUL OR POWERFUL, BUT NOT BOTH

Indeed, we hear that some among you are disorderly [that they are passing their lives in idleness, neglectful of duty], being busy with other people's affairs instead of their own and doing no work.
2 THESSALONIANS 3:11

When bad things happen to us or when we feel like life isn't fair, it's so easy to want to turn inward and feel sorry for ourselves. However, self-pity is not productive—it actually prevents us from growing and moving forward.

Take a moment and reflect on the following questions: How do you respond to disappointments? How much time do you spend feeling sorry for yourself?

Self-pity was a hard thing for me to give up. For years, I used it to comfort myself when I was hurting. However, self-pity is a major trap, and it's one of Satan's favorite tools to prevent us from moving forward. We can't truly be free until we let self-pity go.

One day, the Lord clearly spoke to my heart and said, "Joyce, you can be pitiful or powerful, but you cannot be both."

Second Timothy 1:7 says that God has given us a spirit "of power and of love and of a sound mind" (NKJV). Clearly the Lord does not want us to be pitiful; He has enabled us to be powerful! His Spirit is within us, and God wants us to tap into the power that is already ours.

When you feel those emotions of self-pity rising within you, check your thinking. Then go to God and ask for help to access the spirit of power and of love and of a sound mind that is within you.

PRAYER FOR TODAY: *God, give me the strength to change my thinking and let go of these thoughts of self-pity. I have so much to be thankful for, and I know that You are on my side through everything. Amen.*

DAY 145: DO YOUR OWN THINKING

We destroy arguments and every lofty opinion raised against the knowledge of God, and take every thought captive to obey Christ.
2 CORINTHIANS 10:5 ESV

Do you think about what you're thinking about? Learning to regularly take inventory of our thoughts is essential to having a good life. Instead of being "unthinking" people, we can train ourselves to think about what's going on in our minds.

It was a glorious revelation for me when I realized I don't have to think about just anything that comes into my mind. I can choose my thoughts and do my own thinking—on purpose. I can deliberately choose to think positive, faith-filled thoughts that line up with God's Word.

If your mood begins to sink or you have a bad attitude, take an inventory of your current thoughts, and you will very likely find the culprit. Negative thinking not only makes you upset and bitter, but it also prevents God from working in your life. We receive from God through faith, and faith is always positive.

You don't have to sit by passively and let the enemy fill your mind with poisonous and destructive thoughts. Instead, you can learn to recognize them, and with God's help, you can think about something else that will be beneficial.

Make a decision to think and say the right things—things that line up with the Word of God.

PRAYER FOR TODAY: *God, help me recognize when my thoughts aren't my own so that I can take them captive and replace them with thoughts that are beneficial. Help me think with the mind of Christ! Amen.*

DAY 146: LOOK HOW FAR YOU'VE COME

For it is by free grace (God's unmerited favor) that you are saved (delivered from judgment and made partakers of Christ's salvation) through [your] faith. And this [salvation] is not of yourselves [of your own doing, it came not through your own striving], but it is the gift of God.

EPHESIANS 2:8

Whether it's God's love, salvation, forgiveness, or the many promises in His Word, there's nothing we can do to earn these things. He wants to give them freely to us by His grace.

For years, I dealt with such guilt and condemnation after I would do something wrong. I repented and asked the Lord to forgive me, but I couldn't let it go. I felt like I needed to pay for what I had done by feeling bad about myself.

It took a change in my thinking to simply receive what God wanted to give me: His forgiveness.

In the process, the Lord also helped me to see the importance of having a positive self-image. We shouldn't always focus on everything we do wrong and how far we have to go; we should look at how far we have come!

We must realize that we can never deserve God's blessings—we can never be worthy of them. We can only humbly accept and appreciate them and be in awe of how good He is and how much He loves us.

PRAYER FOR TODAY: *God, thank You for Your grace. I don't deserve Your blessings, yet You freely give them to me. Help me receive them by faith. Amen.*

DAY 147: UNIQUELY YOU

I praise you, for I am fearfully and wonderfully made. Wonderful are your works; my soul knows it very well.

PSALM 139:14 ESV

Jealousy, envy, and comparison with others are mindsets that will never lead us in a positive direction. If we are not secure in our God-given worth and value as individuals, we will mistakenly look to others as a benchmark for our own success.

I used to compare myself to my pastor's wife, who was gentle, sweet, and nice to everyone. Why couldn't I be more like her? I also compared myself to my neighbor, a homemaker who grew her own vegetables and sewed her family's clothes. In reality, the more I focused on comparing myself to other people, the more inadequate I felt.

Learning that I am an individual—that God has a unique, personal plan for my life and that I don't need to compare myself with anyone else—has been one of the most valuable and freeing truths God has helped me understand.

God has made you to be unique, with your own strengths and abilities, and there is no one who can be a better you than you. So set your mind to appreciate the gifts in others, and decide to trust God with yourself. It may take time and persistence, but tearing down this mental stronghold will lead to greater contentment and fulfillment in your life.

PRAYER FOR TODAY: *God, help me stop comparing myself to others. Being jealous all the time is making me miserable! I want to be happy with myself and who You created me to be: uniquely me. Amen.*

DAY 148: THE STORIES WE TELL

But he said to me, "My grace is sufficient for you, for my power is made perfect in weakness." Therefore I will boast all the more gladly of my weaknesses, so that the power of Christ may rest upon me.

2 CORINTHIANS 12:9 ESV

The stories we tell ourselves about what is happening to us can significantly impact our beliefs, our emotions, and how we perceive and respond to our experiences.

For example, we can experience setbacks as permanent failures, or we can see them as opportunities for growth. When faced with financial challenges, we can say that we'll never get ahead, or we can believe that better days are right around the corner. When a relationship hits a snag, or an unexpected illness catches us by surprise, we can think, *I can't do this—it's just too hard*, or we can believe that this too shall pass, and we can do whatever we need to do because God is with us.

Getting upset about our problems never changes them. However, choosing to adopt a positive attitude can. We can magnify our problems, or we can choose to magnify the Lord, who is good! Second Corinthians 12:9 tells us that God's strength is made perfect in our weaknesses. This means that God will show Himself strong through us when we go through difficult times.

No matter what we are going through, we can decide to trust God, lean on Him, and have and enjoy a fulfilling life with Him.

PRAYER FOR TODAY: *God, thank You for reminding me that the story I tell myself about what I am going through is as important as what I am going through. Change my perspective to see opportunities, not challenges. Amen.*

DAY 149: ANYBODY CAN CHANGE

A new commandment I give to you, that you love one another: just as I have loved you, you also are to love one another.

JOHN 13:34 ESV

When I was working through the trauma of my past, Dave's belief that God could change me was a key factor in my healing. I only felt love from him. Sadly, most of the time I couldn't receive it, but that didn't stop him from being who he was. He kept offering love, and he remained joyful.

Similarly, God keeps giving even if we have not yet learned how to receive, and we can learn to do the same thing in our relationships with other people. Even if you don't see any change yet, you can continue believing that God is working.

If you're struggling with someone who you think will never change, begin to fill your mind with thoughts like *I believe God is working and all things are possible with Him*. You will feel better, and your attitude toward the person will be much better.

We cannot change people—only God can. We are only responsible for fulfilling the law of Christ, which is to love. We can be satisfied in knowing we are doing what God is asking of us, even if we don't see immediate results.

Your thoughts, attitudes, and actions can play an important role in someone's transformation. Let God use you. Start believing that anybody can change.

PRAYER FOR TODAY: *God, I have heard amazing stories of how You have changed people. Help me not give up on the people I love and keep believing that with You all things are possible. I will keep doing what You have called me to do: love. Amen.*

DAY 150: THINK HEALTHY

But they who wait for the Lord shall renew their strength; they shall mount up with wings like eagles; they shall run and not be weary; they shall walk and not faint.

ISAIAH 40:31 ESV

Dealing with sickness is one of the most difficult things in life. It not only affects our bodies but also takes a toll on us mentally and emotionally.

When we're sick, the enemy likes to bombard our minds with negative thoughts like *You're never going to get well* or *It's just going to keep getting worse.*

However, we can stop wrong thoughts by filling our minds with the right thoughts from God's Word. Hebrews 4:12 says, "the Word that God speaks is alive and full of power." Thinking and speaking His Word literally breathes life into our situations!

Years ago, when I was battling cancer, God put it on my heart to fill my mind with affirmations from His Word, then speak them out loud as often as I could. I would think and say: "God, I know that You love me. I believe that all things work out for good for those who love You and are called according to Your purpose. I put my trust in You, and I will not fear" (Romans 8:28, 35–39; Joshua 1:9; Proverbs 3:5).

The truth is that all of our thoughts—good or bad—have an effect on our physical bodies. So, we need to choose to think about ourselves and our situations according to God's Word, which promotes health and wholeness.

PRAYER FOR TODAY: *God, renew my strength as You renew my mind. I don't want to believe this is the end for me. I want to believe that You have more for me. Help me focus on hope. Heal me from the inside out. Amen.*

DAY 151: A POSITIVE LIFE BEGINS HERE

Do not be conformed to this world (this age), [fashioned after and adapted to its external, superficial customs], but be transformed (changed) by the [entire] renewal of your mind [by its new ideals and its new attitude], so that you may prove [for yourselves] what is the good and acceptable and perfect will of God, even the thing which is good and acceptable and perfect [in His sight for you].
ROMANS 12:2

Whether you realize it or not, your thoughts, words, and attitudes have a tremendous impact on your relationships. A positive attitude will attract friends and make you so much more enjoyable to be around. Likewise, someone with a negative attitude is fighting an uphill battle if they hope to make and maintain quality friendships.

Today's key verse was life-changing for me. How? When we fill our minds with God's Word and learn to think like He thinks, these positive, faith-filled thoughts flow through our words and attitudes to the people around us.

I don't think negative people even realize how their attitude affects their relationships. I sure didn't. But the truth is, anyone who is happy and positive quickly discovers that being with a negative person doesn't bring them joy.

So I ask you: Are you a good friend? Are you the kind of person other people want to be around?

PRAYER FOR TODAY: *God, I want to be the kind of person that people want to be around. Help me to be a good friend and to show love to the people I meet. Show me when I am being negative so that I can turn my thoughts around. Amen.*

DAY 152
TWO WAYS TO WAIT

Guard and keep yourselves in the love of God; expect and patiently wait for the mercy of our Lord Jesus Christ (the Messiah)—[which will bring you] unto life eternal.

JUDE 1:21

When we're waiting for a breakthrough, we can wait either passively or expectantly.

A passive person is willing to sit around, waiting to see if something good will happen. After a short time, however, they give up, saying, "I've waited, but nothing's happened." The expectant person, on the other hand, believes the answer is always just around the corner, due to arrive any minute. They wake up every morning expecting their breakthrough, saying, "Today could be the day!"

When a woman is pregnant, we say that she is "expecting." She carries inside of her the promise of a baby, and even though she can't hold it yet, she knows it's there. The moment she learns of her pregnancy, she begins to plan for her baby's arrival because she knows the promise will be fulfilled—it's just a matter of time! She will wait as long as it takes. In fact, she prefers that the baby doesn't come early, because she knows it will be healthiest if it comes at full term.

Just like that expectant mother, God wants us to wait for our breakthrough with excitement and anticipation—to expect it to happen at just the right time and to not give up until we see it.

PRAYER FOR TODAY: *God, help me be like that expectant mother who is excited for this season because she knows that something amazing is coming. Help me trust You to bring my breakthrough at just the right time, which could be today. Amen.*

DAY 153: BUILD EACH OTHER UP

Do not let any unwholesome talk come out of your mouths, but only what is helpful for building others up according to their needs, that it may benefit those who listen.

EPHESIANS 4:29 NIV

First Thessalonians 5:11 tells us to encourage one another and build each other up. Encouragement is something people desperately need. But we can't encourage and uplift others if we are always negative, down, and discouraged ourselves.

Encouraging people is not a natural gift for me, but years ago I made a commitment to God to start doing it on purpose. Most days, I ask the Holy Spirit to show me who I can encourage.

Think about the people and friends you will see today, and ask God to put something in your heart that you can say to them that will be uplifting.

It can be as simple as saying something positive to someone you work with or letting them know how much you appreciate them. Sometimes I will take a moment to tell someone how much God loves them and wants to bless them.

Have you ever thought someone looked nice or did a great job at something, but didn't tell them? Tell them! You never know what a person is going through. A genuine compliment could make a profound impact on their outlook.

Our words have the power to heal, inspire, and uplift, and by sharing encouragement, we can make the world a brighter and more hopeful place.

PRAYER FOR TODAY: *God, show me who I can encourage today, and give me a special word that would lift their spirits. Let encouragement flow from my lips to everyone I meet. Amen.*

DAY 154: TRUST MORE, STRESS LESS

Commit your way to the Lord [roll and repose each care of your load on Him]; trust (lean on, rely on, and be confident) also in Him and He will bring it to pass.

PSALM 37:5

Research shows that the majority of mental, physical, and behavioral illnesses come from our thought lives. There is no doubt that the mind and body are connected!

For instance, we can actually stress ourselves out just by the way we think. So often, we believe our circumstances are to blame for our unhappiness; however, it's the way we think about our circumstances that usually causes worry, stress, and unhappiness.

Stress has been proven to cause issues like muscle tension, headaches, breathing irregularities, increased heart rate, and gastrointestinal problems—and that's only a few of the symptoms!

The good news is God has given us the answer for worry and stress. What's His prescription? Trust Him in every situation.

Trusting God is the greatest stress reliever in the world, and our minds play an important role in the process. We have a choice and the answer is found in Proverbs 3:5. We can rely on our own insight and understanding—endlessly thinking about our problems, trying to figure everything out ourselves—or we can choose to adopt a trusting attitude that says, "God, I don't know what to do about this situation. If You want me to do something, I ask You to show me. Meanwhile, I'm going to trust You and enjoy my life while You work on my problems." Amen!

PRAYER FOR TODAY: *God, thank You for giving me guidance from Your Word about how my thought life affects every area of my life. Help me trust You more and stress less. Amen.*

DAY 155: RENEW YOUR MIND

And try to learn [in your experience] what is pleasing to the Lord [let your lives be constant proofs of what is most acceptable to Him].

EPHESIANS 5:10

Through His death and resurrection, Jesus offers us a new way of living. But to fully walk in that new life, we must allow our thinking to be renewed according to God's truth.

Romans 12:2 says, "Be transformed (changed) by the [entire] renewal of your mind [by its new ideals and its new attitude]." But let's look at the second half of this verse. It says: "so that you may prove [for yourselves] what is the good and acceptable and perfect will of God."

God has a good, acceptable, and perfect plan for us, but we won't experience it by thinking the way the world thinks. We are changed as we learn to renew our minds and think the way God thinks. That is entirely possible because God has equipped us with the mind of Christ (1 Corinthians 2:16).

So, when life throws you a curveball and you're tempted to get stressed out, you can choose positive, faith-filled thoughts from God's Word. You can think, *The Lord is going to take care of this. It doesn't matter what it looks like—I believe God is working!*

The truth is, God knew about your problem before you ever experienced it, and He already has a plan for your solution. In the meantime, you can choose to put on the mind of Christ and choose faith-filled thoughts.

PRAYER FOR TODAY: *God, thank You for having a solution for what I am going through. While I might not see it yet, I need Your help to trust Your good plan and good purpose for me. I want to choose to trust You. Amen.*

DAY 156: CHOOSE PEACE

Peace I leave with you; My [own] peace I now give and bequeath to you. Not as the world gives do I give to you. Do not let your hearts be troubled, neither let them be afraid. [Stop allowing yourselves to be agitated and disturbed; and do not permit yourselves to be fearful and intimidated and cowardly and unsettled.]

JOHN 14:27

Years ago, when my children were young, I would sit at our kitchen table and spend hours looking at our bills, worrying about how we would pay them. Dave, on the other hand, would be sitting on the floor in the TV room, letting the kids put curlers in his hair.

I would say, "Dave, how can you have fun at a time like this?" And he would answer, "Joyce, we've prayed about it, and we're doing everything we know to do. I refuse to be miserable with you." Dave was right. I was allowing myself to get upset and waste time I could have been spending with my children.

In John 14:27, Jesus says He gives us His peace, but "not as the world gives do I give to you." The peace Jesus gives us is not dependent on external circumstances but is rather a fruit of the Spirit that we can cultivate through our thoughts, actions, and attitudes. This requires a willingness to let go of worry, fear, stress, and negativity and to choose peace instead.

Choosing peace doesn't mean ignoring or denying the challenges we face; rather, it's about facing them knowing that we can trust the One who holds all things together (Colossians 1:17).

PRAYER FOR TODAY: *God, I don't want to miss any more of my life by worrying about things I can't do anything about. Help me choose the peace that You have freely offered. I know this isn't a one-time thing, so help me choose peace again and again. Amen.*

DAY 157: HOW TO FEEL HAPPIER

And put on the new self [the regenerated and renewed nature], created in God's image, [godlike] in the righteousness and holiness of the truth [living in a way that expresses to God your gratitude for your salvation].

EPHESIANS 4:24 AMP

No matter what is going on in your life today, if you will choose happy, hope-filled thoughts based on God's Word, you will feel happier. Our thoughts are intricately connected to our feelings, so if we want to feel better, we need to think better.

It's like putting gas in a car. If we use the correct fuel, our cars will run well. But if we use the wrong fuel, they may not run at all. In the same way, when we choose our thoughts carefully, our quality of life will improve in amazing ways!

Take a moment to reflect. What types of things have you been mentally focusing on? How do these thoughts connect to the way you feel emotionally and even physically?

You see, nothing good comes from thinking critical, negative thoughts, but something good always comes when we think according to God's plan for our lives.

Ephesians 4:22–24 tells us that the way to *put off* your old life and *put on* the new is to constantly renew your mind and attitude. That begins with filling our minds with God's Word then choosing to think and speak the positive, faith-filled things He says about our lives.

PRAYER FOR TODAY: *God, give me the desire to spend time in Your Word and the wisdom to understand it as I read it. I want to fill my mind with what You say about me, and I am ready to have the good life You want me to have. Amen.*

DAY 158: START YOUR DAY RIGHT

Let the morning bring me word of your unfailing love, for I have put my trust in you. Show me the way I should go, for to you I entrust my life.

PSALM 143:8 NIV

Did you know that you can jump-start your day by thinking and speaking good things on purpose as one of your first acts in the morning? Each morning, I encourage you to meditate on God's Word and speak out things like:

"This is the day God has made, and I am going to enjoy it!" (Psalm 118:24).

"Today, I am strong and energetic" (Isaiah 40:28–31).

"I have favor with God and man everywhere I go" (Luke 2:52).

"God is working on my problems, and I can wait patiently because His timing is perfect" (Psalm 31:15; 37:7; 46:1).

"I can handle whatever comes my way today through Christ, who is my strength" (Philippians 4:13).

Remember, a negative mind and mouth will produce negative moods and attitudes. But when you set your mind in an uplifting direction, it will have a good effect on your entire day.

PRAYER FOR TODAY: *God, I want to start my day in the right direction. Help me focus on Your words and Your thoughts for the day. This is the day that the Lord has made, and I will rejoice and be glad in it. Amen.*

DAY 159: ONE STEP AT A TIME

He drew me up out of a horrible pit [a pit of tumult and of destruction], out of the miry clay (froth and slime), and set my feet upon a rock, steadying my steps and establishing my goings.

PSALM 40:2

If you desire greater emotional stability and the ability to maintain a consistent good attitude no matter what your circumstances are, then make it a goal and don't give up until you have reached it.

Breaking down big goals into smaller steps can make them feel much more achievable. Don't sabotage yourself with discouraging words—saying and thinking that you will never change, that you will never be able to be happy because of what you are going through, that you will always be on an emotional roller coaster. Instead, break it down to one day at a time. Say, "Today I will have a good attitude. When something unexpected comes up, I will keep my cool. I will laugh when the devil tries to steal my joy. I can do this, one day at a time!"

A walk begins with one step and then another and another. Each step forward, no matter how small, brings you closer to where you want to be. No matter how long your journey seems, if you take enough steps in the right direction, you will eventually arrive at your desired destination and truly have the life you've always wanted.

PRAYER FOR TODAY: *God, I don't want my emotions to control me. Teach me how to be consistent and stable in my moods and attitudes. Remind me that even baby steps are steps in the right direction and worth celebrating. Amen.*

DAY 160
A REVELATION OF GOD'S LOVE

For God so greatly loved and dearly prized the world that He [even] gave up His only begotten (unique) Son, so that whoever believes in (trusts in, clings to, relies on) Him shall not perish (come to destruction, be lost) but have eternal (everlasting) life.

JOHN 3:16

The most important message I can ever share with someone is that God loves them and has a good plan for their life. We all need to have a revelation about God's love for us. Until we do, we'll struggle to have genuine love, joy, and peace in our everyday lives.

The good news is, if you've been hurt in the past, you don't have to spend your life being miserable, angry, bitter, resentful, or full of self-pity, hurting others. Through a personal relationship with Jesus Christ, you can receive complete healing in your soul—your mind, will, and emotions. God can restore your life and heal you, making your life better than it was before.

God always had a plan for my life, and He has redeemed me. He has taken what Satan meant for harm and turned it into something good (Romans 8:28). He has taken away my shame and given me a double reward and recompense (Isaiah 61:7).

God's truth has set me free and has restored my soul. I am living proof that nothing is too hard for God. And no matter what you've been through or how bad you're hurting, there is hope through Jesus Christ!

PRAYER FOR TODAY: *God, thank You for loving me. Thank You for dying for me. Thank You for planning a good life for me from the very beginning. Help me trust You and cling to hope as You heal me from the inside out. Amen.*

DAY 161
HEALING FOR THE BROKENHEARTED

The Spirit of the Lord God is upon me, because the Lord has anointed me to bring good news to the poor; he has sent me to bind up the brokenhearted, to proclaim liberty to the captives, and the opening of the prison to those who are bound.

ISAIAH 61:1 ESV

Many people seem to have it all together outwardly, but inside they are hurting. If you could see the thoughts they have about themselves or feel the pain in their hearts caused by others, you would realize they aren't truly enjoying the good life God has planned for them.

Isaiah 61 says the Lord came to heal the brokenhearted and to help those who are crushed and broken on the inside. He wants to give us joy instead of mourning, beauty for ashes, praise instead of despair—and through it all, restore our hope.

Whatever you're going through or whatever has happened in your past, I want you to know that God can restore your life. I can say this with certainty because He has truly restored mine. In fact, He has taken what the enemy meant for harm and worked it out for my good (Genesis 50:20).

Psalm 34:18 says, "The Lord is close to those who are of a broken heart." God sees every hurt, every trial, and every disappointment. And if you let Him, He can make all things new. He can take the bad thing that happened and work it out for your good.

PRAYER FOR TODAY: *God, You know I don't have it all together. You know the secret places of my heart that ache with hurt and disappointment. You know the mess that is in my mind. Please be near me and heal my heart. Amen.*

DAY 162: BEAUTY FOR ASHES

To console those who mourn in Zion, to give them beauty for ashes, the oil of joy for mourning, the garment of praise for the spirit of heaviness; that they may be called trees of righteousness, the planting of the Lord, that He may be glorified.

ISAIAH 61:3 NKJV

You don't have to live stuck in the pain of your past. You can trade in your pain for God's promise. You can have beauty instead of ashes.

Jesus came "to heal the brokenhearted, to proclaim liberty to the captives, and the opening of the prison to those who are bound; to proclaim the acceptable year of the Lord, and the day of vengeance of our God; to comfort all who mourn... to give them *beauty for ashes*, the oil of joy for mourning, the garment of praise for the spirit of heaviness" (Isaiah 61:3 NKJV, emphasis mine).

You were never meant to live a life defined by words like *ashes*, *mourning*, or *heaviness*. Jesus died to give you a life of beauty, joy, and praise!

God can restore whatever you've lost. And He wants to bring forth something beautiful, even in the most unlikely places.

When we come into a relationship with Christ, a divine exchange happens. He gives us joy for mourning, praise instead of depression, righteousness instead of guilt, hope instead of despair, and more. Thank God for His Word and His promises!

PRAYER FOR TODAY: *God, give me the strength to cling to Your Word today and hold on to hope. I know that it will get better, but right now it is hard! Thank You for reminding me that nothing is too hard for You and You make beauty in unlikely places. Amen.*

DAY 163 — HEALING IS A PROCESS

Therefore humble yourselves under the mighty hand of God [set aside self-righteous pride], so that He may exalt you [to a place of honor in His service] at the appropriate time.

1 PETER 5:6 AMP

If you are dealing with a hurt or disappointment today—big or small—please know that God loves you and He wants to help you. Your situation has not been overlooked by Him. He knows exactly where you are and exactly what you are going through.

The healing process isn't easy. It takes time, a commitment to studying God's Word, and prayer. However, the Lord is faithful, and as you trust Him, He will bring healing, growth, and new life.

Start by admitting you need God's help. God helps the humble (1 Peter 5:5–7)! We need to let God take us apart and then put us back together again.

As we renew our minds according to the Word, we will trust God more completely and believe what He says more than what others say about us, more than our feelings, and more than our circumstances. That's when we live in His beauty, filled with His love, free from the prisons of our past, and healed in our souls.

God loves you more than you can comprehend, and He wants you to be free to walk in His good plans for your life. Take time every day to study His Word. Pray and cast your cares on Him, because He cares about you and wants what is best for you.

PRAYER FOR TODAY: *God, I need You. I need Your help. Heal my heart and any broken places. Make me who You want me to be. Amen.*

DAY 164: ROOTED IN LOVE

May Christ through your faith [actually] dwell (settle down, abide, make His permanent home) in your hearts! May you be rooted deep in love and founded securely on love.

EPHESIANS 3:17

God wants us to enjoy our lives (John 10:10), but you cannot enjoy your life if down deep on the inside you're ashamed of who you are.

Isaiah 54:4 says, "Forget the shame of your youth and remember no more" (NIV).

It is inspiring and encouraging to know the Lord can help you forget the harm of your past and bring you to a place where you won't remember those hard times!

Ephesians 3:17 says that we can be "rooted" in God's love. Like plants, some of us have to get transplanted. If you got started in the wrong pot, so to speak, Jesus will transplant you. Instead of being rooted in shame or anything else, you can get rooted and grounded in His love.

God created us to be loved. He wants to love us, He wants us to love each other, and He wants us to love and accept ourselves. Without this foundation of love and acceptance, you can't have joy and peace.

You need to know that you are valuable, unique, loved, and special. When this is your foundation and your roots, you will produce good fruit such as self-control, faithfulness, goodness, kindness, goodness, patience, peace, joy, and love.

PRAYER FOR TODAY: *God, why is it so hard to like myself? Help me see that it's not prideful to like who I am, because You created me. Give me the desire to study Your Word and see what You say about me so that I can get rooted in Your love. Amen.*

DAY 165: THE FAITH TO FORGIVE

Do not repay evil with evil or insult with insult. On the contrary, repay evil with blessing, because to this you were called so that you may inherit a blessing.

1 PETER 3:9 NIV

One of the greatest gifts we can give ourselves is the willingness to forgive. Learning to forgive quickly is key to controlling our emotions rather than allowing them to rule us.

Forgiveness is God's path to emotional healing and spoils the enemy's plan to destroy our relationships. It disarms the sting of bitterness, invites the peace of God, and brings healing power to our souls.

Forgiveness is simply a choice you make to trust God to be the judge, not you. When you give God control over the situation, that opens the door for God's love, power, favor, and peace to flow in your life. Forgiveness is a choice; it is not a feeling.

God has given us His grace to be good to people—even to people who aren't being good to us. He has given us the power to pray for our enemies and not be mad at people who have hurt us or attacked us (Matthew 5:44).

It takes courage and faith to forgive. But if you ask God, He will generously supply His grace and everything you need to obey Him, and He will lead you into a place of emotional freedom.

PRAYER FOR TODAY: *God, help me always quickly and completely forgive anyone who hurts me. I want to be able to forgive others just as You have forgiven me. Thank You for giving me everything I need to fully extend forgiveness. Amen.*

DAY 166: NO ORDINARY COMFORT

Let your steadfast love comfort me.

PSALM 119:76 ESV

Scripture tells us that as a young man, Joseph had great dreams for his life. But his older brothers resented him and sold him into slavery, and he was taken to Egypt. However, Joseph refused to give up. He found great favor with his master, Potiphar, and was eventually put in charge of Potiphar's entire household.

Years later, Potiphar threw Joseph in jail for a crime he didn't commit. But Joseph still didn't give up. In fact, the Lord eventually gave him an opportunity to interpret a dream for Pharaoh, who then promoted him to the role of highest official in Egypt!

When we refuse to give up, the greatest tragedies of our lives can actually turn out to be the greatest blessings. Your problems may never completely disappear, but your attitude and response to those problems can make all the difference for you and so many others.

When you are hurting, I encourage you to run to God—the "[Source] of every comfort" (2 Corinthians 1:3). Spend time in His Word, talk to Him in prayer, and choose to worship Him, even when you don't feel like it.

God's comfort goes far beyond any ordinary kind of comfort. He is the only One who can carry you through the pain and turn things around in your favor.

PRAYER FOR TODAY: *God, I need You to carry me through hard times, and although it isn't easy, Your Word says that You will work it together for my good. I'm trusting You. You did it for Joseph, and You'll do it for me. I need Your comfort today. Amen.*

DAY 167: RESTORE AND RECOMPENSE

For I, the Lord, love justice. I hate robbery and wrongdoing. I will faithfully reward my people for their suffering and make an everlasting covenant with them.

ISAIAH 61:8 NLT

If you've ever been robbed of or lost things that are rightfully yours, I have good news for you: God is a God of restoration, and He wants to restore everything the enemy has stolen.

God desires to not only repay us but also bring us back to what He originally intended—to the plans He had in mind for us before the foundation of the earth. The Bible calls it "recompense" (Isaiah 61:7–8). This means that God Himself will pay us back what is owed us and more.

Isaiah 61:7 says, "Instead of your [former] shame you shall have a twofold recompense...they shall possess double [what they had forfeited]; everlasting joy shall be theirs."

The word *recompense* here means "reward." God wants to reward you and honor you for the things you have been through.

If you trust God and do things His way, He will see to it that you are repaid for every injustice ever done to you. You will receive double what you have forfeited or lost, and everlasting joy will be yours!

PRAYER FOR TODAY: *God, please give me the strength to do things Your way. Help me believe that You have a plan for me and that it's not too late for me to have it. I want everlasting joy. I want peace. I want to trust You to not only restore to me what is owed but also to double it. Amen.*

DAY 168: THE BUSINESS OF DEBT COLLECTING

And the Lord turned the captivity of Job and restored his fortunes, when he prayed for his friends; also the Lord gave Job twice as much as he had before.

JOB 42:10

Job lost everything. He lost his children, his livestock, his livelihood, and his health. His wife turned against him, and so did his friends. Yet Job refused to curse God. Though he struggled deeply, he did not give up hope. He even prayed for the people who hurt him.

His faithfulness and his prayers led to his restoration. After he prayed for his friends, the Bible says God restored his fortunes and gave him twice as much as he had before.

Joel 2:25–26 says, "I will restore or replace for you the years that the locust has eaten...you shall eat in plenty and be satisfied and praise the name of the Lord, your God."

Restoration and blessings can follow even the darkest times.

Be like Job and turn the business of debt collecting over to the Lord Himself—He is the only One who can do the job properly. As you place your trust in Him, He will collect your debts and repay you for all your past hurts.

PRAYER FOR TODAY: *God, I know You are asking me to pray for the people who have caused me pain, but it is difficult. I surrender my will to Yours and ask for Your help to do it because, above all else, I want to be obedient to You. Help me trust that if You ask me to do it, it is because it is the best thing for me. Amen.*

DAY 169

PEACE AND PRAYER

And the peace of God, which surpasses all understanding, will guard your hearts and your minds in Christ Jesus.

PHILIPPIANS 4:7 ESV

Only God can change people from the inside out, and He does it in His timing. So, when someone is mistreating you or causing you pain, pray for them and then choose to be an example of peace and stability.

Maintain a calm delight in their presence. Assure them that you love them, but you're not going to let their decisions dictate your quality of life. In other words, don't become codependent on someone else's behavior.

Even if you don't see how they could ever change, don't give up hope! Remember that abuse or pain from the past is most likely causing a lot of their anger or difficulties. Pray and continue to pray that they will see the truth and begin to walk in the light.

Matthew 7:7 says, "Keep on asking and it will be given you; keep on seeking and you will find; keep on knocking [reverently] and [the door] will be opened to you."

I have seen amazing changes in people through the power of persistent prayer. Our sincere prayers give God an open door to work diligently in their lives, and He loves and changes them in His own way.

Be committed to keep praying and thanking God that He is working in the lives of people, even if you aren't yet seeing results.

PRAYER FOR TODAY: *God, grant me the strength to be an example of peace to the people around me and not let my attitude be affected by theirs. I know that I can't change others, but You can! Help me show them that a life with You will help them find true joy and peace. Amen.*

DAY 170: THE HOME OF GOD

Do you not know that your body is the temple (the very sanctuary) of the Holy Spirit Who lives within you, Whom you have received [as a Gift] from God? You are not your own.

1 CORINTHIANS 6:19

When you become a Christian, God comes to live inside your heart. You become the home of God, and He has access to all that you are and think and do.

God wants access to your mind. He wants you to think about things that are noble, pure, trustworthy, and admirable (Philippians 4:8). He wants access to your heart's desires. He wants you to want what He wants, and He wants you to be happy when others are blessed. He wants access to your words. He wants you to have conversations that are pleasant and encouraging (Colossians 4:6). He wants access to your friends list, because who you spend time with will influence how you live and think and act.

When you become the home of God, He becomes a constant presence in your life, leading, guiding, and comforting you. You can align your thoughts with His thoughts, your actions with His actions, and your values with His values. You can have a personal relationship with Him.

God lives in your heart and loves, understands, sees, and hears you. He wants to live in unity with you and to be the center of everything you do.

PRAYER FOR TODAY: *God, I haven't always been the best "housekeeper." Thank You for Your grace and for coming into my home, my life. I want to give You access to every room in my life so that You can show me who You want me to be in body, mind, and spirit. Amen.*

DAY 171: NO RESPECTER OF PERSONS

For God shows no partiality [undue favor or unfairness; with Him one man is not different from another].

ROMANS 2:11

Scripture says that God is no respecter of persons (Romans 2:11). That means what He does for one person, He will also do for another. It is God's will for *all* of us to be blessed.

You may be in a spot in your life right now that seems too big or painful to overcome. Maybe you're dealing with the pain of a failed relationship, suffering from an emotional wound, or living in debt that has accumulated over the years.

If so, I want you to know that God loves you and He wants to help you. Even if it seems like God is helping everyone else instead of you right now, don't quit, and don't give up! Persevere and keep doing what He's telling you to do, because He has a plan for you and will get you to where you're supposed to be.

It's important to remember that we don't typically get into our messes overnight—they are usually the result of years of difficult circumstances or even bad choices made by ourselves and other people. So, we can't expect to get our lives straightened out overnight.

Yes, God is a miracle-working God, and He can fix our problems in a moment if He wants to. But it usually doesn't happen that way. He often leads us out of our problems little by little, helping us to learn and grow in the process.

PRAYER FOR TODAY: *God, teach me what I need to learn from what I am going through. Grow me in this season. From now on, when I see someone else get blessed, I am going to be happy for them, and I am going to believe that I'm next. What You did for them, You'll do for me. Amen.*

DAY 172
OBEDIENCE LEADS TO BLESSINGS

Don't you realize that you become the slave of whatever you choose to obey? You can be a slave to sin, which leads to death, or you can choose to obey God, which leads to righteous living.

ROMANS 6:16 NLT

When it comes down to it, the way we get out of trouble is through learning how to make right choices. And if we make wise decisions according to what God tells us to do, we'll have what He says we can have.

Deuteronomy 30:19 says, "I have set before you life and death, the blessings and the curses; therefore choose life, that you and your descendants may live."

It's a simple message. God is saying, "Do what I tell you to do, and you'll be blessed!" When we obey God's direction for our lives and trust Him, He blesses us.

Whatever mess you are in, if you are determined to do what's right and follow God's Word, then you will see good results. Your financial situation can be turned around. Your marriage can change and improve. You can have a healthy body. You can have peace and joy. You can have a great relationship with God!

A big part of this is not giving up. Seeing God's good plan come to pass in your life requires commitment, diligence, dedication, and perseverance. But it's worth it!

He will bless you—spiritually, emotionally, physically, financially, and in every other way if you learn to make wise choices.

PRAYER FOR TODAY: *God, thank You for giving me the freedom to choose. I need Your wisdom to make wise choices. Today I choose obedience, trusting that You have a good plan for me. Amen.*

DAY 173
A LITTLE AT A TIME

And all of us, as with unveiled face, [because we] continued to behold [in the Word of God] as in a mirror the glory of the Lord, are constantly being transfigured into His very own image in ever increasing splendor and from one degree of glory to another; [for this comes] from the Lord [Who is] the Spirit.

2 CORINTHIANS 3:18

When we're born again, God plants a seed of everything He is in our spirit. For instance, Galatians 5:22–23 says, "The fruit of the Spirit is love, joy, peace, patience, kindness, goodness, faithfulness, gentleness, self-control" (ESV).

All of these things already exist within you because of your relationship with God. Our part is to cooperate with Him to cultivate and develop His character in our lives so we can become more like Him.

It all begins by spending regular time in God's Word. His Word changes how we think and how we act. It changes how we see God, ourselves, and the world around us. I am convinced that the answer to every problem can be found in God's Word.

Second Corinthians 3:18 says we "are constantly being transfigured into His very own image in ever increasing splendor and from one degree of glory to another."

The Lord changes us little by little. None of us will ever be perfect until we get to heaven, but as long as we're here on this earth, God desires for us to continually learn and grow.

PRAYER FOR TODAY: *God, thank You that Your Word has the power to change me. Give me the desire to spend time in Your Word so that I can grow to behave more like You and represent You in the world. I want my mind, mouth, mood, and attitude to reflect You. Amen.*

DAY 174

MOVE PAST THE PAST

But Jesus looked at them and said, With men this is impossible, but all things are possible with God.

MATTHEW 19:26

Everyone deals with emotional pain to some degree. Whether it's a difficult relationship, an addiction, abuse, or even depression, past hurts can cripple us and prevent us from moving forward. But regardless of what's happened in our past, God still wants us to have a great future.

Our enemy, Satan, wants us to believe we cannot get past our past. He wants us to "park" right where we are, believing that our past pain has permanently damaged God's future for us.

If that's where you are, I want you to know that we serve the God of the impossible—He can fix the unfixable and bring dead things back to life (Matthew 19:26)!

One of the most powerful things we can do is change our attitudes. Instead of focusing our thoughts on what went wrong or what we don't have, we can choose to maintain positive, grateful attitudes—attitudes that focus on God's blessings and all of the great things He is doing in our lives. This shift in mindset will help us move past our past and on to the great things He has planned for the future!

PRAYER FOR TODAY: *God, I don't want to live stuck in the pain of my past any longer. Help me move forward and to see all that You are doing in my life. Thank You for giving me a brighter future! Amen.*

DAY 175
MORE LIKE HIM

For those God foreknew he also predestined to be conformed to the image of his Son, that he might be the firstborn among many brothers and sisters.

ROMANS 8:29 NIV

Throughout our lives, God continually works with us and helps us grow from one level to the next. We gradually become more like Him as we spend more time with Him.

It is important to remember that when God deals with us—when the Holy Spirit convicts us of something—we can't do it on our own. It is only through God's strength that we can change. It's only through our faith and spending time with Him that we can become more like Christ.

God loves you tremendously. There's nothing you can ever do to make Him love you more than He does right now! Growing and changing isn't about trying to be "perfect" or earning God's love and approval. We should want to change because He loves us, not in order to get Him to love us. The Lord loves you too much to let you stay where you are. I've learned that when God shows us areas of our lives that need to change, He's doing it out of love—He loves us enough to help us change.

Just like He created the caterpillar to transform into a beautiful butterfly, God wants to take you through a process of transformation to make you more like Him!

PRAYER FOR TODAY: *God, thank You for shining a light on the areas where You want to help me grow. I know I need to change, but I also know You are the only One who can change me. I'm relying on Your grace and strength to help me as I do my best to obey what You've shown me. Amen.*

DAY 176: CHRIST'S AMBASSADORS

We are therefore Christ's ambassadors, as though God were making his appeal through us. We implore you on Christ's behalf: Be reconciled to God.

2 CORINTHIANS 5:20 NIV

While we're in the growing process, it's important to stay encouraged and realize that our spiritual growth reaps tremendous benefits for ourselves and others. Yes, God wants each of us to accept Jesus Christ so we can spend eternal life with Him in heaven. But He also wants us to spiritually grow and mature so we can have a supernatural impact here on earth.

Today's scripture says, "We are therefore Christ's ambassadors, as though God were making his appeal through us." In other words, we are here to show Jesus to the world. In fact, each one of us has a distinct sphere of influence—people we can each reach for Christ who nobody else can. That's why Jesus says it's so important for you to "let your light shine before others" (Matthew 5:16 NIV).

God wants to help us rise above the circumstances in our lives. He desires for us to have His joy and peace on the inside—even when everything on the outside isn't perfect. When others see that your joy is not dependent on your circumstances, they will be drawn to you. They will want to know the source of your peace, which opens the door for God to make His appeal through you.

PRAYER FOR TODAY: *God, I feel the weight of responsibility when I read this text today, knowing that I am here on this earth to represent You. Help me grow and mature in my faith. Thank You that You are always with me and that I don't have to do this alone. Amen.*

DAY 177

RESTORATION AND WHOLENESS

Restore us, O God; cause Your face to shine on us [with favor and approval], and we will be saved.

PSALM 80:3 AMP

God is a God of restoration and wholeness. We see it all throughout the Bible. John 3:16 says, "God so loved the world that He gave His only begotten Son, that whoever believes in Him should not perish but have everlasting life" (NKJV).

Second Corinthians 5:17 says that as new creations in Christ, "old things have passed away; behold, all things have become new" (NKJV), and verse 21 says we become the righteousness of God in Christ.

Luke 19:10 says: "The Son of Man has come to seek and to save that which was lost" (NKJV). Notice this doesn't say "who was lost," but "that which was lost." Jesus came to save us from our sins and to restore whatever was lost.

It could be loss of a good childhood, confidence, acceptance, or something that was stolen from you. Whatever needs to be restored to wholeness spiritually, mentally, emotionally, and physically, Jesus can bring healing to that part of your life.

In His Word, you will find everything you need to discover restoration and wholeness and to be the person you were created to be. The key is to consistently study the Bible, read good books that will help you understand the Bible, and develop a personal relationship with God.

PRAYER FOR TODAY: *God, I don't ever want to take for granted all the ways You love me. I can't thank You enough for how much You care about me and all You have done for me. Thank You for helping me grow into the person You created me to be. Amen.*

DAY 178: LIFE AS GOD HAS IT

In Him was Life, and the Life was the Light of men.

JOHN 1:4

The Greek word for "life" used in many parts of the New Testament is *zoe*, which means, in part, "life as God has it."

Think about this: *life as God has it*. What does it mean? Is God worried? Is He anxious about anything that's happening in the world? Is He frightened? No! God is perfect and holy. He is always peaceful, joyful, and confident. And He wants us to have this life through our relationship with Christ.

So many people are not living the life God has for them. They are anxious and worried about their situations, they don't have peace, and they aren't joyful.

I know what this is like because I used to be a miserable Christian. I was angry most of the time and was very hard to get along with. I didn't have any peace, and I was not enjoying my life. When I finally got tired of being miserable and was desperate to have peace, I cried out to God for help and got serious about my relationship with Him, and He began changing me.

When you spend time with God, your life will change in amazing ways because God is a Redeemer and He wants you to have "life as He has it."

PRAYER FOR TODAY: *God, I want life as You have it. I want Your peace, Your joy, Your confidence. I want to enjoy this life that You have given me. Thank You for desiring to be in a relationship with me and for helping me to be more like You. Amen.*

DAY 179: THE WORD OF GOD

Every Scripture is God-breathed (given by His inspiration) and profitable for instruction, for reproof and conviction of sin, for correction of error and discipline in obedience, [and] for training in righteousness (in holy living, in conformity to God's will in thought, purpose, and action).

2 TIMOTHY 3:16

Hebrews 4:12 holds the key to a radical transformation in our spiritual lives: "the Word that God speaks is alive and full of power [making it active, operative, energizing, and effective]."

John 1:1 tells us that Jesus is the Word of God. So, when we spend time studying the Word, we're spending time with God. He works in our hearts, making us more like Jesus in our thoughts, attitudes, and behaviors.

I want to encourage you to be diligent with your personal Bible study time. Attending church weekly can provide valuable insights, but God has so much more that He wants to say to you. By dedicating time to Your relationship with Him, He will take you into a deeper and more personal exploration of the Scriptures.

God loves you unconditionally, and He wants to help you. He wants you to be whole in Christ and enjoy the great life He's planned for you. Allow God's Word to permeate your heart, and you will have the abundant life He has for you. I urge you to spend some time each day receiving God's love.

PRAYER FOR TODAY: *God, bring the Word alive to me in a new way. I ask for Your grace to not just read the truth but to put it into practice. Change my heart as I dig into the Scriptures. Give me a fresh revelation of who You are. Thank You for the promise that if I seek You I will find You. Amen.*

DAY 180 — PRISONERS OF HOPE

Return to the stronghold [of security and prosperity], you prisoners of hope; even today do I declare that I will restore double your former prosperity to you.

ZECHARIAH 9:12

Today's verse is not the only scripture that says God will give us double for our trouble, but this passage shows us that there is a part we play in this, too—God wants us to be "prisoners of hope" so that He can bless us.

We have to keep an attitude that allows God to work in our lives. God doesn't work through negative attitudes. God doesn't work through entitled or passive or self-pitying attitudes. God can only work where there is faith, and before you have faith, you have to have hope.

Hope is a positive attitude that has nothing to do with your circumstances. It is an expectant outlook that something good is going to happen in your life. Being a prisoner of hope means being so locked up in hope that you believe without a doubt that something good is going to happen in your life. Believe that God can change whatever needs to be changed, that with His help you can do whatever you need to do, and that there is no situation too big for God to handle.

If you will keep a determined, steadfast attitude, filled with hope, it will be impossible for you not to be a winner in life. God has a double blessing in store for you, prisoner of hope!

PRAYER FOR TODAY: *God, I refuse to give up hope. Help me keep trusting while I wait for things to change. I know that You have a plan, a double blessing, and I'm going to keep believing until I receive it. Amen.*

DAY 181
WHEN YOUR ATTITUDE NEEDS SAVING

For by your words [reflecting your spiritual condition] you will be justified and acquitted of the guilt of sin; and by your words [rejecting Me] you will be condemned and sentenced.

MATTHEW 12:37 AMP

When Jesus died to save us, He wanted to save all parts of us and make us whole. And that includes our attitude!

Many people need to get their attitude saved—because every time something doesn't go the way they want it to go, their first response is a bad attitude. When we don't get what we want, our emotions flare up, and instead of doing what the Word says, we follow how we feel. We think wrong, and then what we think comes out of our mouths.

Words are containers for creative and destructive power. I can say, "Something good is going to happen to me," or I can say, "Nothing good ever happens to me." Either way, I'm likely to get what I say.

With our thoughts, our words, and our attitudes, we either give God permission to work in our lives or we give the enemy permission to work in our lives.

One of the best things we can do is learn to discipline ourselves to think before we speak. When something doesn't go the way we want it to, instead of defaulting to being negative, have your mind set ahead of time that you are going to praise God anyway and trust that He has something even better in mind for you.

PRAYER FOR TODAY: *God, You know that it is hard for us to keep positive attitudes when things don't go the way we think they should. Help me to discipline my mind, to think before I speak, and to keep trusting and believing in You. I want to keep the door open for You to work. Amen.*

DAY 182: SPEAK IN FAITH

And whatever you ask for in prayer, having faith and [really] believing, you will receive.

MATTHEW 21:22

Several years ago, we had a piece of property to sell. We were believing to sell it, and someone showed a lot of interest in it. They said they needed time to think about it and scheduled a day to let us know one way or another. Well, that day came and there was no call all morning. The hours ticked by, getting close to the end of the business day, and we still hadn't heard anything.

I remember driving down the road and thinking, *God, I've been telling myself this was a done deal, but now we haven't heard from them.* The Lord just so simply said to me, "The day's not over, is it?"

When it got to be about six in the evening, I opened my mouth, but instead of saying what I was thinking (which was *He's never going to call, and he's not going to buy it!*), I spoke in faith and said, "We are going to hear from this man today, and he is going to buy this house." Within thirty minutes, we got the call, and he bought the house!

Now, I know God doesn't always work things out the way we expect, but I believe He honors our trust in Him, especially when we choose faith over fear.

PRAYER FOR TODAY: *God, I know that the enemy wants me to doubt that You are going to come through, but I'm not taking the bait. I know You will answer my prayer in Your way as I trust in You. Amen.*

DAY 183: TAKE YOUR OWN ADVICE

Listen to advice and accept instruction, that you may gain wisdom in the future.

PROVERBS 19:20 ESV

Why is it that when someone else doesn't get what they want, we can say, "Just trust God and believe that He has something better in mind for you," but when it happens to us, we have a hard time doing what we tell others to do?

It's easy when we're looking on from a distance to have the right answer for everybody else: "Your breakthrough is coming!" "God works all things together for good." "Trust God and His timing." "Pray about it!" "Give it to God!" But we're not as good at applying those answers to our own lives because when we are hurt, disappointed, or not seeing results, our emotions get involved and our minds are clouded.

The truth is, if we would simply do what we would tell somebody else to do in the same situation we're in, we'd have victory. Because it's not that we don't know the answers; it's just that we don't always apply them to ourselves.

When a situation arises that tests your faith, take a step back and think about what you would say to a friend who was going through it. Distancing yourself from your emotions will help you act in faith rather than frustration.

PRAYER FOR TODAY: *God, thank You for giving me the answers I need. Help me apply them to my life. Teach me to respond out of the truth I know and not from my feelings in the moment. Amen.*

DAY 184

HOPE IN THE UNSEEN

For in this hope we were saved. Now hope that is seen is not hope. For who hopes for what he sees?

ROMANS 8:24 ESV

Hope is having a happy anticipation that something good is going to happen. We don't hope for what we already know, what we already have, what we can already see. We hope for what we cannot see, what we cannot feel, but what we believe God will do.

Hope says, *Something good is going to happen to me; something good is going to happen to my friends; something good is going to happen at my job; something good is going to happen in this nation; something good is going to happen in the Church.*

There is too much negative talk in this world. There may be a lot of wrong things going on, but we're not going to change them by simply talking about things the way they are. We effect change by speaking out of our faith, believing that with God all things are possible. He calls things that don't exist as if they already exist (Romans 4:17), and we can do the same.

God can get you the job you need. God can give you favor with people. God can open doors that no man can shut. God is a miracle-working God, but you have to expect Him to work and to do something great in your life, something you can't see yet, but that you hope for. Faith is a powerful force, but it must be released by praying, speaking in faith, and taking God-inspired action.

PRAYER FOR TODAY: *God, You know the desires of my heart. Thank You for working behind the scenes to bring about the thing I am hoping for the most. Give me faith to keep praying and believing. I know that You will do something great in my life. Amen.*

DAY 185: ENJOY THIS LIFE

[What, what would have become of me] had I not believed that I would see the Lord's goodness in the land of the living!
PSALM 27:13

According to the Bible, we will one day live in heaven, but the Bible also says that Jesus came so that we might have and enjoy life while we are here. I grew up in an abusive and dysfunctional home, so God had to teach me how to enjoy life and that it is His will for us to do so.

God wants to bless us, and He will as long as we keep Him first in our lives.

Only you can decide to enjoy your life here on earth. Only you can decide that you are going to stop being negative and believe the positive. You can even enjoy your life while you are in the midst of difficult circumstances.

I used to hate being around happy people. I found them so annoying. But now I am one of those annoying happy people! But I didn't get that way by accident. I decided that I didn't want to be miserable anymore. I decided to choose joy.

I grabbed hold of the scripture that says, "Cheer up! I have overcome the world" (John 16:33 WEB), because if Jesus died so that I could "cheer up," then the best thing I can do for Him is to enjoy my life.

PRAYER FOR TODAY: *God, I am looking forward to seeing You in heaven one day, but until my time comes, I long to enjoy this life and all that You have for me. Open my eyes to see Your goodness in the land of the living. Amen.*

DAY 186: SPEAK BLESSINGS

You will be blessed when you come in and you will be blessed when you go out.

DEUTERONOMY 28:6 AMP

Learning to speak life-giving words has been a lifelong journey for me, and every bit of progress has come straight from God and His Word. He loves you so much, and He'll help you grow in this area, too.

One of the best ways you can use your words is to speak blessings over everything around you. These are faith-filled words that can bring life to others and your situation. Some of the first words I say when I get up in the morning are "God, I bless this day in Jesus' name. I bless my husband, my children, my friends, my work, our partners, and myself. I'm blessed because of Jesus, and I'm living in the blessings of God." It really helps me start my day with the right attitude.

The Bible tells us to speak life, not death (Proverbs 18:21). By speaking life and blessings, we can contribute to the fulfillment of God's purposes in our lives and the lives of others.

Let's use our words wisely and intentionally, speaking blessings over ourselves, our loved ones, and everything around us. In doing so, we can sow seeds of positivity, hope, and encouragement that have the potential to yield a bountiful harvest of blessings in return.

PRAYER FOR TODAY: *God, help me grow in the area of using my words to speak blessings and life over myself and the people I love. Continue to teach me the power of my words. Thank You for Your loving correction that leads me in the way I should go. Amen.*

DAY 187: TRUTH IS LIKE A HAMMER

Is not My word like fire [that consumes all that cannot endure the test]? says the Lord, and like a hammer that breaks in pieces the rock [of most stubborn resistance]?

JEREMIAH 23:29

Jeremiah 23:28 says, "Let the one who has my word speak it faithfully" (NIV). The Amplified Classic version of Jeremiah 23:29 says the Word is "like a hammer that breaks in pieces the rock [of most stubborn resistance]."

Speaking God's Word out loud has transformed my life in countless ways. For example, many years ago, after I had tried and failed several times to stop smoking, God started challenging me to speak out the truth that I was free from it (John 8:36; Romans 8:2). As I did what God put in my heart to do each day, God gave me His grace to quit, and I've been free ever since! I started saying, "I don't smoke cigarettes anymore" while I was still smoking.

Sometimes you have to hit an obstacle many, many times before it cracks open, so keep hitting your problems with the hammer of God's Word. Speak it out loud, over and over again. Eventually, it will break down the hardest things you're facing, because God's Word always accomplishes what it was sent to do (Isaiah 55:11). The more you hear yourself say it, the more you will believe it.

There is great power in our words. We harness that power by speaking the truth of God's Word out loud, over and over, until we see the fruit of our words.

PRAYER FOR TODAY: *God, there is nothing too hard for You. Thank You that You have already overcome this thing I'm facing. I am free! I am free! I am free! Amen.*

DAY 188: BE THANKFUL AND SAY SO

O give thanks to the Lord, for He is good; for His mercy and loving-kindness endure forever! Let the redeemed of the Lord say so, whom He has delivered from the hand of the adversary.

PSALM 107:1-2

Take a few minutes every day to thank God for everything you can think of—from hot water, to food, to a roof over your head. And thank people when they do things for you.

Psalm 107:1–2 says, "Give thanks to the Lord, for He is good... Let the redeemed of the Lord say so."

This simple practice makes a huge difference when we're waiting for a breakthrough. When we thank God that He's working on that situation behind the scenes, it helps us remember and trust that He's actively involved in our lives and that freedom is coming. When we thank Him for all the blessings we do have, it helps us keep a positive attitude and enjoy the wait. When we shift our focus from what we lack to what we have, it helps us be content in every situation. When we are not only thankful, but we are thankful and say so, we can encourage others and improve our relationships.

God has already given us all so much, but He's not going to give us more to complain about. So, focus on what you have to be thankful for... and say so!

PRAYER FOR TODAY: *God, I am thankful for this day. I am thankful for my life. I am thankful for a roof over my head and food in the fridge. I am thankful for the ability to read Your Word. Remind me to live with gratitude and help me thank You and others throughout my day. Amen.*

DAY 189: WHAT'S IN YOUR HEART?

Above all else, guard your heart, for everything you do flows from it.
PROVERBS 4:23 NIV

The Bible has a lot to say about your heart. It's not talking about your physical heart; it's referring to what's going on inside of you—your thoughts, motives, and desires. These "hidden" things are important because they eventually come out through your words, attitudes, and actions.

If you have a healthy spiritual heart, it leads to a healthy life. But if your spiritual heart isn't healthy, the life you live won't be all that it could be.

Just like it's possible to have a *physical* heart murmur, I believe we can also suffer from a *spiritual* heart murmur. We can get into a habit of complaining or "murmuring" about the things we aren't happy with in life. These murmurs are often the result of jealousy, resentment, or a lack of gratitude.

The truth is God can never bless us to the degree He wants until we learn how to truly be happy for other people. If all we can do is complain about what others have and what we *don't* have, it just keeps us stuck in the same place.

So, I want to ask you today: What is in your heart? Is it full of murmuring and complaining? Or is it filled with praise and thanksgiving for God?

PRAYER FOR TODAY: *God, there is some stuff in my heart that shouldn't be there. Rid my heart of all the murmuring and complaining. Fill it with praise and thanksgiving. You are a good, good Father. Amen.*

DAY 190: THE ROAD OF THANKSGIVING

All the Israelites murmured [in discontent] against Moses and Aaron; and the whole congregation said to them, "Oh that we had died in the land of Egypt! Or that we had died in this wilderness!"
NUMBERS 14:2 AMP

The Bible tells us that because of their unbelief and bad attitudes, the Israelites literally wandered around in the wilderness for forty years. They complained when they were hungry, and so God supernaturally provided them with manna every morning. Although they were satisfied for a little while, they grew tired of the manna and grumbled because they wanted meat instead (Exodus 16:11–16).

It's easy to read about the Israelites and think, *How could they be so ungrateful?* However, we often do the very same thing! We can pray to have children then later complain about the hard work that comes with caring for them. Or we can desire a bigger house and then get upset because we have to spend more time cleaning it.

God's blessings don't travel on the backs of complaints. When we are thankful, however, it opens the door for God to answer our prayers and bring blessings into our lives. God's blessings travel on the road of thanksgiving.

PRAYER FOR TODAY: *God, thank You for all the blessings in my life! Forgive me for the times I haven't been thankful, especially for the things I prayed and asked You for. From now on, help me travel the road of thanksgiving! Amen.*

DAY 191

WHAT YOU SAY

How precious to me are your thoughts, O God! How vast is the sum of them!

PSALM 139:17 ESV

What you say about yourself, both to yourself and to other people, is more important than what anyone else says about you.

You will never get beyond your opinion of yourself. And if that's something you struggle with, I encourage you to read Psalm 139 and see what God thinks of you. It says you are fearfully and wonderfully made, known and loved by God, and created with intention and purpose.

In your home, in your car, or wherever you are by yourself, you can declare God's truth over yourself.

For you to live fully in the wonderful future God has for you, you will have to learn how to talk about yourself, and to yourself, in the right way. If you will learn how to talk to yourself the way God intended, it won't make any difference what anyone else says to you or about you.

The Word of God should be the most important thing in all our lives. Set your mind to believe what God says about you and then speak that over your life and the lives of your loved ones.

PRAYER FOR TODAY: *God, what You think of me is important. It is humbling that You think I am wonderful, that You took such care to create me, and that You even think of me at all. Help me see myself through Your eyes. Amen.*

DAY 192

PROSPER IN EVERY WAY

Dear friend, I hope all is well with you and that you are as healthy in body as you are strong in spirit.

3 JOHN 2 NLT

In the Amplified Classic version, 3 John 2 says, "Beloved, I pray that you may prosper in every way and [that your body] may keep well, even as [I know] your soul keeps well and prospers." God says, "I want you to have all of the blessings I have for you that you are spiritually mature enough to handle."

In other words, the more deeply rooted you are in Christ, the more fruit of the Spirit (love, joy, peace, patience, kindness, goodness, gentleness, faithfulness, self-control) you'll be able to produce.

Being rooted in Christ means cultivating a deep, personal relationship with God through prayer and studying His Word. It involves surrendering to His will, embracing His unconditional love, and trusting Him completely. It means understanding that we are valued, accepted, and cherished by God.

Get your roots planted deeply in God and in His love. Spend time with Him, talking with Him and studying His Word, so you will learn how to live by the leading of the Holy Spirit, not by your feelings, what you think, or what people tell you. Live instead by the Word of God.

PRAYER FOR TODAY: *God, I want to live by Your leading, not by my feelings. I know this is a process, but I'm committed to it. Open my mind to understand the Scriptures so that I can grow in my knowledge of You. Amen.*

DAY 193: PLANTING SEEDS

The rain and snow come down from the heavens and stay on the ground to water the earth. They cause the grain to grow, producing seed for the farmer and bread for the hungry.

ISAIAH 55:10 NLT

In Isaiah 55:10–11, God compares His Word to rain and snow that water the earth, causing plants to bud and flourish. Similarly, when God speaks His Word into our lives, it has the potential to bring forth spiritual growth, renewal, and fruitfulness.

God's Word never returns void. It always produces fruit. It brings healing to the brokenhearted, comfort to the grieving, guidance to the lost, and hope to the hopeless.

When you plant a seed in the ground of God's kingdom through speaking and believing His Word, you can help nurture its growth by continuing to speak in agreement with what He has said. You don't want to kill your seed by saying negative things about what you've planted, making it null and void. You want His Word to prosper in your life.

If you are seeking breakthrough in your marriage, relationships, finances, work, or any other area of your life, then believe God's promises for you and speak life!

Whatever you're trusting God for, begin speaking with faith, as someone who believes God is already at work. I often say, "God is working in my life. I may not see it, but God is working!" Even when you talk about your difficulties, you can do so in a way that reflects hope.

PRAYER FOR TODAY: *God, I believe You are working it all out for my good. Thank You for the seeds of blessing that You have led me to speak over my life. Help them grow and flourish. Amen.*

DAY 194: THE NARROW PATH

But small is the gate and narrow and difficult to travel is the path that leads the way to [everlasting] life, and there are few who find it.
MATTHEW 7:14 AMP

The secret to having a great life is making one right decision after another, thinking one right thought after another, speaking one right word after another, and choosing one good attitude after another. The devil will fight you on this, but hold firm and keep it up!

To receive all of God's promises, we can't be ruled by our emotions or our circumstances. We can't just do what we want based on how we think or feel. We will have to choose God's way even when it's hard, even when we are tired, even when it looks like things will never change.

We can't overcome a lifetime of bad decisions by making one good decision. But every right decision we make—whether it's a thought, word, action, or attitude—slowly changes our lives for the better.

This doesn't mean we have to be perfect. God knows we'll miss it sometimes—but what He's looking for is a heart that keeps turning back to Him.

Keep pressing on. Decide to stay on that narrow path even when it's difficult. Because when you do, you're sowing seed for the greatest harvest of your life. You're going to become who God created you to be!

PRAYER FOR TODAY: *God, I can't change the past, but with Your help, I choose to make better choices going forward. Keep me on the narrow path, especially when it's hard, because I know that is Your will for my life. I receive Your promises. Amen.*

DAY 195: YOU CAN CHOOSE RIGHT EVEN IF YOU FEEL WRONG

So put to death and deprive of power the evil longings of your earthly body [with its sensual, self-centered instincts] immorality, impurity, sinful passion, evil desire, and greed, which is [a kind of] idolatry [because it replaces your devotion to God].

COLOSSIANS 3:5 AMP

We can't always help how we feel, but we can do something about what we think. We can do something about what we say. And we can do something about how we act.

I know from personal experience that you can feel totally wrong and still choose to do what's right. And when we do what's right—even when we don't feel like doing it—we grow stronger in our faith, and eventually our feelings catch up with our decisions and behavior.

The key is to not walk according to the flesh, which is human nature without God. Colossians 3:5 says, "Put to death, therefore, whatever belongs to your earthly nature: sexual immorality, impurity, lust, evil desires and greed" (NIV).

Every time you give in to your flesh, you are feeding it. But when you submit to the Holy Spirit and do what's right, you are starving the old nature, killing it, and putting on your new nature (2 Corinthians 5:17).

We might want everything to be easy, but we often grow the most through the hard things that God brings us through. And He wants us to have the best life possible.

PRAYER FOR TODAY: *God, give me strength to choose what's right even when I feel wrong. I trust Your Word and believe that the more I starve my old nature, the more my new nature will grow. I don't want anything to come between us. Help me lay these things down at the altar. Amen.*

DAY 196
COUNT YOUR BLESSINGS

Bless (affectionately, gratefully praise) the Lord, O my soul, and forget not [one of] all His benefits.

PSALM 103:2

What we focus on has the ability to make us either happy or miserable. We can either dwell on the negative things in life or choose to magnify the good. When we choose to be thankful, it releases a new level of faith, hope, and joy. We become happier, and we bring more joy to those around us.

The old saying "Count your blessings" is terrific advice. I think it's easy to get used to all of the wonderful things God does for us and take them for granted. That's why it's so powerful to take time each day to thank Him for the blessings in our lives—big and small.

I've made a habit of being thankful. As I go about my day, I'll thank God for His help with my work, the beautiful day He has provided, and even the coffee I get to drink. I praise Him for the people He has placed in my life and for the strength He gives me to keep on going when I feel too busy or overwhelmed.

Practice being a person of gratitude. Choose to count your blessings and give thanks. Voice your thankfulness to God for the wonderful things He does for you each and every day. You will be happier, and your blessings will increase.

PRAYER FOR TODAY: *God, I want to become a person who celebrates the positive in every situation. Teach me to make a habit of being thankful. I never want to take for granted all that You are doing in my life. Amen.*

DAY 197: PAINFUL TRUTHS

I will give you a new heart and put a new spirit in you; I will remove from you your heart of stone and give you a heart of flesh.
EZEKIEL 36:26 NIV

The most painful truth I ever had to face was that I was selfish, self-centered, hard to get along with, manipulative, and controlling. It was a hard truth, but if I hadn't faced the truth about myself and my attitudes, I wouldn't be doing what I'm doing for God today. I can truly say that I have received the Word of God, and the truth has set me free!

A friend of mine told me how she had to face the truth about her bad temper. She discovered that she could control her temper in front of people she wanted to impress, but in front of her husband and other people she knew would put up with her, she would let herself get mad. When she faced the truth, she realized that she needed to respect people and allow God to do a work in her.

Facing the truth God might be speaking to you can be hard at times, but it is a critical part of growing and experiencing the breakthrough God has for you.

Is there a truth you need to face about yourself—about your moods or your attitudes?

Don't let emotions get in the way of what God wants to do. It's a new day, you're a new creation, and God has a good plan for your life.

PRAYER FOR TODAY: *God, I know it's going to hurt, but I've got to do this if I'm going to move forward. So, show me the hard, painful truth. Show me where I need to change. And give me the courage to walk it out. Amen.*

DAY 198: THE CHRISTIAN WALK

Finally, then, brothers, we ask and urge you in the Lord Jesus, that as you received from us how you ought to walk and to please God, just as you are doing, that you do so more and more.

1 THESSALONIANS 4:1 ESV

When I think about my life the day I first became a Christian compared to now, I'm in awe of what God has done in my life. I'm a completely different person today.

But it didn't happen overnight, and I'm still learning and growing in my relationship with God every day. I know He has more for me, and I believe He has more for you, too. But to experience that, we have to do some walking.

In 2 Corinthians 5:7, we're told to "walk by faith" (NKJV). In Ephesians 5:2, we're told to "walk in love" (NKJV). In 1 John 2:6, we're told to walk as Christ walked. In 1 Thessalonians 4:1 we're told to "walk so as to please and gratify God." Ephesians 5:8 says we are to "walk as children of Light," and verse 15 says "to look carefully then how you walk." And Galatians 5:16 says to walk in the Spirit.

Walking is basically a combination of steps. In the Christian walk, those steps are our choices. And when you walk with God, it means you use your free will to make choices in your mind, mouth, moods, and attitudes that line up with the will of God.

PRAYER FOR TODAY: *God, help me walk by faith, not by sight. Align my thoughts with Yours, and help me speak the words You want me to speak and to maintain an attitude that glorifies You. Amen.*

DAY 199: RELEASE YOUR FAITH

So then faith comes by hearing, and hearing by the word of God.
ROMANS 10:17 NKJV

It's important to understand that your faith can't work unless you release it. Just having faith in and of itself doesn't do any good.

You can have money in the bank and still starve to death. You can have food in the refrigerator and go hungry. You can have a coat in your closet and still go out and freeze.

Having something is no guarantee that you're going to use it. In the same way, you have to use your faith in order for it to work!

So, how do you release your faith? First, pray according to God's promises in His Word. Second, say what His Word says. And third, do what you believe God wants you to do based on His Word.

Pray it, say it, and do it. The more you lean on God and His Word, the more pressure you take off yourself. Faith gives you the power to trust God.

It's because of what Christ has done for you—as a gift to you—that you can live by faith, releasing it and experiencing all He has for you.

PRAYER FOR TODAY: *God, I surrender. Nothing works when I try to do it on my own. I need You. Increase my faith to trust You more. I want to pray it, say it, and do it when it comes to my faith. Amen.*

DAY 200: KNOW WHAT IT SAYS

Heaven and earth will pass away, but my words will not pass away.
MATTHEW 24:35 ESV

I encourage you to confess the Word of God out loud throughout the day and meditate on it as the Holy Spirit prompts you. Each time a thought comes to your mind that does not agree with God's Word, confess the truth of God's Word out loud, and you will find the wrong thought disappears.

Can we confess things that we can't find a chapter and verse for? Yes, I believe we can, as long as we are reasonably sure that we're declaring God's will for our lives and not just what we want.

For instance, just because someone confesses over and over that they want a sports car doesn't mean it will show up. The point of our confessions is to speak God's Word over our lives and say what He says about us.

While the Bible may not specifically mention our exact situation, it does contain wisdom and direction for every area of our lives. That is one reason why it's so valuable to read, study, and know what God's Word says.

Get in agreement with Him and become His mouthpiece, declaring the good things He has in store for you.

PRAYER FOR TODAY: *God, I don't always understand what is going on in my life, and I don't always see You working, but I believe that You are. I trust what Your Word says, so help me confess it daily. Not my will but Yours be done. Amen.*

DAY 201: PRAYER COMES FROM THE HEART

Be not rash with your mouth, and let not your heart be hasty to utter a word before God. For God is in heaven, and you are on earth; therefore let your words be few.

ECCLESIASTES 5:2

Prayer is important because it demonstrates our dependence on God. Prayer is simply communication with God—talking to Him and listening to what He has to say to you.

Prayers do not have to be long or eloquent to be powerful. The enemy has tried to give us this mentality that we have to pray a certain way to make it "work."

But the Bible says just the opposite. In Ecclesiastes 5:2, Solomon, the wisest man on earth, said, "Let your words be few." Prayer that touches God is sincere and comes from the heart. Praying a long time is certainly good, too, but I think it is important to know that a prayer doesn't have to be long to be effective.

John 15:5 says that when we are connected to God, we will bear abundant fruit. But when we are cut off from a close personal relationship with Him, we can do nothing. We experience the power of prayer through personal relationship with Him as we put our trust in Him.

Staying connected to the heart of your heavenly Father keeps your mind focused on just how much you need God's love and grace to make it through each day.

PRAYER FOR TODAY: *God, thank You for the closeness You offer me and for the freedom to come to You in prayer at any time. Help me continually seek You with a sincere heart, trusting that it is not about doing it perfectly but about being genuine. Guide me in understanding the true power of prayer. Amen.*

DAY 202: GUARD AGAINST SELF-PITY

Do not be deceived, God is not mocked; for whatever a man sows, that he will also reap.

GALATIANS 6:7 NKJV

It's easy to fall into the trap of self-pity when facing challenges, but dwelling on it won't make things better or speed up your breakthrough. It does not honor God, and it will just make you miserable while you are waiting.

When you're tempted to wallow in self-pity, remember that facing your pain is part of the process of getting to your breakthrough. If you must go through it anyway, you may as well do what you can to enjoy the journey!

It won't be easy, but you can stop feeling sorry for yourself. I've learned from experience that self-pity is a total and complete waste of time.

Shifting your focus to helping others can be a powerful way to overcome self-pity. Look for opportunities to make a difference—through acts of kindness, volunteering, or simply offering support and encouragement.

The Bible shows us that we will sow what we reap, and as you sow blessing and grace into the lives of others, you will reap the blessings and grace of God in your life (Galatians 6:7).

PRAYER FOR TODAY: *God, when I'm tempted to say "Woe is me," or "What about me?," help me redirect my thoughts toward others. Put people in my path who need encouragement, support, and care. Teach me to shift my focus away from myself and to trust You to work it out in Your own way and timing. Amen.*

DAY 203: YOU CAN'T TRUST YOUR FEELINGS

The heart is deceitful above all things, and it is exceedingly perverse and corrupt and severely, mortally sick! Who can know it [perceive, understand, be acquainted with his own heart and mind]?
JEREMIAH 17:9

Without God, human nature often leads us to do whatever we feel like doing. Oftentimes, the reason our lives get in such a mess is that we're living according to what we think, want, and feel instead of choosing to do the will of God.

But here's the good news: Through your faith in Christ, you have a new nature! Second Corinthians 5:17 says, "Therefore, if anyone is in Christ, the new creation has come: The old has gone, the new is here!" (NIV)

Your soul—your mind, will, and emotions—doesn't tell you anything about God. It only focuses on what you want. But as a born-again child of God, you are a new creation in Christ, with the Holy Spirit dwelling within you. You can be led by the Holy Spirit, and through obedience to His leading, you can learn to enjoy the good life Jesus died for you to have.

Jesus shows us this in John 10:10: "I came that they may have and enjoy life, and have it in abundance (to the full, till it overflows)."

If you're not experiencing joy and fulfillment, you might be missing out on God's best. Embrace your new nature and let the Holy Spirit guide you to live abundantly.

PRAYER FOR TODAY: *God, thank You for the new life You died to give me. Help me honor You by placing my trust in You above my feelings. I want to fully embrace all that You have for me in this life. Amen.*

DAY 204
WITH GOD, CHANGE IS POSSIBLE

Love endures with patience and serenity, love is kind and thoughtful, and is not jealous or envious; love does not brag and is not proud or arrogant.

1 CORINTHIANS 13:4 AMP

The quickest way to sabotage a relationship is to look at the other person and think or say, "You will never change." Thankfully, God always believes we can change and continues to work in us. We would be more patient and long-suffering with people and their flaws if we purposely thought, *God is patient with me, so I will be patient with you.* Instead of giving up on people, we can choose to pray for them.

It's remarkable that Dave stayed by my side during the early years of our marriage. No matter what he did, I wasn't happy. I couldn't be happy, even when circumstances were going my way, because everything going on inside of me was wrong. My thoughts and attitudes were all wrong, and they controlled my moods and behaviors.

When I asked Dave how he managed to stay with me, he said, "I knew that God could change you!" His faith in God's ability to change me not only kept our marriage together but was a key factor in my own healing. Although I didn't yet know how to trust God, He used Dave's faith to help me.

God can use you in the same way—to be an example of His love and patience in your relationships.

PRAYER FOR TODAY: *God, thank You for Your never-ending patience with me. Help me show that same patience to others, trusting that You are at work in their lives just as You are at work in mine. Amen.*

DAY 205: SIGNIFICANCE

To the praise of the glory of His grace, by which He made us accepted in the Beloved.

EPHESIANS 1:6 NKJV

One of our deepest human needs is to feel significant. We want to know that we matter, have value and a purpose. Feeling accepted by others plays a crucial role in fulfilling this need.

We can accept or reject someone without saying a word. A look of disbelief, a doubtful furrow of the brow, or a dismissive headshake can all convey disapproval or lack of respect.

To truly make others feel significant, we must first shift our mindset. Recognizing that people don't need to think like us allows us to be more accepting in both our words and our expressions. God loves and accepts all of us, and He desires that we do the same thing with one another.

When someone has a totally different opinion from ours, we can choose to think, *I respect your right to your opinion, and I realize that God made us all different for a reason.* If we think that way, we will talk and behave in a way that makes others feel accepted and as significant as God says they are.

PRAYER FOR TODAY: *God, thank You for making us all different. Help me remain open to learning from others and appreciating their unique gifts and perspectives. Teach me to see that, despite our differences, each person is created in Your image and adds valuable variety to my life. Amen.*

DAY 206: WHAT DO YOU THINK OF ME?

Now am I trying to win the favor of men, or of God? Do I seek to please men? If I were still seeking popularity with men, I should not be a bond servant of Christ (the Messiah).

GALATIANS 1:10

Do you ever get caught up in worrying about what others think or say about you? I think most of us do at times. It's natural to want people to like us, think well of us, and accept us. However, if we're not careful, we can let this concern take over and distract us from God's plan for our lives.

Once, a neighbor asked me if I was going to participate in our neighborhood cleanup day that year. I declined, knowing my reason was valid, yet I couldn't help but be concerned about her opinion of me for not helping.

God's Word instructs us to focus on pleasing Him rather than people (Galatians 1:10; Ephesians 6:6). When I find myself preoccupied with others' opinions, meditating on these scriptures helps me realign my focus.

What we think about other people is more important than whatever they may be thinking about us. I am not responsible for anyone else's thoughts, but I am responsible before God for mine.

PRAYER FOR TODAY: *God, remind me that my goal is to please You, not people. When I find myself worrying about others' opinions or judgments, help me to immediately take those thoughts captive and to remember that I am responsible for my own thoughts, not anyone else's. In Jesus' name, amen.*

DAY 207
HOW TO THINK ABOUT PEOPLE

Be careful how you think; your life is shaped by your thoughts.
PROVERBS 4:23 GNT

How we think about people when we are not with them determines how we will treat them when we are. Before meeting with anyone, even a friend for coffee, think of the things you enjoy and appreciate about them. Turn these thoughts into prayers of gratitude, thanking God for bringing that person into your life.

Relationships are a major part of our lives, and I pray that we will always remember the impact our thoughts have on them. Cultivate a mindset of positivity and gratitude toward everyone. We all have faults and weaknesses, but thankfully, with God's help, we can focus on each other's strengths and give no entrance to the negative.

By choosing your thoughts carefully, you can ensure that you treat others as God intends. Aim to leave people feeling uplifted and valued after spending time with you. Remember that people don't always remember what we say, but they do remember how we made them feel, and that starts with our thought lives.

PRAYER FOR TODAY: *God, thank You for the relationships that You have brought into my life. Help me think positive thoughts about others in advance, so that I may overflow with Your love and make those around me feel valued. Amen.*

DAY 208 — WORRY LESS, TRUST MORE

Do not let your hearts be troubled (distressed, agitated). You believe in and adhere to and trust in and rely on God; believe in and adhere to and trust in and rely also on Me.

JOHN 14:1

Some years ago, I had to face the fact that although I said "I trust God," my mind proved that I really didn't. I wanted to trust Him, but the truth was that I worried and felt fearful and anxious in many situations. Being honest with myself was the first step toward addressing these negative mental habits that were hindering my faith. With God's help, I have come a long way toward the goal of trusting Him completely.

There is no doubt that our thoughts and our stress levels are closely connected. Stress can affect our physical and emotional health in many ways—from headaches and muscle tension, to panic attacks and ulcers, to anxiety, depression, and trouble sleeping.

When we worry, we are searching for answers to our problems and attempting to control our circumstances. However, the truth is that we are never in control—God is. Instead of worrying about things we cannot control, we should learn to control our worry.

Worry only compounds our problems, but as our scripture for today reminds us, we reduce stress by increasing our trust in God.

PRAYER FOR TODAY: *God, help me be honest with myself about my anxious thoughts. I recognize that worrying only worsens my situation. I want to trust You with my life and all the details of it. Help me believe the best in every situation and trust You more each day. Amen.*

DAY 209: FIGHT TO THE FINISH

I have fought the good (worthy, honorable, and noble) fight, I have finished the race, I have kept (firmly held) the faith.

2 TIMOTHY 4:7

It is important for us to never give up, because we need to give God our faith to work with. God promises to fight for us (Exodus 14:14), but we must remain in the fight to receive all He has for us. The Bible tells us to wait on God, and that means to hope in Him, believing that something good is going to happen in your life.

Second Timothy 4:7 says, "I have fought the good fight, I have finished the race, I have kept the faith" (NKJV). You must keep the attitude that you are not only going to stay in the fight, but that you are going to stay the course until the end. You are going to finish your race. You are going to fulfill your destiny.

Without a never-give-up attitude, the devil will seek to rob us of what Jesus died to give us. Satan doesn't want you to experience even a fraction of it. But God wants you to have all of it—not a little of it, not half of it, not eighty percent of it. He wants you to have everything that Jesus died for you to have, and you will get it if you keep a fight-to-the-finish attitude.

PRAYER FOR TODAY: *God, thank You for all that You have given me and for the greater blessings You want to bestow in my life. Help me fight, even when it is hard, even when I want to give up, even when I am not seeing breakthrough, because I know that blessings will come. Strengthen my resolve and adjust my attitude so I can embrace the full measure of Your promises. Amen.*

DAY 210: FACE THE TRUTH

However, when He, the Spirit of truth, has come, He will guide you into all truth; for He will not speak on His own authority, but whatever He hears He will speak; and He will tell you things to come.
JOHN 16:13 NKJV

It's impossible to get to the place you want to be if you don't face the truth about where you are right now. Only the truth can set you free, and it's usually the truth about *you*, not someone else, that frees you.

John 16:13 says, "When He, the Spirit of truth, has come, He will guide you into all truth." You can know the truth because the Holy Spirit will guide you into it.

The Holy Spirit doesn't condemn you. He convicts you of your sin so you can repent, receive God's forgiveness, and keep going forward. And He reminds you that through Christ, you are "the righteousness of God in Him" (2 Corinthians 5:21 NKJV).

We need the Holy Spirit to reveal truth, exposing any lies we've believed and guiding us to align our lives with God's will. This is what it means to be "transformed into the same image from glory to glory...by the Spirit of the Lord" (2 Corinthians 3:18 NKJV). This is how you get to the place of total and complete freedom in your life in Christ.

PRAYER FOR TODAY: *God, thank You for sending the Holy Spirit to guide us into the truth about ourselves. Open my eyes to the lies I have believed, and help me embrace the Holy Spirit's conviction so I can make changes needed in my life. Amen.*

DAY 211: ASKING FOR WISDOM

If any of you is deficient in wisdom, let him ask of the giving God [Who gives] to everyone liberally and ungrudgingly, without reproaching or faultfinding, and it will be given him.

JAMES 1:5

Trials come for different reasons. They are from Satan, but God uses them to teach us, to grow or test our faith, and to shape us into the likeness of Jesus. God will always work something good out of our trials if we love Him and want His will.

Today's scripture tells us that if any of us is lacking wisdom, we can ask God for it and He will give it to us "liberally and ungrudgingly, without reproaching or faultfinding." If you need to know what to do amid your trials and tribulations, you can pray, "God, give me wisdom," and He will! He will never say, "You got yourself into this mess; now get yourself out." If you pray for wisdom, He will give it to you.

James 1:6 tells us, however, that we must ask "in faith" and "with no wavering (no hesitating, no doubting)." You can't go to church on Sunday believing He will give you wisdom but be doubting He'll do it by Tuesday. Set your mind and keep it set that the Word of God is true and that our generous God will give wisdom when you need it.

PRAYER FOR TODAY: *God, thank You for never blaming or shaming me. Help me turn to you when I need wisdom, rather than trying to navigate difficulties on my own. Give me the wisdom I need to make the best choices for my life today. Amen.*

DAY 212: BE WILLING TO BELIEVE

So, we see that they were not able to enter [into His rest], because of their unwillingness to adhere to and trust in and rely on God [unbelief had shut them out].

HEBREWS 3:19

One of the ways the devil tries to attack us is by filling our minds with doubt and unbelief.

Matthew 13:58 says that when Jesus was in His hometown of Nazareth, "He did not do many mighty works there because of their unbelief" (NKJV). God's miracles in our lives are accessed through faith, and when we are plagued by doubt, we block ourselves from receiving what He has in store.

We might convince ourselves that we can't help but doubt, but that is another lie from the devil. And if we continue to lean on that excuse, we will never get on the other side of doubt and unbelief. When doubt is attacking you, think about all the times God has been faithful to you in the past.

In Hebrews 3:19, it says that the people were not able to enter God's rest "because of their unwillingness to...rely on God [unbelief had shut them out]." Their doubts kept them from God's best. But notice it doesn't say that they were "unable" to trust Him; it says that they were "unwilling" to rely on Him.

The truth is, God would not tell us to have faith, to believe, and to trust and rely on Him if we were incapable of doing so. Choose to be willing to have faith and reject doubt!

PRAYER FOR TODAY: *God, thank You for equipping me with everything I need to have faith in You. Help me to move past my excuses and to get my mind off my doubts and onto who You are and all that You want to do. In Jesus' name, amen.*

DAY 213

FIRST WORDS

Brood of vipers! How can you, being evil, speak good things? For out of the abundance of the heart the mouth speaks.
MATTHEW 12:34 NKJV

The first words that come out of your mouth when you are faced with a challenging situation may set the tone for how the rest of it unfolds. This is exactly why it is so important to get our minds right, because our words reflect our inner thoughts.

When our minds are right, we start off on the right path, and it is easier to respond to circumstances with positive words of faith. We establish a solid foundation that helps us stay focused and move in the right direction.

However, if our minds are clouded with doubt, negativity, and unbelief, our responses will likely be negative as well. Not only will our initial words be negative, but we are setting ourselves up to have to put in more time, energy, and effort to correct our thinking and to overcome obstacles.

Since trials and tribulations are an inevitable part of life, it's better to think and speak positively out of faith right from the onset, so that we can move through them more quickly and enjoy life no matter what comes our way.

PRAYER FOR TODAY: *God, I don't want my trials to last any longer than they have to. Help me think positively so that the first words out of my mouth are words of faith, not fear. Amen.*

DAY 214: CONFESS THE TRUTH

And you will know the Truth, and the Truth will set you free.
JOHN 8:32

God loves you, He chose you, He has a good plan for your life—and He wants all of that to be cemented in your heart. So if you have a hard time agreeing with Him in those areas, start confessing the truth!

Say to yourself, *I am the righteousness of God in Christ. I am made acceptable in the Beloved. God formed me with His own hand, He loves me, and God doesn't make mistakes.* (Read: 2 Corinthians 5:21; Ephesians 1:6; Psalm 139:13–14; Jeremiah 31:3; and Deuteronomy 32:4.)

God doesn't want you to feel inferior to others. He wants you to recognize and embrace the unique gifts He has placed within you and to pursue the opportunities He sets before you.

God loves you and longs to be gracious to you—because He sees Christ in you!

PRAYER FOR TODAY: *God, thank You for putting the truth about me in Your Word. Help me confess these truths and to keep confessing them until they are cemented in my heart. In Jesus' name, amen.*

DAY 215: PRAISE AND MAKE PROGRESS

He is your praise, and He is your God, who has done for you these great and awesome things which your eyes have seen.
DEUTERONOMY 10:21 NKJV

Did you know that it is possible to talk about our problems in a positive, faith-filled way? I think sometimes God wants us to stay quiet about the inconveniences we experience so that we don't complain and remain stuck in the problem. But other times, I think He wants us to speak about our challenges with words of faith so that we can praise and make progress.

For example, you might say, "This isn't easy for me, and I certainly wouldn't have chosen to go through this on purpose, but I believe God is working. I know that if I trust Him and keep a good attitude, He will work it all out for my good."

As you begin to speak in agreement with His Word, God will lift you up above the everyday frustrations you face and cause you to be genuinely joyful, peaceful, and worry-free, regardless of your circumstances.

PRAYER FOR TODAY: *God, I trust that You have a purpose in everything You do. Help me focus on all that You have done and are doing for me. I want real, authentic joy every day, and I know that comes from real, authentic praise and thanksgiving. Amen.*

DAY 216: ARE YOU TRULY THANKFUL?

Do all things without grumbling and faultfinding and complaining [against God] and questioning and doubting [among yourselves].
PHILIPPIANS 2:14

Did you know that complaining is a sin? It causes many people a great deal of problems in their lives and destroys the joy of anyone listening.

In Ephesians 4:29, the apostle Paul instructs us: "Let no foul or polluting language, nor evil word nor unwholesome or worthless talk [ever] come out of your mouth." At one time, I didn't know this included complaining, but now I have learned that murmuring and complaining pollute our lives. They are considered an evil report to God and are certainly "worthless talk," because complaining has never changed anything except to make a bad attitude worse.

We need to ask ourselves: How quick are we to become impatient and begin to complain when stuck in traffic or while waiting in checkout lines? How quick are we to spot and point out the faults of others? Do we complain about our jobs when we should be thanking God for His provision?

Truly thankful people don't have time to complain because they are too focused on appreciating the blessings they have.

PRAYER FOR TODAY: *God, help me express thankfulness all of the time. Teach me to take the sins of the mouth seriously and avoid anything that might offend or separate me from You. I want to start each day with gratitude in my heart and on my lips. Amen.*

DAY 217

AT THE ONSET

Withstand him; be firm in faith [against his onset—rooted, established, strong, immovable, and determined], knowing that the same (identical) sufferings are appointed to your brotherhood (the whole body of Christians) throughout the world.

1 PETER 5:9

All of us will deal with disappointments from time to time—that's part of life. However, if we let it, our disappointment can lead to discouragement, and discouragement can lead to despair and depression.

I've said this for years: If you don't let the devil impress you with what he does, then he can't oppress you, and if he can't oppress you, then he can't depress you. When depression attacks, we usually feel like giving up, but how we respond to it makes all the difference.

One of the most important things we can do is resist the devil at "his onset" (1 Peter 5:8–9). It's so important to resist the feeling of depression immediately, because the longer we allow it to remain, the harder it is to resist.

While we can't control all of our circumstances and won't be completely free of pain or disappointment, we don't have to let today's struggles ruin our hope for tomorrow.

PRAYER FOR TODAY: *God, there are times when I feel like giving up, like I can't do it anymore, like things will never be good again. The next time that happens, help me rebuke the devil at his onset. Remind me not to be impressed by him, because the battle is Yours and You've already won. Amen.*

DAY 218: A SPIRITUAL ISSUE

You will show me the path of life; in Your presence is fullness of joy, at Your right hand there are pleasures forevermore.

PSALM 16:11

I realize that depression may be the result of a physical or chemical imbalance, and I don't want to discount these causes. However, for a great number of people, depression is a spiritual issue, and the Bible gives us great instructions on how to fight it.

Philippians 4:4 says, "Rejoice in the Lord always [delight, gladden yourselves in Him]; again I say, Rejoice!"

Praising the Lord in the midst of our pain is the greatest thing we can do. Why? Because when we choose to fix our attention on God and rejoice in the good things He has done, we make Him bigger than our problems.

Psalm 16:11 says that in God's presence there is "fullness of joy." When we worship God, we invite His presence into our lives, allowing Him to replace our discouragement with His joy and peace. This shift brings hope and breathes new life into our situations.

PRAYER FOR TODAY: *God, help me see if my moods are a spiritual issue, one that can be overcome through coming into Your presence and rejoicing. Thank You for the promise that You will show me the way to joy and contentment. Help me trust Your path for my life. In Jesus' name, amen.*

DAY 219
THE RIGHT WORD AT THE RIGHT TIME

A man has joy in making an apt answer, and a word spoken at the right moment—how good it is!

PROVERBS 15:23

Did you know that you are a person of influence? God has placed you where you are and gifted you to share the gospel in a unique way. Just as the Holy Spirit encourages you to become all God has designed you to be, you can build up the people you encounter each day. You can impact them in a way that will encourage them to feel better about themselves and who God created them to be.

We have the ability to make a difference in the world just by speaking the truth and offering encouragement. It's very inexpensive to give a compliment: "I like your shirt" or "God loves you" or "You are really good at what you do." Just a few properly chosen words at the right time can change a person's life for the better.

Ask the Holy Spirit to help you form a habit of adding value to everyone you meet through the words that you speak.

PRAYER FOR TODAY: *God, I have never thought of myself as an influencer, but I want you to use me to bring the right words at the right times to encourage others. Help me to see opportunities everywhere and to open my mouth to encourage others on a daily basis. Amen.*

DAY 220: THE REST OF GOD

Casting the whole of your care [all your anxieties, all your worries, all your concerns, once and for all] on Him, for He cares for you affectionately and cares about you watchfully.

1 PETER 5:7

If you are living your life always waiting to see how you feel or what you think before you decide what you will say or do, you won't have rest—you'll have stress! But if you give all of your worries, all of your concerns, and all of your cares to God, you can stand on His Word and declare what He says is true: "God cares for me, God watches out for me, and God has got this, so I have nothing to fear."

Hebrews 4:3 says that when we trust and rely on God, we will enter His rest. When we are truly in the rest of God, we know that He will take care of whatever situations we are facing. We don't know how He will do it. We don't know when He will do it. But we're not worried about any of that, because we know He will do it.

When you can release your concerns about when or how God will move the mountain in front of you, that's when you are truly experiencing His rest.

PRAYER FOR TODAY: *God, thank You for Your unwavering caring and protection over my life. Help me lay down my burdens at Your altar. Thank You that I can trade my worries for Your rest. In Jesus' name, amen.*

DAY 221
DEFEATING DOUBT AND UNBELIEF

[For Abraham, human reason for] hope being gone, hoped in faith that he should become the father of many nations, as he had been promised, so [numberless] shall your descendants be.

ROMANS 4:18

Abraham was an old man with no children, which meant that if he died, his inheritance would go to one of his servants. Yet he "hoped in faith" because God had promised him that he would become the "father of many nations" through a child of his own.

Romans 4:19 says that Abraham was impotent and that Sarah was well past the age of childbearing. They needed a miracle, and nothing else would do!

Verses 20–21 say: "No unbelief or distrust made him waver (doubtingly question) concerning the promise of God, but he grew strong and was empowered by faith as he gave praise and glory to God, fully satisfied and assured that God was able and mighty to keep His word and to do what He had promised."

When doubt, unbelief, and distrust attack your mind, fight back with the same weapons that Abraham used: faith and praise and glory to God.

PRAYER FOR TODAY: *God, thank You for Your Word and for the examples from the fathers of our faith on how we can overcome doubt and unbelief. I want the faith of Abraham that doesn't weaken or rely on human reasonings. Strengthen my faith, Lord. Amen.*

DAY 222
REMEMBER HIS FAITHFULNESS

Sing to Him, sing praises to Him; meditate on and talk of all His wondrous works and devoutly praise them!

1 CHRONICLES 16:9

When we talk about praising God, we aren't just talking about lifting our hands and singing. Praise also is an opportunity to dwell on, be thankful for, and recount God's goodness in your life.

Dave and I will often praise God for what He has done in our ministry by remembering those early days. We started out in the unfinished basement in our home. I can remember three or four ladies praying in the basement with me and laying the foundation in the Spirit for what God is doing right now. I can remember a few friends finishing that basement for us so we could have office space. I remember our first van with the rusty wheel wells and bald tires and the little bubble trailer we pulled behind it so that we could do conferences in nearby cities. And I praise Him for His faithfulness as He has grown this ministry for His glory.

What has God done for you? How have you seen His hand at work in your life? When challenges come your way, instead of focusing on your problems, focus on your victories. Think about and talk about all of the ways God has come through for you in the past. He has done it before, and He will do it again!

PRAYER FOR TODAY: *God, thank You for everything You have done for me. As I go about my day, help me remember Your faithfulness and goodness so I can praise You for it. I don't ever want to forget all you have walked me through in the past. Put someone in my path today who I can tell about Your mighty deeds. Amen.*

DAY 223

SPEAK GOD'S WORD FAITHFULLY

The prophet who has a dream, let him tell his dream; but he who has My word, let him speak My word faithfully. What has straw in common with wheat [for nourishment]? says the Lord.

JEREMIAH 23:28

Second Corinthians 10:4 tells us that we are in a war, but our weapons are not physical, they are spiritual. In order to battle in the spiritual realm, we have to have spiritual weapons. Your spiritual weapons include praise and worship, the Word of God—which Ephesians calls the sword of the Spirit—and speaking words of faith and truth. As Jeremiah says, we are to speak God's Word faithfully.

Jesus was led by the Spirit into the wilderness to be tempted by the devil, and He fought back with the weapon of the Word by quoting Scripture back at the devil. Jesus is our example in all things, so we should study and know the Word, not just for intellectual knowledge but so that we can speak it faithfully against the enemy's attacks.

When was the last time you spoke the Word of God out loud? Whatever you are going through, there is a scripture for it. Find it and speak it out loud over your life.

PRAYER FOR TODAY: *God, thank You for equipping me with all the weapons I need for this battle. Help me remember that Your Word is more powerful than the enemy. Hide Your Word in my heart so that it is there, ready to be spoken, when I need it! Amen.*

DAY 224: WHAT ARE YOU THINKING?

But there is another power within me that is at war with my mind. This power makes me a slave to the sin that is still within me.
ROMANS 7:23 NLT

A war is raging within you between your flesh and your spirit, and your mind is the battlefield. The devil loves to invade our thoughts and confront us with things like worry, doubt, confusion, depression, anger, and condemnation. He likes to argue with us about why our faith won't work. But 2 Corinthians 10:5 says that we can take those thoughts captive and make them obedient to Christ.

We can't always help what thoughts come into our minds, but we can choose what we do with those thoughts. We can choose to dwell on them. We can choose to speak them and give them creative power to come into existence. Or we can choose to immediately refute them. In order to do so, you will need to know God's Word, and that requires dedication to studying and reading on a regular basis.

When a thought arises, immediately ask yourself, *Is this from God?* If it isn't, don't give it a second thought! Say the opposite of what the devil has told you. Use the Word of God as your weapon to combat the enemy's lies.

PRAYER FOR TODAY: *God, help me immediately recognize when the thoughts in my mind are not from You so that I can take them captive. Bridle my tongue when I am tempted to speak words of doubt, worry, or condemnation. Instill in me a passion for Your Word so that I can effectively combat the enemy's tactics with Your truth. Amen.*

DAY 225 — AN INDISPENSABLE WEAPON

Therefore take up the whole armor of God, that you may be able to withstand in the evil day, and having done all, to stand firm.
EPHESIANS 6:13 ESV

Ephesians 6 in the Message version says, "God's Word is an indispensable weapon" (vv. 13–18). That means knowing the Word of God—and speaking the Word of God—is vital to your ability to overcome the enemy's tactics.

For example, when the devil tries to bury you under guilt and condemnation, if you know the Word, you can declare, "It is written: 'There is therefore now no condemnation for those who are in Christ Jesus'" (Romans 8:1 ESV).

When the enemy tries to tell you that you cannot overcome your past, remind him of the truth: "I am not my past. The Word says that I can forget everything that lies behind me and reach out for what is ahead because I am a new creation, created in Christ Jesus for good works" (Philippians 3:13; 2 Corinthians 5:17; Ephesians 2:10).

When Satan plants a seed of fear in your heart and mind, the Word will remind you: "God did not give us a spirit of timidity (of cowardice, of craven and cringing and fawning fear), but [He has given us a spirit] of power and of love and of calm and well-balanced mind and discipline and self-control" (2 Timothy 1:7).

By immersing yourself in the Word, you equip yourself with the full armor of God, enabling you to stand firm against any attack.

PRAYER FOR TODAY: *God, thank You for giving me everything I need to overcome fear, doubt, and unbelief. Thank You for giving us Your Word, which is a wellspring of truth. When the enemy attacks, help me turn to Your Word as my first line of defense. Amen.*

DAY 226: MEDICINE FOR YOUR SOUL

He sent His word and healed them, and rescued them from their destruction.

PSALM 107:20 AMP

The Word of God possesses incredible healing power—it's like spiritual medicine for your soul. Just as antibiotics heal infections in your body, God's Word has the inherent power to mend and restore your life.

God doesn't want you to read a chapter of the Bible a day out of obligation or because you are afraid that He will get mad at you if you don't. He wants you to hunger for the Word, just like your body hungers for food. He wants you to understand that there is life in His Word. I love God's Word. It comforts me, and it has healed my soul.

The Word of God will renew your mind. It will teach you how to think, how to act, and how to live. To truly benefit from it, you need to embrace it with love. If you don't have that desire, pray for a deeper hunger for His Word and for a revelation of its life-giving power.

PRAYER FOR TODAY: *God, ignite a deep hunger for Your Word within me. Open my mind and heart to its transformative benefits. And when I open Your Word, help me understand all that You are saying to me. Renew my mind and teach me how to think, speak, and act according to Your will. In Jesus' name, amen.*

DAY 227: GOD LOVES YOU

And I am convinced that nothing can ever separate us from God's love. Neither death nor life, neither angels nor demons, neither our fears for today nor our worries about tomorrow—not even the powers of hell can separate us from God's love.

ROMANS 8:38 NLT

When I first started preaching publicly, I prayed that God would speak something powerfully through me. I wanted those first messages to be *big*. And He said to me, "Tell my people I love them." I thought that was a simple message that everyone learned as kids in Sunday School, but God said to me, "Not all people know I love them. If they did, they would act a lot differently from the way they do."

The Bible says that perfect love casts out fear (1 John 4:18). When we truly comprehend God's love, fear loses its grip. We realize that because God is for us, no one and nothing can stand against us.

The world tells us that love is earned, deserved, and contingent on our behavior. When we apply that definition and distorted view of love to our relationship with God, it's no wonder we struggle to live out our faith properly!

The foundation for everything else in our Christian walk is dependent on us having a deep knowing that God loves us unconditionally and that there is never anything we can do that will separate us from that love.

PRAYER FOR TODAY: *God, thank You for loving me. Help me fully grasp, deep down in my heart, that Your love for me is real, unconditional, and everlasting. Let this be the foundation for all that I do, think, and say. Amen.*

DAY 228

HOW TO GET OUT OF A BAD MOOD

Either make the tree good and its fruit good, or make the tree bad and its fruit bad, for the tree is known by its fruit.

MATTHEW 12:33 ESV

Everything begins with a thought. If we allow negative, unkind thoughts to fill our minds, they will produce bad, negative fruit. The fruit we are talking about here is our words, our actions, our moods, and our attitudes. If you are in a bad mood and you want to change it, the first thing you should do is ask yourself what you are thinking about.

Negative thoughts may be fueling your bad mood. When you dwell on those thoughts, when you keep thinking about the unfair thing that happened to you or replaying over and over in your mind something you said or did that you shouldn't have, you will stay stuck in that bad mood.

But here's the good news: You can change your mood by changing your thoughts! Positive thoughts are like a healthy tree that produces good fruit in the form of a good mood, a positive attitude, and kinder words.

The more we immerse ourselves in God's Word and open ourselves up to the Holy Spirit's guidance, the more we will reflect Christ in our character—through our kindness, love, and the way we live.

PRAYER FOR TODAY: *God, thank You for showing me how to get out of a bad mood! Help me put this message into practice. I want to be like the good tree that produces good fruit. Thank You for being so loving, gracious, and kind to me—not to mention patient—as I learn Your truths. Amen.*

DAY 229
A CALM AND PEACEFUL ATMOSPHERE

A calm and undisturbed mind and heart are the life and health of the body, but envy, jealousy, and wrath are like rottenness of the bones.

PROVERBS 14:30

Our thoughts, words, and attitudes influence the atmosphere around us. Thoughts become words, attitudes, body language, facial expressions, and even moods—each contributing to the environment we create. This atmosphere can be hectic and stressful, or it can be calm, positive, and even enjoyable.

We all have people we enjoy being around—people we feel comfortable with, whether the house is a mess, traffic is backed up, or there is a long wait at our favorite restaurant. As God's Word says, they are "calm and undisturbed" by the things of life. But we also have people we don't enjoy being around—people who drain us, who make us feel anxious and stressed, who bring a chaotic atmosphere with them regardless of their circumstances. In other words, people we try to avoid!

God's desire for us is that we would create a positive, peace-filled atmosphere for ourselves and those around us through the thoughts we think, the words we speak, and the moods and attitudes that follow.

PRAYER FOR TODAY: *Father God, I come to You in the name of Jesus and ask You to help me be calm and undisturbed, the kind of person that people want to be around. Enable me to have peace in the middle of the storm and experience joy regardless of external circumstances. Amen.*

DAY 230

HOW TO DEFEAT YOUR ENEMIES

And David said, "The Lord who delivered me from the paw of the lion and from the paw of the bear will deliver me from the hand of this Philistine." And Saul said to David, "Go, and the Lord be with you!"

1 SAMUEL 17:37 ESV

When David faced Goliath, he was full of conviction and courage. Despite King Saul's doubts about David's youth, size, and experience, David confidently recounted how God had showed up for him previously, giving him the strength to kill a lion and a bear that threatened his herd. He was certain that God would show up for him again.

As David confronted Goliath, the giant mocked him for showing up with only a slingshot and some smooth stones from the riverbed. Yet David boldly said:

> You come to me with a sword and with a spear and with a javelin, but I come to you in the name of the Lord... This day the Lord will deliver you into my hand...that all the earth may know that there is a God in Israel... For the battle is the Lord's, and he will give you into our hand (1 Samuel 17:45–47 ESV).

The way to defeat our enemies is to open our mouths and proclaim the Word of God. Our victory begins with a declaration of faith that God is able.

PRAYER FOR TODAY: *God, put Your Word in my mouth so that I can declare it in the face of my enemies. When I am intimidated and tempted to remain silent, let David's example inspire me to speak with confidence and faith. Amen.*

DAY 231

YOUR ATTITUDE, YOUR CHOICE

Let this same attitude and purpose and [humble] mind be in you which was in Christ Jesus: [Let Him be your example in humility].
PHILIPPIANS 2:5

God's desire for us is that we learn to live with a positive attitude of faith and hope. Our minds, mouths, and attitudes belong to us—no one should do our thinking for us—therefore, we have the power to maintain a positive outlook regardless of our circumstances.

You can start by thinking and confessing biblical truths like:

I will not quit. I will not give up. I am committed to pressing on to the finish line, living in victory, and bringing glory to God. I want to learn to think right. I want to learn to talk right. I want to learn to have a good attitude. I want to learn to walk in love and be a blessing to everybody everywhere that I go. I don't just want to go through the motions. I love God, and I am expecting good things in my life!

When faced with negative situations, a positive attitude invites God to work and transform those circumstances. Be fervent in your faith and outlook and watch how God will turn things around.

PRAYER FOR TODAY: *God, thank You for giving me the mind of Christ. Jesus is my example in all things, and I ask You to help me be like Him in my thoughts, words, moods, and attitudes. Jesus trusted and hoped in You, regardless of His circumstances, and with Your help I can do the same. Amen.*

DAY 232
WHAT'S ON YOUR MIND?

Therefore let us, as many as are mature, have this mind; and if in anything you think otherwise, God will reveal even this to you.
PHILIPPIANS 3:15 NKJV

Do you ever replay a conversation over and over in your mind, overthinking what you said or how you said it or what the other person must have thought of you?

How much time do you spend thinking about what happened to you ten, thirty, or even fifty years ago?

Did you do something recently that you think offended God, and you can't stop thinking about it?

Have you ever had a job or a relationship that ended badly, and you still get emotional when you think about it, when you drive past that workplace, or when you see that person in public or on social media?

God wants you to be fully present, embracing this moment and everything that He has for you now. Yet, we often find ourselves mentally and emotionally trapped in the past, burdened by what has happened to us rather than being hopeful for the future.

We can't place our hope in the past, but we can trust God to redeem it. So let's be people of hope today.

PRAYER FOR TODAY: *God, I realize now that I can't change the past. Not only can I not change the past, but I cannot be open to what You have for me in the present if I'm stuck back there in what I did and what was done to me. Help me let go of the past, and help me be a person of hope. Amen.*

DAY 233

HE WILL REWARD YOU

But when you do a charitable deed, do not let your left hand know what your right hand is doing, that your charitable deed may be in secret; and your Father who sees in secret will Himself reward you openly.

MATTHEW 6:3-4 NKJV

Every time God asks you to give up something, do something hard, or do something that challenges your flesh and you do it, He takes notice. He sees your obedience, understands the difficulty, and is faithful to care for you. God honors our right choices, our obedience, and our decision to choose Him over our immediate feelings.

You may have a job or a ministry that keeps you behind the curtain, out of the public eye, where the things you do often seem to be overlooked or go unappreciated. Someone else might even get the credit for things you do. Rest assured, God sees everything you are doing, and He will not forget your faithfulness.

Keep an attitude of expectation and trust that God will encourage you. His peace, His presence, and His promises are often the first signs of His reward.

PRAYER FOR TODAY: *God, sometimes I just want to know that I am appreciated and that what I am doing is making a difference. Would You do something today to show me You are with me and that living in obedience to You matters? Thank You, Father. Amen.*

DAY 234

FOR YOUR BENEFIT

Now [in Haran] the Lord said to Abram, Go for yourself [for your own advantage] away from your country, from your relatives and your father's house, to the land that I will show you.

GENESIS 12:1

In the book of Genesis, God asks Abram to leave everything behind—his family, his land, and his inheritance—for the land that God would show him. In return, God said, "Your reward shall be exceedingly great" (Genesis 15:1).

God may be asking you to leave something behind—a relationship, a job, your hometown, a life of sin or addiction, an excess of worldly "stuff." If He is, know that it is for your own advantage because He has something better for you, somewhere better for you, or someone better for you. But first you have to let go of the thing He tells you to leave behind.

Whatever you are going through right now may seem impossible, but if you will stick with it and walk through it with a godly attitude out of love for God, He will honor your faithfulness. His reward may not look like what you expect, but it will be "exceedingly great" in His eyes.

Don't miss what God has for you by giving up somewhere in the middle or holding too tightly to the things He is asking you to let go of. I think we can go through anything if we keep the right attitude: *There is a reward on the other side of this trial.*

PRAYER FOR TODAY: *God, I know in my mind that everything You ask me to do is for my own benefit, but sometimes it's hard to keep a good attitude! Teach me to obey immediately and to trust that You always have my best interests at heart. Give me the strength to let go of what You don't want me to have. In Jesus' name, amen.*

DAY 235 — PROMOTION IS COMING

Whoever believes and has decided to trust in Him [as personal Savior and Lord] is not judged [for this one, there is no judgment, no rejection, no condemnation]; but the one who does not believe [and has decided to reject Him as personal Savior and Lord] is judged already [that one has been convicted and sentenced], because he has not believed and trusted in the name of the [One and] only begotten Son of God [the One who is truly unique, the only One of His kind, the One who alone can save him].

JOHN 3:18 AMP

The enemy often opposes you most when God is preparing something significant in your life. As a result, he will pull out all the stops to distract you or make you doubt God's plan.

Rejection is one of the ways the enemy will do this. If you've ever been turned down for a date, denied a home loan, dismissed when you've offered an idea, or excluded from a friend's party, you know the pain of rejection.

Rejection is so difficult. It can make us feel disappointed, ashamed, angry, or unworthy. But we don't have to stay there! The enemy often uses rejection to discourage us and keep us from stepping confidently into God's plan. But when we renew our minds with truth—like John 3:18 and Ephesians 1:6—we remember that in Christ, we are never rejected but fully accepted in the Beloved!

PRAYER FOR TODAY: *Father, help me overcome rejection when it happens to me. Help me always believe the best of people and not assume they are rejecting me when that might not be the case at all. Let me be more concerned about how I am treating others than I am about how they are treating me. Amen.*

DAY 236

REMEMBER LOT'S WIFE

Remember [what happened to] Lot's wife [when she looked back]!
LUKE 17:32 AMP

Jesus tells us in the Gospels to "Remember... Lot's wife." What is it that we are supposed to remember about her?

Genesis 19:26 says, "Lot's wife looked back, and she became a pillar of salt" (NIV).

Despite being warned, Lot's wife looked back at Sodom and Gomorrah as she fled, and it immobilized her. She turned into a pillar of salt and could never move forward. Her fixation on the past prevented her from moving forward. Like her, if we can't let go of what lies behind—past hurts, disappointments, pain, or even the "good ol' days"—we can't move forward into all that God has for us.

We cannot fully embrace the future God has for us if we are constantly looking back. To move forward, we must release our grip on the past. We cannot advance while lamenting missed opportunities or dwelling on past injustices.

Jesus tells us to remember Lot's wife so that we will learn from her mistake—so that we will look forward with optimism and hope, with gratitude and expectancy, learning from what lies behind so that we can better embrace what is yet to come.

PRAYER FOR TODAY: *God, thank You for gently and patiently teaching me that when I trust You, everything will turn out better than expected! Help me release my anxieties and regrets about the past so that I can move forward into all that You have prepared for me. Amen.*

DAY 237: A LIFELONG PROCESS

But grow in the grace and knowledge of our Lord and Savior Jesus Christ. To him be the glory both now and to the day of eternity. Amen.

2 PETER 3:18 ESV

If you build a house the right way, it will take a lot longer than you expect, and it won't be done until it's done. In the same way, God wants us to trust Him and be patient.

Most things that are worthwhile take longer than we think. They are harder than we think. They cost more than we thought they would. And we can be tempted to cut corners, hurry ahead, or give up before we get to the finish, but if we will press on, we will see a great reward.

The Christian life is no different. If you really want to have victory, you must be willing to make progress little by little. You have to be willing to keep the faith even when you aren't seeing results. You must be willing to lay down the things that no longer serve you, and that will be harder and more costly than you think.

Do you truly want the mind of Christ? Do you truly want your mind, mouth, moods, and attitudes to glorify Him with every thought, every word, every action? Spiritual maturity is a journey, and I encourage you to enjoy the journey rather than being overly focused on the destination.

PRAYER FOR TODAY: *God, grant me the strength and patience to grow in Your grace and knowledge each day. When I grow tired of the process, be my source of encouragement. Remind me that everything worth having requires perseverance and that if I don't give up, I will see the victory. In Jesus' mighty name, amen.*

DAY 238

GET UP!

When Jesus noticed him lying there [helpless], knowing that he had already been a long time in that condition, He said to him, Do you want to become well? [Are you really in earnest about getting well?]

JOHN 5:6

In this story, there were many people lying by the pool of Bethesda, waiting for the angel to stir up the water so that they could be healed.

Jesus noticed one man who had been there for thirty-eight years. Scripture says that he had "a deep-seated and lingering disorder" (v. 5). Only the first person to get in the water when the angel stirred it up was healed, and he had never been first. Jesus asked the man if he truly wanted to get better. The man replied with excuses: No one would help him, and someone else always got ahead of him.

Jesus is the most compassionate person who ever walked the face of this earth, but He didn't respond with "That's terrible! What can I do for you?" Instead Jesus responded with a directive: "Get up!" (v. 8). Jesus, full of compassion, addressed the man's excuses directly, challenging him to rise above his situation. Jesus wanted the man to take a step of faith, and when he did, he was healed.

If you need a miracle, ask God for help and do your part. Remain in faith, keep a positive attitude, praise God, be thankful, be obedient, and do anything God is asking you to do.

PRAYER FOR TODAY: *God, thank You for the reminder that I am responsible for my attitudes and my actions and that I have the power to get up. Give me the desire to be whole and the strength to take the first step toward change today. Amen.*

DAY 239
ENJOY THE PROGRESS YOU HAVE MADE

Jesus said to him, If I want him to stay (survive, live) until I come, what is that to you? [What concern is it of yours?] You follow Me!
JOHN 21:22

God changes us from one degree of spiritual maturity to another even more mature level. But it is important to learn to enjoy the progress you have made instead of worrying about how far you have to go. God has been changing me for almost fifty years, and He is still changing me.

The person next to you may be at a level of maturity beyond where you are, but that shouldn't take away from you enjoying where you are. You could be happy praying fifteen minutes a day and know that God is happy with you, but when you hear about someone else who prays for three hours a day, you suddenly feel frustrated and upset. That is the enemy speaking! The devil wants us to compare ourselves to others so that we become jealous and covetous, but those are sins because they prevent us from enjoying what God is doing in us right now.

God has a personal plan for you, and you have your own personal relationship with Him, so stop looking around at other people and keep your eyes on God. I believe Jesus is saying to us today essentially what He said to Peter in John 21: "Don't concern yourself with what God is doing in others. *You* follow *Me*!"

PRAYER FOR TODAY: *God, thank You for what You are doing in my life. Help me to stay focused on my own path and to not be distracted by others. Teach me to appreciate and enjoy the blessings of the present moment, knowing that Your plan for me is perfect. Amen.*

DAY 240

SIT, STAND, WALK, RUN

All athletes are disciplined in their training. They do it to win a prize that will fade away, but we do it for an eternal prize.
1 CORINTHIANS 9:25 NLT

The Bible says in Ephesians 2:6 that we are seated in heavenly places with Christ Jesus. When we are seated with Jesus, that means we have entered His rest. Hebrews 4 says that we enter that rest through faith and believing.

After you have learned how to sit with Jesus, you can begin to stand against the enemy (Ephesians 6:11). Standing against the enemy means that you can resist him and not give him victory. I used to get upset every time the enemy came against me with trials of any kind, but I don't anymore, because I know it is a useless waste of energy. When I realized I was letting him win in my mind and it was affecting my moods, I quit getting so worked up, because I can choose to trust God and know He will work it out for my good.

Once you know how to rest in God and begin to stand against the devil, you can learn how to walk as Jesus walked: walk in faith, walk closely with God, and walk in love (Ephesians 5:2).

When you can stay in His rest, stand against the enemy, and walk in love, only then can you run your race (1 Corinthians 9:24). Keep the attitude that this is a process and every day you are making progress toward the finish line.

PRAYER FOR TODAY: *God, thank You for showing me that progress is more important than perfection! Help me stick with the process and to be as disciplined as an athlete and as gracious with myself as a parent watching a child learn to sit, stand, walk, and finally run. You are that gracious heavenly Father for me. Amen.*

DAY 241

DAILY INVENTORY

Teach us to number our days, that we may gain a heart of wisdom.
PSALM 90:12 NIV

On average, we are awake for sixteen hours a day. At the end of each day, it is a good exercise to ask yourself, *What did I do with my time today?*

You can take a daily inventory by creating a timeline: First, I made coffee. Then, I spent time with God. Next, I went to work. At lunch, I ate with some coworkers. On the way home, I got stuck in traffic. For dinner, I cooked a meal. This evening, we watched TV together as a family, and, after putting the kids to bed, I read for a while and then went to sleep.

You can also take a daily inventory by asking questions such as *How much time did I spend worrying today? Did I spend my day being concerned about what others thought of me? Did I spend it upset, depressed, and feeling sorry for myself? Did I have good fellowship with others, or was the time spent on gossip? How much of my day was spent doing something that was fruitful?*

As I get older, I am aware that I have less and less time on this planet, so it has become even more important to me to not waste any more of my time on thoughts, conversations, or actions that don't move me closer to Christ. This simple practice can help you see where your time is going and guide you to make any needed adjustments.

PRAYER FOR TODAY: *God, in the name of Jesus, help me make my days count. When I get off track, redirect me to things that add value to my life and to the lives of others. Amen.*

DAY 242: HOPE FOR YOUR CHILDREN

Thus says the Lord: Restrain your voice from weeping and your eyes from tears, for your work shall be rewarded, says the Lord; and [your children] shall return from the enemy's land. And there is hope for your future, says the Lord; your children shall come back to their own country.

JEREMIAH 31:16–17

This is a special devotion for those raising children or anyone who has ever raised a child, especially if the child isn't currently walking with the Lord.

These scriptures were written by God and preserved for you so that you can think on them, meditate on them, and speak them out loud. Especially if you are worried about your children and their futures, read Jeremiah 31:16-17 out loud, and let it remind you of God's heart and His faithfulness.

Whenever fear or doubt creeps in about your children, return to these scriptures. Shout them at the enemy. Speak them over your family. Hide them in your heart. Believe that there is hope for your children. God can redeem the years. He can take a situation that seems hopeless and turn it around in an instant. Enter His rest, knowing He has a plan for your children.

PRAYER FOR TODAY: *God, I intercede for parents today everywhere who are worried about their children. Help us to trust that Your hand is upon our children and that You are ordering their steps. Help us to believe Your Word that says there is hope for them and that they will return to You. In Jesus' name, amen.*

DAY 243
DON'T WORRY ABOUT ANYTHING

Don't worry about anything; instead, pray about everything. Tell God what you need, and thank him for all he has done.

PHILIPPIANS 4:6 NLT

Most people live complicated lives that leave them frustrated, confused, weary, and worn out. But life does not have to be this way! One of the "simplest" ways to simplify your life is to quit worrying.

If you're thinking that it sounds easier said than done, know that there is hope. Whenever God instructs us to do something, He also gives us the ability to do it. Today's verse says it clearly: "Don't worry about anything." Therefore, we know that if you pray and ask God for the strength to stop worrying, you can trust that He will help you and begin to renew your mind with His peace. The more you trust God the less you will worry.

Practice living one day at a time. Give yourself—your thoughts, your conversations, every part of you—to the day at hand. Instead of worrying, believe God and watch Him work on your behalf. You can develop a calmer, more peaceful mind with His help.

The Message version of this verse says it beautifully: "It's wonderful what happens when Christ displaces worry at the center of your life." Wonderful indeed!

PRAYER FOR TODAY: *God, I am tired of living anxious and stressed-out. Thank You for Your Word, which tells me that I don't have to worry. Transform my mindset and help me trust You more each day so that, instead of worrying, I can wonder at Your marvelous works. Amen.*

ONE DAY AT A TIME

So do not worry or be anxious about tomorrow, for tomorrow will have worries and anxieties of its own. Sufficient for each day is its own trouble.

MATTHEW 6:34

How do you approach life? Do you look at all the things coming in the future and start to panic or worry? Or do you live life one day at a time, refusing to borrow trouble from tomorrow?

We can paralyze our minds if we try to think about too many things at once. If you have six projects that you need to finish this week, and you let your mind start thinking about the details of each one, you will feel pressured. You may even feel so overwhelmed that you aren't able to concentrate on any of the projects, and you don't end up getting anything done! It isn't the projects pressuring you, however, but thinking about all of them at once instead of focusing on the one that needs to get done today.

Jesus tells us in Matthew 6 to take life one day at a time and to let tomorrow worry about itself. That is good advice! God will give you the grace you need for tomorrow when tomorrow comes, so focus on enjoying and fully engaging with today.

PRAYER FOR TODAY: *God, help me live life one day at a time, not wasting today on worries about tomorrow. Help me to prioritize my tasks, to see what needs to be done today, and to give myself to that. In Jesus' name, amen.*

DAY 245: FIX YOUR EYES ON JESUS

Fixing our eyes on Jesus, the pioneer and perfecter of faith. For the joy set before him he endured the cross, scorning its shame, and sat down at the right hand of the throne of God.

HEBREWS 12:2 NIV

So much of our happiness has to do with our focus—what we're dwelling on in our minds. That's why when we put our focus on God and all of the great things He does for us, it breathes hope into our thoughts, our moods, and our entire day.

When we give thanks, we make God bigger in our eyes, and suddenly our problems seem smaller!

Take a few moments right now to thank God for His goodness, love, and faithfulness. Then thank Him for a couple things in your life that you're grateful for—whether it's your family, your career, or even your cup of coffee in the morning.

Instead of focusing on the negative, instead of constantly focusing on anything and everything that is not going as planned, we can choose to remember the good things He's doing and celebrate them.

Do you want to make this day and every day better? Then choose to focus on the good! As you do, your perspective will change, and you'll suddenly feel so much better about life.

PRAYER FOR TODAY: *God, help me focus on the good things that You are doing in my life, because when my mind is fixed on You, everything changes for the better. Amen.*

DAY 246: HEALTHY HABITS

This will bring health to your body and nourishment to your bones.
PROVERBS 3:8 NIV

Have you been in a bad mood lately? Today's scripture reminds us that living in line with God's wisdom brings health. Sometimes our habits and lifestyle contribute to our moods and poor health. Here are some practical tips to improve both:

- Leave margin in your schedule so you don't have to rush from one thing to the next. This also allows you to stay in peace if you end up wanting to give something more time than you previously planned.
- Take time to do things you enjoy. There will always be work that needs to be done, so waiting until you "have time" to enjoy life means that you never will.
- Have a plan, but decide ahead of time that you won't get upset if your plan is interrupted for valid reasons. Take a deep breath, tell yourself *We are shifting gears*, and give yourself to the new plan.
- Make healthy choices when it comes to the food you eat. Your body needs the proper nutrition in order to function at its peak performance.
- Have a regular bedtime. A good night's rest can be the biggest determining factor between a good mood and a negative one.
- Give yourself permission to say no when you need to—and not feel guilty about it!

PRAYER FOR TODAY: *God, help me see where I need to make changes in my life in order to be happy, healthy, and whole. I want to enjoy my life and be a joy to be around, and I need Your help. In Jesus' name, amen.*

DAY 247
START AND END YOUR DAY WITH SOLITUDE

And after He had dismissed the multitudes, He went up into the hills by Himself to pray. When it was evening, He was still there alone.

MATTHEW 14:23

Our culture is obsessed with busyness, with doing things and getting things done. Somehow, we think that busyness makes us important. Yet, God's love for us isn't dependent on our productivity. He values our moments of solitude and quiet just as much. In fact, Jesus often went off by Himself to pray.

Taking even just a few minutes of solitude in the morning can help you get ready to face the day with the proper attitude. You don't know what the day will hold, but inviting God into it and starting off on the right foot, with a peaceful heart and a clear mind, will prepare you to handle whatever comes with grace.

Likewise, taking a few minutes of solitude at the end of the day can restore your soul to a restful place, where you can let go of any built-up stress, thank God for all the ways you saw Him at work in your life, and ready yourself for a good night's sleep.

Schedule solitude into your day and notice how it improves your mind, mouth, mood, and overall attitude.

PRAYER FOR TODAY: *God, forgive me for equating my worth with my busyness rather than with who You've created me to be. Show me where I have become addicted to noise and activity, and help me prioritize quiet time alone and with You. In Jesus' name, amen.*

DAY 248: HAVE YOU LOST YOUR MIND?

And who of you by worrying and being anxious can add one unit of measure (cubit) to his stature or to the span of his life?
MATTHEW 6:27

Have you ever said, "I feel like I'm losing my mind"? The truth is, you have lost your mind if you have given up the control of your thoughts to an enemy who is bent on killing, stealing, and destroying (John 10:10). The good news is that you can reclaim your peace by choosing to focus on positive thoughts intentionally.

Our thoughts affect our emotions, and we can upset ourselves or calm ourselves down by choosing what to think about. We can think about everything that could possibly go wrong, or we can choose to get our minds off of ourselves by inviting a positive friend out for lunch, listening to happy music, or encouraging someone else.

God did not create you to be a worrier. Worry is thinking about your problem over and over—and it's a complete waste of time and energy! Nor does God expect you to change your mind, renew your thoughts, and think like He thinks without any help. He wants us to be totally dependent on Him rather than being independent. We need His help every step of the way, and He is always ready to help you—just ask!

PRAYER FOR TODAY: *God, thank You for reminding me that worrying is a waste of time and energy. I have tried to manage my anxiety on my own, but I need Your help. Give me the strength to do whatever needs to be done without fear. I trust You, Lord. Amen.*

DAY 249: CONFESS YOUR BELIEFS

For with the heart a person believes (adheres to, trusts in, and relies on Christ) and so is justified (declared righteous, acceptable to God), and with the mouth he confesses (declares openly and speaks out freely his faith) and confirms [his] salvation.

ROMANS 10:10

This passage from Romans teaches us that to be saved, we must believe in our hearts and confess with our mouths. The heart and the mouth (believing and speaking) work together.

This principle is echoed throughout the Psalms and Proverbs. Proverbs 3:1-3 tells us not to forget God's laws but to write them on the tablet of our hearts. In Psalm 45:1, David said that his tongue was like the pen of a ready writer. So, symbolically, your heart is the tablet, and your tongue is the pen.

In other words, when we confess God's Word out loud, we write it on our own hearts, and it becomes more firmly established both in our hearts and in the earth. God's Word is forever settled in heaven (Psalm 119:89), and each time we speak it, we affirm its truth in our lives. Believe and confess; confess and believe!

PRAYER FOR TODAY: *God, in the name of Jesus, help me trust You with all that I am and with my whole heart. Give me the boldness to speak Your Word openly and to confess my faith freely so that I may firmly establish Your truth in my heart. Amen.*

DAY 250: HOLD FAST YOUR CONFESSION

Inasmuch then as we [believers] have a great High Priest who has [already ascended and] passed through the heavens, Jesus the Son of God, let us hold fast our confession [of faith and cling tenaciously to our absolute trust in Him as Savior].

HEBREWS 4:14 AMP

The scripture above tells us to "hold fast" our confession of faith in Jesus. Another translation tells us to "hold firmly to the faith we profess" (NIV).

If there were no danger of drifting from our confession of faith, we could hold it loosely, at arm's length, trusting that it would always be there. But the author of Hebrews tells us to hold fast, to hold our confession of faith firmly in our grasp, because spiritual opposition is real.

Satan will try to steal our confession by putting wrong thoughts in our minds, hoping the thoughts will produce wrong words that will come out of our mouths. He will tell us that confessing the Word does no good, that it changes nothing. He will distract us from spending time in God's Word or cause us to feel lazy and not want to confess the Word even though we know it will benefit us if we do. Satan fights anything that will produce good results in our lives.

Don't make it easy for the devil. Hold firm to your faith and boldly confess the promises of God's Word.

PRAYER FOR TODAY: *God, thank You for Your Word, which instructs me in how to live and encourages me to fight the good fight of faith. Strengthen my resolve to resist the devil's schemes and deepen my desire to study and confess Your Word daily. Amen.*

DAY 251

WHAT GOES IN VS. WHAT COMES OUT

It is not what goes into the mouth that defiles a person, but what comes out of the mouth; this defiles a person.

MATTHEW 15:11 ESV

Old Testament Jewish law required the Jews to not eat foods that were considered to be unclean. But when Jesus came to earth, He said that what comes out of the mouth (words) defiles, not what goes into the mouth (food).

In the United States, we are obsessed with food: fine dining, fast food, farm to fork, diet food, supplements that take the place of food, protein shakes, going vegan, eating clean... the list goes on and on. And now we even have "foodies," people who eat as a hobby, not as a necessity. Every celebration we have is centered around food. But to Jesus' point: What would happen if we took as much care about what comes out of our mouths as what we put in them?

Many people don't realize the power of their words. Because of that, they do not use caution regarding what they say about themselves, their future, their finances, their children, other people, and probably hundreds of other topics. The Bible says, "Death and life are in the power of the tongue" (Proverbs 18:21). Since that is true, we should certainly put more thought into the words we speak than we do the foods we eat.

PRAYER FOR TODAY: *God, I ask for forgiveness for the words I have spoken that did not reflect Your will. Please help me be more mindful and intentional with my speech, starting today. In Jesus' name, amen.*

DAY 252: BEING POSITIVE TAKES CONSCIOUS EFFORT

But his delight and desire are in the law of the Lord, and on His law (the precepts, the instructions, the teachings of God) he habitually meditates (ponders and studies) by day and by night.

PSALM 1:2

Positive confession of the Word of God should be an ingrained habit of every believer. If you have not yet begun to develop this important habit, start today. Look up scriptures about what God says about you, and begin meditating on them and speaking them out loud: "I am the righteousness of God in Jesus Christ. I prosper in everything I lay my hand to. I have gifts and talents, and God is using me. I operate in the fruit of the Spirit. I walk in love. Joy flows through me" (2 Corinthians 5:21; Deuteronomy 28:8; 1 Peter 4:10; Galatians 5:22-23; Ephesians 5:2; John 15:11).

If negative thinking, speaking, and behaving have been a natural part of your disposition for a long time, you will have to make a conscious effort to get your life in line with what God says about you. But don't lose heart!

James 3:2 says that "we *all* often stumble and fall and offend in many things" (emphasis mine), but the one who "never says the wrong things" is perfect. Since none of us is perfect, we know that choosing to say the right things over the wrong things will be something we have to work on for as long as we live. We may never be perfect in this life, but we can make progress!

PRAYER FOR TODAY: *God, help me get my mouth in line with the truth of what You have done for me and what Your Word says about me. I know it will take effort on my part, but it will be worth it to make positive confession a habit in my life. Help me recognize when I've made progress. Amen.*

DAY 253: REJOICE AND BE GLAD

Rejoice in the Lord always [delight, gladden yourselves in Him]; again I say, Rejoice!

PHILIPPIANS 4:4

Many serious things are going on in this world, and we need to be aware of them and prepared for them. But at the same time, because of the Spirit of God in our lives, we can learn to relax and take things as they come without getting nervous and upset about them. Thankfully, with God's help, we can learn how to enjoy the good life He has provided for us through the death and resurrection of His Son, Jesus Christ. We do not need to worry or be afraid. God is in control!

Twice in Philippians 4:4–7, the apostle Paul tells us to rejoice. He urges us not to fret or have any anxiety about anything but to pray and give thanks to God—not *after* every difficulty is over, but *in everything*.

In spite of all the troubling things going on around us, we can maintain positive, joyful attitudes. Our daily confession can be based on Psalm 118:24: "This is the day the Lord has made; I will rejoice and be glad in it."

PRAYER FOR TODAY: *God, no matter what challenges I face today, I thank You that I can rejoice and be glad. Thank You that my joy is not found in my circumstances—my joy is found in You. Help me keep this joyful attitude in everything and at all times. Amen.*

DAY 254
BE WISE AND INNOCENT

I am sending you out like sheep among wolves. Therefore be as shrewd as snakes and as innocent as doves.

MATTHEW 10:16 NIV

Today's scripture tells us how to keep our mind right so that we can cultivate and enjoy the relationships that God wants to give us without falling victim to people who aren't concerned with our best interest. The passage tells us to be wise like snakes while also being innocent like doves.

People who are innocent but not wise usually open their hearts to others without knowing whether they are trustworthy. They don't use reasonable caution in relationships and often end up being hurt or betrayed. In contrast, people who are wise in some areas yet not innocent in their thoughts may be overly suspicious of others, always expecting people to take advantage of them. They may end up with few deep, meaningful relationships or even with no true friends at all.

Being out of balance in either direction is not God's plan for us, so He sent the Holy Spirit to help us be appropriately wise and appropriately innocent at the same time so that we can develop healthy, balanced relationships with others.

PRAYER FOR TODAY: *God, thank You for the gift of Your Holy Spirit to help me discern when to trust others and when to be cautious. It amazes me that I can have the mind of Christ! I long to have healthy relationships with other believers, and I ask for your wisdom to show me which relationships to invest in. In Jesus' name, amen.*

DAY 255: WORDS OF FAITH

Agree with God, and be at peace; thereby good will come to you.
JOB 22:21 ESV

If we want God's will for our lives, then our words need to agree with His Word. After we pray for specific needs in our lives, it's so important to follow up with words of faith and say what God says.

For instance, if you're praying for personal guidance in a crisis, don't go to lunch with your friends and say, "My situation is hopeless, and I have no idea what I'm going to do." Speak words of faith! Choose to say things like "I may not know how this is going to turn out yet, or what to do next, but I know God is working in my life, and He will show me which direction to go when it is time."

Or if you're praying for a health concern, don't go around saying, "Why am I always sick? I feel like I will never get well." Instead, choose to say faith-filled words like "God is in control, and He is the Lord my healer! He is a miracle-working God, and it is His desire that I be made well."

Our words have a powerful spiritual impact and should align with God's promises.

PRAYER FOR TODAY: *God, help me to align my words with Your truth and to follow my prayers with words of faith. In Jesus' mighty name I pray, amen.*

DAY 256: GOD APPROVES OF YOU

Before I formed you in the womb I knew [and] approved of you [as My chosen instrument], and before you were born I separated and set you apart, consecrating you; [and] I appointed you as a prophet to the nations.

JEREMIAH 1:5

We have an enemy, Satan, who wants to constantly fill our minds with negative thoughts. He wants us to continually focus on our weaknesses, meditate on them, and then speak them out of our mouths.

I've heard countless stories of people who were repeatedly told they were dumb or stupid when they were growing up. Their parents convinced them they would "never amount to anything in life." A teacher told them they weren't gifted in an area, so they shouldn't even try. Or maybe other kids were making fun of them for the way they looked or talked or laughed.

If we don't recognize these lies from the enemy and replace them with truth from God's Word, we begin to believe these things about ourselves, agreeing with the lies.

Research shows that we believe what we think and say about ourselves more than what anyone else says about us. That's why it's so important for us to purposely meditate on the good things about ourselves. We need to actively look for the good, and then choose to think about it and speak it out loud.

PRAYER FOR TODAY: *God, help me align my thoughts with Your truth about me, not the lies that the enemy wants me to believe. You don't make mistakes, so obviously You created me this way on purpose. Thank You for loving me just the way I am. Amen.*

DAY 257
KEEP SPEAKING

For she kept saying, If I only touch His garments, I shall be restored to health.

MARK 5:28

The Gospels tell the story of a woman who had "an issue of blood" for twelve years. She spent all she had on doctors, but her condition only grew worse. When she heard about Jesus, she decided to push through the crowds, determined to receive healing.

Mark 5:27–29 (ESV) says, "She...came up behind him in the crowd and touched his garment. For she said, 'If I touch even his garments, I will be made well.' And immediately the flow of blood dried up." Of all the people surrounding Jesus, this woman was the one to receive healing. She not only believed Jesus could heal her, but she released her faith *through what she said*.

The Amplified Bible, Classic Edition version of this text says that, as she approached Jesus, she "kept saying" that if she touched Him she would be healed. If your faith waivers, *keep saying* what God says. If you don't immediately see results, *keep releasing* your faith through the words of your mouth.

God will give you the faith to believe even before you see results. *Keep speaking* until you get your breakthrough. Then praise Him for your victory!

PRAYER FOR TODAY: *God, give me faith to believe the good plan that You have for my life. Give me boldness and courage to speak in faith. Give me confidence to keep speaking even when my voice shakes. I believe that You are who You say You are and You will do what You say You will do. Amen.*

DAY 258: ACTIVATE GOD'S PROMISES

For [if we are] in Christ Jesus, neither circumcision nor uncircumcision counts for anything, but only faith activated and energized and expressed and working through love.

GALATIANS 5:6

When we *say* what God says and *do* what God says to do, then we can *have* everything God says we can have. Make it a daily practice to confess God's promises over your life, such as:

- "I can do all things through Christ, who strengthens me" (Philippians 4:13).
- "God loves me, and He will never leave me or forsake me" (Romans 8:39; Hebrews 13:5).
- "God wants me to prosper and have hope" (Jeremiah 29:11).
- "I am a believer, not a doubter" (Mark 5:36).
- "I never get tired or grow weary when I study the Word, pray, minister, or praise God; I am alert and full of energy." (2 Thessalonians 3:13; Isaiah 40:31).

Whatever you're praying for, I encourage you to multiply your faith and release it through the words you speak. Study and learn God's Word, and begin to say the good things He says about you. Your words contain tremendous power, and they can activate all of God's incredible promises for your life.

PRAYER FOR TODAY: *God, thank You for showing me how to activate my faith and receive Your promises. Grow my desire to study Your Word so I will know what words to speak that will glorify You and open the door for me to receive all that You have for me. Amen.*

DAY 259

JOY IN THE MORNING

For His anger is but for a moment, His favor is for life; weeping may endure for a night, but joy comes in the morning.

PSALM 30:5 NKJV

God created us with tear glands and the ability to cry, which must mean there will be times in life when we need to weep. In the Bible, Hannah wept because she was brokenhearted over not having a child (1 Samuel 1:7).

When David and the men with him discovered the Amalekites had burned the city of Ziklag and taken everyone in it captive, they raised their voices and wept until they had no more strength to weep (1 Samuel 30:4). David also wept when his son became deathly ill (2 Samuel 12:21–22). Even Jesus wept over the grief of his friends Mary and Martha regarding the death of Lazarus (John 11:35). He was compassionate toward their sorrow even though He knew He was going to raise him from the dead.

God wants us to bring our pain to Him, and tears are certainly part of the process of healing in our souls. However, God did not create us to remain in a season of sadness indefinitely. God's Word promises that there is a time for everything: "a time to weep, and a time to laugh; a time to mourn, and a time to dance" (Ecclesiastes 3:4 ESV).

No matter what you are going through right now, ask God to help you deal with it in a healthy way. Cry when you need to, but keep in mind that the season of sadness will come to an end. As you walk with God, He will lead you into great joy.

PRAYER FOR TODAY: *God, guide me to find healing through expressing my feelings, while always holding on to Your promise of joy. Amen.*

DAY 260

BEAR GOOD FRUIT

When you bear (produce) much fruit, My Father is honored and glorified, and you show and prove yourselves to be true followers of Mine.

JOHN 15:8

God desires that we bear good fruit on a regular basis. Doing good, being creative, helping others, accomplishing goals, praying for others, being friendly, and offering encouragement are all simple ways to bear good fruit.

How often do we think something positive about someone but neglect to say it out loud? You and I have the ability to make someone else's day better by speaking words that reflect God's heart and letting them hear through us the good things He sees in them: "I like your hair." "What a great outfit!" "You are so thoughtful." "That was very generous of you." "What good manners you have!" "You have a beautiful voice." "That was a smart choice." "I'm impressed by how you handled that!" "The house looks great." "This meal is delicious!"

It's easy to notice flaws, but you can ask God to help you see the good in others. Soon you will find yourself in the habit of looking for the positive traits in others, and it will become natural for you to compliment the people around you.

Bear good fruit that will honor God by speaking positive things out loud.

PRAYER FOR TODAY: *God, show me how I can bear good fruit in my life that honors You. Open my eyes to the good in others, and open my mouth to share it with them. Thank You for working through me to encourage others and show them that they are loved by You. Amen.*

DAY 261

REMEMBER WHEN

I will remember the deeds of the Lord; yes, I will remember your miracles of long ago.

PSALM 77:11 NIV

God told the Israelites to remember how He redeemed and delivered them from slavery (Deuteronomy 24:18). After Esther saved the Jewish people from Haman's wicked plot to kill them, the people declared that every year they would have a two-day feast to remember what God had done for them through her (Esther 9:27–29). When David was dealing with depression, he purposely remembered a time when he had success (Psalm 42:4–5).

There are many instances recorded in the Bible when God instructed His people to remember, recount, and recall His mighty acts and the things He had done for them, because when they didn't, they ended up in sin and disobedience.

When we fail to remember, we lose appreciation. We become selfish and independent and are prone to worry and be upset. Remembering the good things in life and how God has proven Himself over and over will keep us on the happy path of gratitude. Our minds will be hopeful, thankful, joyful, healthy, and positive when we choose to remember God's promises and all that He has already done for us.

PRAYER FOR TODAY: *God, thank You for everything You have done for me in the past. Help me remember the ways You have shown up for me, opened doors for me, and answered my prayers, so that I can be encouraged in the future, knowing that You can and will do it again. Amen.*

DAY 262: MEMORIES

I press on toward the goal to win the [supreme and heavenly] prize to which God in Christ Jesus is calling us upward.

PHILIPPIANS 3:14

Have you ever paid attention to how memories affect you?

Some memories put a smile on your face. You are immediately in a good mood. You might even laugh out loud.

Other memories have the oppositive effect. They can make you feel tense, angry, or afraid. You might clench your fists or your teeth at the thought of what you had to endure. And if you allow your thoughts to stay there, that memory can ruin your entire day.

That is why the apostle Paul said that one of his greatest aspirations was to forget what was behind him and to press toward the future (Philippians 3:12–14). He didn't want the memories of what he had done—how he had persecuted Christians—to rob him of what God had for him going forward: leading others to a closer walk with Christ.

If a memory causes your mood to drop, take it captive immediately and replace it with what God says about you. Don't give the devil a foothold by allowing him to keep you stuck in the past. God has a good plan for your future.

PRAYER FOR TODAY: *God, thank You for giving me a future and a hope. Help me recognize immediately when my mood drops and if my thoughts are the cause of it. Speak the truth of Your Word into my heart to replace anything negative within me. In Jesus' name, amen.*

DAY 263: THE RIGHT ORDER

[That you may really come] to know [practically, through experience for yourselves] the love of Christ, which far surpasses mere knowledge [without experience]; that you may be filled [through all your being] unto all the fullness of God [may have the richest measure of the divine Presence, and become a body wholly filled and flooded with God Himself]!

EPHESIANS 3:19

The book of Ephesians has just six chapters in it. The first three chapters are about who we are in Christ, the amazing things Jesus has done for us, how much He loves us, and our relationship with God. Chapters 4–6 are about how we are to behave as Christians.

This order is significant and purposeful. *First*, God wants to develop a relationship with us in which we understand how much He loves us. *Then*, He wants us to change our thoughts, words, and actions so that we will think, speak, and act as He would have us think, speak, and act.

When we do this in the right order, changing our thoughts, words, and behavior becomes not something we feel we *have to do* to earn God's love, but something we *want to do* because He already loves us, and we love Him in return.

So, if you find yourself struggling to change in any of these areas—mind, mouth, mood, or attitude—the key is not in trying harder. The key is to develop your relationship with Him.

PRAYER FOR TODAY: *God, forgive me for the times that I have felt I had to earn Your approval. Lavish me with Your love and grace. Help me to receive it, to trust it, to want more of it, and, in time, to bear fruit from it. Amen.*

DAY 264: WHEN ANGRY

When angry, do not sin; do not ever let your wrath (your exasperation, your fury or indignation) last until the sun goes down. Leave no [such] room or foothold for the devil [give no opportunity to him].

EPHESIANS 4:26–27

Did you read today's verses? They don't say, "Don't get angry" or "If you ever get angry." They say, "When [you are] angry." *When*, not *if*!

We're all going to be angry at times, but it's not feeling anger that's a problem. The problem comes when we fuel our angry emotions with wrong thoughts, which then lead us to act on those feelings.

Self-control is a fruit of the Spirit that's given to us to help us manage ourselves (Galatians 5:23). This means that when we feel a certain way, we can choose not to act on it if we know it's against the Word of God.

Second Corinthians 10:5 instructs us to take every thought captive into the obedience of Christ *before* it becomes a stronghold in our minds. In other words, we can choose what we are going to think and dwell on. Instead of thinking wrong thoughts, we can take a stand and, with God's help, refuse to allow the situation to get out of control.

God is greater than our emotions, and we can trust Him to be our Vindicator while we walk in peace.

PRAYER FOR TODAY: *God, I need Your help. I know being upset is not going to get me anywhere. With Your grace and strength, guide me to control my feelings and trust You to handle the situation that stirred my anger. Amen.*

DAY 265: PRAY ABOUT EVERYTHING

You desire but do not have, so you kill. You covet but you cannot get what you want, so you quarrel and fight. You do not have because you do not ask God.

JAMES 4:2 NIV

Revelation 5:8 says that the prayers of God's people are laid before Him. Prayer is one of the greatest privileges we have, because it is literally talking to God and laying before Him whatever is on your heart. You can pray anytime, anywhere, about anything, and He will hear you.

God is ready to act on our behalf—and He can accomplish more in a moment than we could in a lifetime on our own—but we have to do our part and pray. James 4:2 says that we don't have because we haven't asked. In other words, if we don't pray, our prayers cannot be answered.

If you are struggling with a negative attitude, bad mood, anxiety, or worried thoughts, remember that Philippians 4:6–7 says to pray about everything and God will exchange your worries for His peace.

Learn to "pray at all times" (1 Thessalonians 5:17 GNT): daily, regularly, and immediately when you are anxious or worried or have a need. God is always available to help you the moment you call upon Him.

PRAYER FOR TODAY: *God, continue to give me revelation on this topic of prayer. Help me understand that You want to hear from me at all times and that I am never an inconvenience. Forgive me for the times I have worried instead of praying and receiving Your peace. Teach me how to pray without ceasing. In Jesus' name, amen.*

DAY 266: THE POWER TO TREAD

Behold, I give unto you power to tread on serpents and scorpions, and over all the power of the enemy: and nothing shall by any means hurt you.

LUKE 10:19 KJV

What kind of mood did you wake up with today? A good mood? A bad mood? A depressed mood? An ecstatic mood? Were you just feeling kind of moody?

No matter how you started the day, you have the power to talk yourself into a good mood and out of a negative one. No one else has that power but you.

The enemy will try to attack your moods. He will try to get you stuck on the pain of your feelings. And he'll try to get you to talk about them: "I woke up in a bad mood today" or "Leave me alone; I feel depressed" or "I don't know what's wrong with me; I'm just in a bad mood."

When the enemy attacks, attack back! Instead of saying what he wants you to say, shout at him: "I will not get in a bad mood!"

God has given us the "power to tread" on the enemy. That means we have the authority to resist him, rather than letting him control us.

The devil is not going to go away. You will always have to stand against him and his tactics on a regular basis, and you will have to resist him, which is why God has given us the power to tread on our enemy.

PRAYER FOR TODAY: *God, thank You for giving me the power to tread on the enemy. Help me talk myself into a good mood each day so that I can fully enjoy the life You've given me. Amen.*

DAY 267

A SURE FOUNDATION

Jesus Christ (the Messiah) is [always] the same, yesterday, today, [yes] and forever (to the ages).

HEBREWS 13:8

Jesus is our model for how to live our lives, and the Bible says that He never changes. He is always the same: yesterday, today, and forever. He is "the Rock" (1 Corinthians 10:4), a "foundation stone...Whoever believes need never be shaken" (Isaiah 28:16 NLT). Another translation says, "Anyone who trusts in [Him] will never be disappointed" (NCV).

Our faith won't be shaken because we believe in the One who never changes. He is dependable. He is reliable. He has proven Himself trustworthy. If He said it, He means it. If He did it, He'll do it again.

God wants us to have that kind of stability in our own lives. He doesn't want us to "wait and see" how we feel to decide if we will follow Him, if we will do the right thing, or if we will show up for people. Others should be able to depend on us—we should be able to depend on ourselves—because our firm foundation is Jesus the Rock.

Don't let the devil tell you how to feel. Don't "wait and see" which way your mood swings. Be stable. Be reliable. Be dependable. Say "I'll be there," and then be there. That's what Jesus would do.

PRAYER FOR TODAY: *God, thank You for being my unshakeable foundation and for proving Your faithfulness repeatedly. Help me be stable like You. Help me be a consistent force to my family and friends—reliable, dependable, and trustworthy. In Jesus' name, amen.*

DAY 268: CALL AND RELEASE

For there is not a word in my tongue [still unuttered], but, behold, O Lord, You know it altogether.

PSALM 139:4

You have a call of God on your life, but if you aren't bearing good fruit, God will not release you into that calling. In other words, your ability is released as you get stability.

God must be able to trust you before He will release you. So, if you lack maturity, He will put you into situations to help you grow—and He won't let you out until He has done a work in you!

Psalm 139:4 says that God knows every word on your tongue before you ever utter it. Verse 5 says that He has His hand upon you. Trust God, and don't get frustrated while you are waiting, because He knows the perfect time to release you into your calling.

That was certainly the case for me. He called me long before He released me because I had so much growing to do in these areas of the mind, mouth, moods, and attitudes. But as I grew, and as my life began to bear good fruit, He opened doors for me, and He will do the same for you.

PRAYER FOR TODAY: *God, thank You for the calling You have put on my life. Help me to lean on You when I find myself in situations I don't want to be in and to believe that You are doing a work in my life. Help me trust that You will open doors when You know that I am ready and will glorify You. Amen.*

DAY 269: BE CONSTANT

And do not [for a moment] be frightened or intimidated in anything by your opponents and adversaries, for such [constancy and fearlessness] will be a clear sign (proof and seal) to them of [their impending] destruction, but [a sure token and evidence] of your deliverance and salvation, and that from God.

PHILIPPIANS 1:28

Today's scripture tells us not to be afraid when the enemy attacks. It says that your "constancy" will be a "clear sign" to the devil that he has lost and "a sure token and evidence" that God is delivering you.

Constancy means you stand firm in your beliefs. You remain steady in your attitude, knowing that God has already won this fight. You don't let your mind drift, your mouth give the devil a foothold, or your mood sink. You keep your focus on the victor, not on being a victim. You do right things even when wrong things are being done to you.

Philippians 1:29 says that not only do we have the privilege to believe in God, but we also have the privilege to suffer for Him. Suffering is part of life, but how we respond to it is up to us.

When you refuse to be intimidated by the enemy and choose to have peace even when your situation isn't peaceful and to have joy even when your circumstances aren't joyful, you are inviting God in to deliver you while simultaneously shutting the door on the devil.

PRAYER FOR TODAY: *God, help me be stable in the storms that are a normal and inevitable part of life. When I am tempted to let my mood sink in defeat, remind me to be constant and fearless. Amen.*

DAY 270: PRAY AGAINST TEMPTATION

When He arrived at the place [called Gethsemane], He said to them, "Pray continually that you may not fall into temptation."
LUKE 22:40 AMP

Today we look at Luke 22:40–44. When Jesus prayed in the garden of Gethsemane, He first asked God to "remove this cup" (v. 42 AMP) from Him. He didn't want to go to the cross if He didn't have to, but He was willing to go if it was God's will.

Verse 44 says that Jesus went to God in prayer a second time in the garden, and this time "He prayed *more intently*; and His sweat became like drops of blood" (AMP, emphasis mine). Jesus was in agony, and He resisted the temptation to follow His feelings *so hard* that He was sweating blood. He even asked a third time, knowing how hard it would be to endure the cross, but He resisted the temptation to follow His feelings and was willing to do God's will no matter what it cost.

Watchman Nee said that emotions are a believer's number one enemy, which is why Jesus told His disciples to pray *continually* that they would not fall into temptation. Temptation will always be part of our lives—the temptation to look at things we shouldn't, say things we shouldn't, do things we know aren't in line with God's will. So, we must pray continually that we will follow God rather than our feelings.

Verse 43 says that God sent an angel to strengthen Jesus. God not only wants us to resist temptation; He will help us, strengthen us, and provide us with a way out (1 Corinthians 10:13).

PRAYER FOR TODAY: *God, in the name of Jesus, give me the strength to follow You instead of my feelings. Anytime I am being tempted, help me resist the temptation and follow Your will always. Amen.*

DAY 271

WHEN GOD SAYS "GO BACK"

Have I not commanded you? Be strong and courageous! Do not be terrified or dismayed (intimidated), for the Lord your God is with you wherever you go.

JOSHUA 1:9 AMP

Have you ever noticed that the armor of God detailed in Ephesians 6 doesn't include anything that covers your back? It includes the sword, the helmet, the breastplate, the belt, the shoes, and the shield. Nowhere on that list is anything to protect your back, because God never intended for us to run away! He has anointed you to go *through* hard times, when needed.

In Genesis 16, a pregnant Hagar wanted to run away when Sarai began to mistreat her, but an angel of the Lord found her and told her to go back and submit to her mistress.

In Exodus 2, Moses fled Egypt after he killed a man. He ran to the wilderness, where he stayed forty years, but an angel of the Lord appeared to him in a burning bush and told him to go back.

In 1 Kings 19, the prophet Elijah hid in a cave to avoid Jezebel, but the word of the Lord came to him and told him to go back.

You won't always be "in the mood" to confront your issues. You won't always "feel like it" when God tells you to stay in the fight, but He may bring you back to it until you learn to trust Him there.

PRAYER FOR TODAY: *God, thank You for being with me wherever I go. Help me keep moving forward. Give me the courage to face what I need to face and stay in the fight until I get it, especially on those days when I feel like running away. Amen.*

DAY 272
WHATEVER YOU DO

Whatever you do [whatever your task may be], work from the soul [that is, put in your very best effort], as [something done] for the Lord and not for men.

COLOSSIANS 3:23 AMP

When our motive for doing things is to get appreciation from people or to be noticed by others, we will end up discouraged. But when our motive is to do our very best for God, we will always be satisfied.

How many times have you wanted to quit something because you felt like no one appreciated what you were doing? Have you ever allowed yourself to get stuck on thoughts like *Does anyone even see me and how hard I'm working?* Have those thoughts ever turned into words like "It sure would be nice to get a little appreciation around here"? If those thoughts have been on your mind and, especially if they have come out of your mouth, they have no doubt caused you to have a bad mood and a bad attitude.

The Bible tells us that we shouldn't be working for human approval, but for God because of His great love for us and in response to our great love for Him. In fact, God wants us to look to Him for acceptance. There may be times when He lets us go through periods of disappointment with people simply so that we will remember that our hope should be in Him.

PRAYER FOR TODAY: *God, I confess that I want to be liked and approved by others. Forgive me for the times that I have sought other people's approval over Yours. Help me remember that You appreciate everything I do when I do it unto You. Amen.*

DAY 273
ONE OF OUR GREATEST TESTIMONIES

And it shall come to pass, that whosoever shall call on the name of the Lord shall be saved.

ACTS 2:21 KJV

The ability to display stability and remain calm in troubled times can be one of our greatest testimonies to a troubled world.

It is "normal" in our society to get aggravated and frustrated when things don't go our way. It is "understandable" when people's words and attitudes worsen under the weight of an overwhelming news cycle. It is "typical" to see moods swing from extreme highs to extreme lows in a culture that is addicted to excitement and adrenaline rushes.

So, when a Christian is able to keep calm and at peace when all natural reasoning says we should be upset, people will take notice. "How can you be calm at a time like this?" "The world seems to be falling apart, yet you seem strangely at peace." "What's your secret?"

You can tell them, "Jesus gave me His peace, so I've decided not to be troubled by the things of this world anymore. I've decided to be peaceful" (John 14:27). And the really good news is, His peace is available for anyone who calls on His name!

PRAYER FOR TODAY: *God, thank You for giving me Your supernatural peace. Help me remain in that peace—not just for my own sake, but as a witness to the world that is so desperate for peace. They won't find what they are looking for until they find You. Use me to point the way. Amen.*

DAY 274
WHAT IT MEANS TO BE PRUDENT

The wisdom of the prudent is to give thought to their ways, but the folly of fools is deception.

PROVERBS 14:8 NIV

In the Bible, being *prudent* means, in part, "being good stewards or managers of the gifts and resources God has given us to use." Those gifts include time, energy, strength, health, and even material possessions. They include our bodies as well as our minds and spirits.

Being a good steward of your mind means giving thought to what you are doing, where you are going, what you are thinking about, and who is leading you.

Amos 5:13 says that a prudent person knows when to keep quiet. Good stewardship of our words is a gift that we all need to work on developing!

King Solomon in all of his wisdom said, "The prudent sees danger and hides himself, but the simple go on and suffer for it" (Proverbs 22:3 ESV). Each of us needs to know our limits and be able to recognize when we are approaching them. Instead of pushing ourselves past what we know we can comfortably handle, we need to listen to and obey what God is telling us to do. If He wants us to stop before we get angry, or take a break before we get frustrated, or think before we say something we will later regret, then we should do so! We must follow His wisdom if we really want to enjoy blessed lives.

PRAYER FOR TODAY: *God, help me be a good steward of my thoughts, words, actions, and attitudes. Teach me to hear from You and to obey Your Word immediately so that I can enjoy my life! Amen.*

DAY 275: ATTITUDE IS IMPORTANT

Get rid of all bitterness, rage and anger, brawling and slander, along with every form of malice. Be kind and compassionate to one another, forgiving each other, just as in Christ God forgave you.
EPHESIANS 4:31–32 NIV

I believe when we maintain positive attitudes, God takes the things the enemy means for our harm and works them out for our good and for the good of other people (Romans 8:28).

My own life is a perfect example. The enemy's plan was to use the years of abuse I suffered to destroy me. If I had chosen to continue responding to my circumstances with a negative attitude of anger and bitterness, he would have succeeded. Instead, I chose to be positive and believe that God's plan to heal and restore me would come to pass. It did, and now He is helping millions of people through my testimony!

You and I always have a choice about our attitudes. Our attitudes belong to us, and nobody can make us have a bad one if we don't want to. When we decide to react to our circumstances with negative attitudes—such as self-pity, resentment, or bitterness—it hinders God from doing everything He wants to do in our lives and keeps us from reaching our full potential.

But choosing to have a positive attitude not only takes the limits off what God can do in and through us; it also helps us see our circumstances from God's perspective and enables us to enjoy our everyday lives.

PRAYER FOR TODAY: *God, help me get my heart right and help me think positive, speak positive, and choose a positive attitude so that You can work in and through me. Show me anything negative within me so that I can cast it down. Amen.*

DAY 276 — A POSITIVE REPORT

Caleb quieted the people before Moses, and said, Let us go up at once and possess it; we are well able to conquer it.

NUMBERS 13:30

Moses sent twelve men as spies into Canaan, and ten of them came back with a negative report. They told all the people about the giants who lived there. They said, "We are not able to go up against the people [of Canaan], for they are stronger than we are" (Numbers 13:31).

The effect of those negative words was amazing. Based on their negative report, the entire nation of Israel refused to go into the land, thereby forfeiting God's promises to them. In the same way, a negative attitude can keep you from realizing the promises of God for your life, because it keeps you from moving forward in faith.

The only two people out of that entire generation who ever entered the Promised Land were the two spies who gave a positive report: Joshua and Caleb. After seeing the same thing that the other ten spies saw, where the other men said, "We are not able," Joshua and Caleb said, "We are well able" (vv. 30–31).

No matter what sort of giants you may be facing, the truth is, "He Who lives in you is greater (mightier) than he who is in the world" (1 John 4:4).

PRAYER FOR TODAY: *God, help me have an attitude of faith. Forgive me for the times that I have focused on the size of my challenges rather than the size of my God. I know that You are greater than anything that will ever come against me. In Jesus' name, amen.*

DAY 277

HOW IS YOUR HEART?

The good person out of the good treasure of his heart produces good, and the evil person out of his evil treasure produces evil, for out of the abundance of the heart his mouth speaks.

LUKE 6:45 ESV

When God sent Samuel to Jesse's house to anoint a new king, Samuel saw Jesse's oldest son, Eliab, and thought, *Surely, he is the one*. But God said to Samuel: "Do not consider his appearance or his height, for I have rejected him. The Lord does not look at the things people look at. People look at the outward appearance, but the Lord looks at the heart" 1 Samuel 16:7 (NIV).

Samuel went through each of Jesse's sons, all of whom looked like they could do the job, but God had chosen none of them. Then Jesse said to Samuel, "There is yet the youngest; he is tending the sheep" (1 Samuel 16:11).

David showed up, and he was handsome, with beautiful eyes, but that's not why God chose him. God saw in David "a man after [His] own heart" (Acts 13:22).

God has given us the ability to peek into each other's hearts through the words that we speak (Luke 6:45). If a person's words are good, positive, and full of praise for the Father, then you know they are a person after God's own heart.

PRAYER FOR TODAY: *God, forgive me for the times that I have judged others based on their outward appearance and for the times that I have put more thought into what I looked like than what I sound like. Help me get my heart right so that the right words will follow. Amen.*

DAY 278: GIVE AN ACCOUNT

But I tell you, on the day of judgment men will have to give account for every idle (inoperative, nonworking) word they speak.

MATTHEW 12:36

Today's scripture tells us that on judgment day we will have to give an account of every word that has ever come out of our mouths. But I don't think we have to wait until that day to see the effects our words have on us.

Proverbs 18:21 says that "death and life are in the power of the tongue" (ESV). Our words have the power to create and the power to destroy. That creative or destructive power doesn't kick in only on judgment day. It happens the moment a word is formed on our tongues and passes through our lips.

Genesis 1 says that God spoke the world into existence ("And God said…and there was…"). Everything that God spoke was immediately created. Because we are created in His image, our words are also containers of power. When we speak words of life, life is created, moods are lifted, joy is experienced, and God is pleased. But the opposite is also true. When we speak words of death, life is destroyed, attitudes sink, depression sets in, and God's heart breaks for His people.

Listen to yourself. Are the words that you speak careless and destructive, or are they filled with life abundant? Your words are so powerful that one right word to a person can change their entire day.

PRAYER FOR TODAY: *God, forgive me for times I've been careless with my words. Help me see how powerful and important they are, and help me choose right words that I am honored to present to You on the day of judgment. Amen.*

DAY 279: SPIRITUAL MATURITY

If anyone thinks himself to be religious (piously observant of the external duties of his faith) and does not bridle his tongue but deludes his own heart, this person's religious service is worthless (futile, barren).

JAMES 1:26

What determines your level of spiritual maturity?

Is it how often you go to church? Is it how many scriptures you have memorized? Is it how long you can pray? Is it determined by the number of people you have led to Christ?

While all of these things are good and important, the Bible says that they don't matter if your words aren't honoring Him. Our words are a reflection of the motives of our hearts, and God cares deeply about both our hearts and why we do things, as well as what we do.

First Corinthians 13:3 says that you can give everything you have to the poor, but if you don't do it in love, it doesn't mean a thing. Today's scripture is making a similar point. You can do all the religious works you want, but your words will reveal your motives, and if they aren't godly, then you are lacking in spiritual maturity.

When you learn to control your mouth, your motives will change. Out of the overflow of your heart, you will want to honor God with holy living and acts of service, and these things will be pleasing to Him.

PRAYER FOR TODAY: *God, I want to make a difference in the world for You, but first I need to get right with You. Show me where I have been trying to earn Your approval, and help me rest in Your love. Amen.*

DAY 280

WORDS OF GRACE

However, brethren, I could not talk to you as to spiritual [men], but as to nonspiritual [men of the flesh, in whom the carnal nature predominates], as to mere infants [in the new life] in Christ [unable to talk yet!]

1 CORINTHIANS 3:1

In Paul's day, the Corinthians were known as being Spirit-led people, yet in today's scripture, Paul tells them they are talking like their mouths still need to be saved.

Paul wants to talk to them about deep, spiritual things—the richness of God's love for all people and growing in Christlikeness—yet he can't because they are like babies still bottle feeding, not yet able to walk or talk in the Spirit.

Their words are filled with envy, jealousy, strife, and discord, and, like baby talk, he can't make sense of them. Paul essentially says, "With all of this arguing, it's as if you are living like people who don't know God" (1 Corinthians 3:3).

Our words are a witness to other Christians and to the world. Are we still speaking out of our old, unsaved selves—with bitterness, anger, fault-finding, and spite (Ephesians 4:31)? Or are we speaking out of mouths that have been saved and brought to a new life with Christ—words that build up and give grace to those who hear (Ephesians 4:29)?

PRAYER FOR TODAY: *God, in the name of Jesus, please bring salvation to my mouth. I want my words to honor You and to reflect Your love and grace, but I need Your help. Amen.*

DAY 281: SHUT OUT WRONG THOUGHTS

But refuse (shut your mind against, have nothing to do with) trifling (ill-informed, unedifying, stupid) controversies over ignorant questionings, for you know that they foster strife and breed quarrels.

2 TIMOTHY 2:23

Today's passage tells us to shut our minds against anything that would lead to an argument. Gossip, judgment, criticism, jealousy—don't even let these things into your thoughts, because they spiral and grow, breeding more and more negativity and strife.

Proverbs 17:14 says: "Starting a quarrel is like opening a floodgate, so stop before a dispute breaks out" (NLT). Once you open a floodgate, there is no putting the water back. The same is true for giving our minds to contentious thinking or opening our mouths to slander and strife—tempers will flare, and a negative comment can grow into a full-blown brawl.

Each time a thought comes to your mind that doesn't agree with God's Word, declare the truth of Scripture out loud, and you will find the wrong thought disappearing. Our minds and our mouths are connected, so when one is wrong, we can correct it with the other. Speaking right words will help us shut our minds against negativity, and thinking right thoughts will help us speak words that glorify God.

PRAYER FOR TODAY: *God, help me stop negative thinking at the door of my mind. Don't let anything that isn't true or from You enter. Keep me from rumors and petty arguments, and help me stay focused instead on things above. Amen.*

DAY 282: IF YOU WANT TO ENJOY LIFE

For let him who wants to enjoy life and see good days [good—whether apparent or not] keep his tongue free from evil and his lips from guile (treachery, deceit).

1 PETER 3:10

Our joy is directly connected to the words we speak. And one of the ways we can instantly increase our joy is to stop talking incessantly about all of our problems and choose to speak words that will nourish our bodies, minds, and spirits in a positive way.

Another way we can instantly increase our joy is to use our words to encourage and bless those around us. If you give others joy with your words, you will increase your own joy! If you want to enjoy your life, let God use you to speak kind words to others. Because the kinder you are to other people, the happier you will be.

Maintaining a thankful attitude is another great thing we can do for ourselves. When you choose to be thankful, you are purposely focusing on the good things God is doing and gaining better perspective on your life. Being grateful invites God's presence and causes us to be more positive and hopeful.

In short, if you want to enjoy life, watch what you say.

PRAYER FOR TODAY: *God, thank You for all that You have done and are doing in my life. I am blessed when I come in and blessed when I go out; I am so very blessed. Put someone in my path who I can be a blessing to today. In Jesus' name, amen.*

DAY 283
AN OBEDIENT ATTITUDE

He who watches the wind [waiting for all conditions to be perfect] will not sow [seed], and he who looks at the clouds will not reap [a harvest].

ECCLESIASTES 11:4 AMP

When the Lord asks us to do something, any of us can be tempted to wait for a convenient season, a time when all conditions are perfect (as the scripture above says), or until we are in the mood. Human nature causes us to hold back sometimes as we walk with God, wanting to wait until following Him won't be difficult. But knowing what to do and not doing it is a sin (James 4:17).

Instead, we need to have the attitude that when God speaks, we will be obedient to Him. When we choose only the easy path or what feels comfortable, we limit the growth and strength God wants to develop in us. But as you face resistance and overcome it, you will build your strength and grow in your faith.

Don't be like the man in Ecclesiastes 11:4 who never plants and therefore never reaps a harvest. Conditions will never be perfect, so waiting for perfection is pointless. Instead, do what God says to do when He says to do it, and you will reap the blessings of obedience.

PRAYER FOR TODAY: *God, help me to follow You and to obey You promptly when You lead me. Help me grow in strength and faith by following Your guidance. Amen.*

DAY 284 — PURPOSEFUL WORDS

I will not talk with you much more, for the prince (evil genius, ruler) of the world is coming. And he has no claim on Me. [He has nothing in common with Me; there is nothing in Me that belongs to him, and he has no power over Me.]

JOHN 14:30

Scary, frustrating, or unexpected circumstances often tempt us to say and do things we would never say or do when things are going well, but we must resist the urge to be critical and negative.

When Jesus was being beaten before He went to the cross, the Bible says that He "opened not His mouth" (Isaiah 53:7). John 14:30 reminds us that even Jesus used self-control to not speak out of His emotions during times of intense stress.

Proverbs 10:19 says, "In the multitude of words sin is not lacking" (NKJV). Jesus was no doubt tempted to give His accusers a piece of His mind, but He never sinned. Jesus chose His words carefully so as not to open the door to the enemy. In that same way, when we exercise self-control and refuse to lash out in anger or fear, the enemy doesn't get his way in our lives.

Jesus calls us to use our words on purpose and reminds us that there will be a time to speak and a time to remain silent (Ecclesiastes 3:7).

PRAYER FOR TODAY: *God, help me discern when to speak up and when to be quiet. Help me choose words on purpose, words that bring life to my situation and glory to Your name. Amen.*

DAY 285

EDIFYING WORDS

The words of a whisperer (gossip) are like dainty morsels [to be greedily eaten]; they go down into the innermost chambers of the body [to be remembered and mused upon].

PROVERBS 18:8 AMP

God not only wants us to have positive thoughts about other people, always believing and looking for the best in them (1 Corinthians 13:7), but He also wants our words about other people to be edifying—and not just for the person that we are talking about, but also for the person we are talking to.

Proverbs 18:8 says that when we talk about one person to another person, our words sink down into the person we are talking to. So, now we have not only influenced our own feelings about someone, but we have also influenced how another person will think and feel when this person shows up or is brought up again in conversation.

It is our human tendency to spread bad news and listen to gossip, but we don't want those words sinking down into the innermost chambers of our bodies, where they can have a harmful effect. Instead, if we are going to speak about others, let us do so with a good report. And if someone offers to tell you something about someone else, tell them you only want to hear it if it's something good.

PRAYER FOR TODAY: *God, teach me to be eager for good news and positive talk instead of gossip. Help me speak words that will edify and continue to edify others as they remember them. In Jesus' name, amen.*

DAY 286

THE SAME POWER

Again He said to me, Prophesy to these bones and say to them, O you dry bones, hear the word of the Lord.

EZEKIEL 37:4

In Ezekiel 37, God led the prophet Ezekiel to a valley of dry bones and instructed him to prophesy to them—to speak the Word of the Lord to them—so they would live. Ezekiel says in verse 10: "So I prophesied as He commanded me, and the breath and spirit came into [the bones], and they lived and stood up upon their feet, an exceedingly great host." Those dry bones turned into a mighty army!

Prophesy to the dry bones in your life! Jesus said that if we have faith, we can speak to the mountain and it will move (Mark 11:23). He didn't say to talk *about* the mountain—but to speak *to* it, believing God's power can bring change. Too often we spend more time talking about our problems than declaring the solutions found in the Word of God.

The Word of God says not only that God is powerful, but that He has filled us with His Spirit. He has overcome the world, and He has made us more than conquerors. The same power that raised Jesus from the dead lives in us, so speak to your mountains with faith in Him.

PRAYER FOR TODAY: *God, I need You, and I am nothing without You. Fill me with Your power so that I can speak to my mountains and cause them to move. In Jesus' name, amen.*

DAY 287

SAY NOT

But the Lord said to me, Say not, I am only a youth; for you shall go to all to whom I shall send you, and whatever I command you, you shall speak.

JEREMIAH 1:7

God came to Jeremiah with a beautiful sentiment about how He knew him before he was formed in his mother's womb (Jeremiah 1:5). God said He approved of Jeremiah, chose him, and set him apart for a purpose before he was ever born.

And Jeremiah responded by essentially saying, "I'm too young!" (v. 6).

Jeremiah was obviously looking at himself, not at what God saw. In his own eyes, Jeremiah was young, inexperienced, and not yet ready for the pressures of a public ministry. And he allowed that to be his confession.

But God responded with "Say not" (v. 7). In other words, don't say "I'm too young." Don't say what you can't do. Don't have a negative confession. Remember who called you, who chose you, who set you apart, and who has known you longer than anyone else. God has a wonderful plan for your life. God is saying, "I know what you are capable of, so you can trust me enough to go where I send you, do what I command you, and say what I tell you to say."

Stop saying what you can't do and start saying what God says.

PRAYER FOR TODAY: *God, help me see what You see in me. Help me keep a positive confession. Give me the courage to follow Your will for my life. In Jesus' name, amen.*

DAY 288

WATER YOUR SEED

You have said, It is useless to serve God, and what profit is it if we keep His ordinances and walk gloomily and as if in mourning apparel before the Lord of hosts?

MALACHI 3:14

The word *tithe* means "a tenth part." In the principle of tithing, the first tenth of your income belongs to God. The law of reaping and sowing (Galatians 6:7) applies to tithing as well, so while it may feel like a sacrifice to tithe, God will give you so much more in return.

Malachi 3:10 says:

> "Bring the whole tithe into the storehouse, that there may be food in my house. Test me in this," says the Lord Almighty, "and see if I will not throw open the floodgates of heaven and pour out so much blessing that there will not be room enough to store it." (NIV)

Verses 13–14, however, say that the people spoke negatively against God and this principle, calling it worthless. Perhaps they didn't see their return as quickly as they wanted.

A negative confession will not make God hurry up. However, I believe you can "water your seed" by confessing what God's Word says.

Don't kill your seed with a negative confession; water your seed with the water of the Word and watch for your harvest to come.

PRAYER FOR TODAY: *God, thank You for pouring out blessings upon me. Give me the desire to plant seeds, and help me speak only positive confessions over them as I water them with Your Word. Amen.*

DAY 289

GO FORWARD IN FAITH

When I am afraid, I will put my trust and faith in You.

PSALM 56:3 AMP

David killed bears and lions with his own hands when he was just a shepherd boy. He fought the giant Goliath with a slingshot and a couple of river stones. The people said that while King Saul killed thousands, David killed tens of thousands.

We might think that David was fearless to do all those things, but he wrote in Psalms that when he was afraid, he put his trust in God. The use of *when* implies that there were times when he felt afraid, but he chose to go forward anyway, in faith, because he trusted in God.

If you've been afraid of something and desire to be free, the time will eventually come when you'll have to face your fear and not run away from it. Like David, you will have to approach it with the following attitude: *I trust God, and I'm going to do it, even if I have to do it afraid.*

The Bible says that God has not given us a spirit of fear, but a spirit of power, love, discipline and a calm mind (2 Timothy 1:7). That means that we don't have to bow down to fear when it strikes. We can move forward in faith and go anywhere that God leads us.

PRAYER FOR TODAY: *God, forgive me for the times when I have let fear stop me. Help me trust in and rely on You as I move forward in faith. Amen.*

DAY 290
A HIGHER ATTITUDE

For as the heavens are higher than the earth, so are My ways higher than your ways and My thoughts than your thoughts.

ISAIAH 55:9

Your attitude determines your altitude in life. So, if you want to go higher, if you want to dream bigger, if you want to see more of God in your life, then you will have to choose with intentionality to think, speak, and act according to His Word.

Instead of having an "I can't do it" attitude, you can choose to think, *I can do all things through Christ* (Philippians 4:13).

Instead of a "This is impossible" attitude, you can think, *Nothing is impossible with God!* (Matthew 19:26).

Instead of an attitude that worries, *What if it doesn't work out?*, you can think, *What if it does work out?* (Hebrews 11:1).

The truth is, any time you follow a dream God puts on your heart, you have a part to play in seeing it happen. You'll have to plan. You'll have to make sacrifices. You'll need to persevere on days when you feel like quitting.

God will equip you with everything you need to see His dream for you come to fruition. And the good news is, when your power seems insufficient, God's power *is* sufficient for you (2 Corinthians 12:9).

PRAYER FOR TODAY: *God, thank You for calling me higher. Thank You for wanting more for my life than I could ever dream up on my own. Give me the courage to step out in faith—to plan, to sacrifice, to persevere—until it happens. Amen.*

DAY 291 — SEATED IN HEAVENLY PLACES

And He raised us up together with Him [when we believed], and seated us with Him in the heavenly places, [because we are] in Christ Jesus.

EPHESIANS 2:6 AMP

The Bible tells us that God not only raised us up when we were dead in sin, but also gave us the very life of Christ and seated us with Him in heavenly places.

When we worry, become anxious, or try to control everything, we aren't living as if we're "seated." In fact, we often say our emotions "rise up" or we describe ourselves as feeling "stirred" or "heated" when anger or frustration takes over. However, being seated in heavenly places is to be at rest, not controlled by our moods but instead trusting God to fight for us.

After Jesus completed the work His Father sent Him to do, God raised Him up and seated Him at His own right hand, waiting for His enemies to become His footstool (Hebrews 10:12–13). In other words, Jesus is now at perfect rest and peace, and if we are seated with Him, then that same rest and peace is available to us.

PRAYER FOR TODAY: *God, I want to take my seat next to You and release the worries of this world. Help me keep my focus on You so that I can stay at rest and peace, enjoying this life and giving myself to the things that You have for me to do. In Jesus' name, amen.*

DAY 292 — BE SLOW TO SPEAK

Understand [this], my beloved brethren. Let every man be quick to hear [a ready listener], slow to speak, slow to take offense and to get angry.

JAMES 1:19

Have you ever instantly regretted something you said the moment it left your mouth? Unfortunately, we can't take back our words, and they often have the power to damage relationships. That's why James offers this three-step advice: (1) Be quick to listen, (2) slow to speak, and (3) slow to get offended or angry.

First, be quick to listen. Listen deeply. Focus on what the other person is truly saying, without forming your response while they're talking.

Second, be slow to speak. Don't immediately jump in with a comeback or answer. Take the time to fully understand what the other person is saying. If something is unclear, ask a clarifying question. Giving space between a statement and a response also shows the other person that you were listening, that you are processing, and that you value their words.

Finally, be slow to get offended or angry. Don't immediately assume the worst. If you respond in anger, you can't take your words back. But if you are slow to speak and slow to take offense, you make room for deeper understanding.

PRAYER FOR TODAY: *God, help me today to be guided by the Holy Spirit in my conversations with others. Help me listen well, believe the best, and use my words to speak life. In Jesus' name, amen.*

DAY 293: GOD'S WILL FOR YOUR LIFE

Therefore do not be vague and thoughtless and foolish, but understanding and firmly grasping what the will of the Lord is.

EPHESIANS 5:17

Ephesians 5:17 tells us that we can understand and firmly grasp God's will for our lives. However, many people complicate this by overthinking, foolishly trying to reason in their own minds, wondering if *this* or *that* is God's will. But Paul writes that those thoughts are foolish and vague.

According to the Bible, God's will is for us to grow up and mature spiritually, to be transformed into the image of Jesus Christ (Romans 8:29), and to have good relationships so we can have good lives that please Him.

If you've had a negative past, it's because the enemy interfered. No matter what you went through or are currently facing, you can choose to think and speak positively about your future, aligning yourself with God's plan.

Scripture tells us that "where there is no vision...the people perish" (Proverbs 29:18), so it's important for you to have a positive vision for your life. No matter what has happened in the past, no matter what is going on right now, you can believe that great things are ahead in your future because that is God's will for you.

PRAYER FOR TODAY: *God, help me to remain positive in my thoughts and to not waste time looking back to the past or worrying about the future. Lead me and guide me toward the bright future You have planned for me. In Jesus' name, amen.*

DAY 294: A LONG LIFE

Those who control their tongue will have a long life; opening your mouth can ruin everything.

PROVERBS 13:3 NLT

Can watching your words actually extend your life? Maybe not in the literal sense we often think of, since only God knows the number of our days (Job 14:5). But you can add quality and peace to your life, however many days you have left, by speaking words that will benefit you and others.

Look at what Solomon, the wisest man who ever lived, had to say about the power of words:

> With his mouth the godless man destroys his neighbor, but through knowledge and superior discernment shall the righteous be delivered (Proverbs 11:9).
>
> There are those who speak rashly, like the piercing of a sword, but the tongue of the wise brings healing (Proverbs 12:18).
>
> A soothing tongue [speaking words that build up and encourage] is a tree of life, but a perversive tongue [speaking words that overwhelm and depress] crushes the spirit (Proverbs 15:4 AMP).

God's Word has the power to strengthen you, helping you use your words wisely and experience a life filled with greater peace and joy.

PRAYER FOR TODAY: *God, please guide and guard my words so that everything I speak brings life, reflects Your love, and conveys Your wisdom and power. In the wonderful name of Jesus I pray, amen.*

DAY 295: DISCIPLINE IS YOUR FRIEND

For the time being no discipline brings joy, but seems grievous and painful; but afterwards it yields a peaceable fruit of righteousness to those who have been trained by it [a harvest of fruit which consists in righteousness—in conformity to God's will in purpose, thought, and action, resulting in right living and right standing with God].

HEBREWS 12:11

Discipline is our friend, not our enemy. It helps us become the people we say we would like to be but cannot become without it and the help of the Holy Spirit.

Discipline is the ability to train, correct, or refine a pattern of behavior. For example, if you want to cultivate positive thoughts—which lead to positive words that yield positive moods and attitudes and ultimately, a joyful life—you'll have to break the cycle of negative thinking and train your mind to hold on to thoughts that are true, uplifting, and aligned with God's Word.

People who think they can make undisciplined choices—following the desires of the flesh instead of the Spirit—and still have a fulfilling life are deceived. As the scripture says, discipline may not seem joyous now, but afterward, you will enjoy the harvest of peace and righteousness.

PRAYER FOR TODAY: *God, please give me Your grace to live a life of discipline and self-control, guided by Your Holy Spirit instead of my own fleshly desires. In Jesus' name, amen.*

DAY 296

FOLLOW MY EXAMPLE

Brethren, together follow my example and observe those who live after the pattern we have set for you.

PHILIPPIANS 3:17

Because Paul's eyes were on eternity, he knew how to remain joyful regardless of his circumstances. His encounter with Christ gave him a profound understanding of God's extravagant love and grace. Through his great faith, Paul believed that God would work all things together for his good—even jail sentences, shipwrecks, and beatings. Therefore, Paul could say with confidence, "Follow my example, live as I live, walk as I walk, do as I do, think as I think." Can you say the same about your life? Should other people follow your example?

God wants you to learn to make the most of every moment and to have a positive influence on the people in your life and the next generation. Paul set a good example for us to learn from. When you make good choices, it will enable you not only to enjoy your own life but to be a powerful example to those around you.

Walk in a manner worthy of your calling. Be an example to others. Leave a legacy of faith. This is pleasing to the Lord!

PRAYER FOR TODAY: *God, I need Your help to live a life that is a good example to others and one that honors You. I am ready and willing to make the changes You reveal to me so that I can walk worthy of my calling and live a life that pleases You. In Jesus' name, amen.*

DAY 297

IT TAKES PRACTICE

But He said, Blessed (happy and to be envied) rather are those who hear the Word of God and obey and practice it!

LUKE 11:28

Changing your words and thoughts is not an easy thing to do, but with God's help, all things are possible.

We have to make a conscious decision to think and speak in a way that honors God. It doesn't come naturally and certainly doesn't happen overnight. In fact, it takes a lot of practice. There will be days when you have setbacks, but you can handle them by starting again.

When babies are learning to walk, they fall many, many times before they gain the confidence to walk. Their parents don't criticize them for falling. They cheer them on and encourage them to keep trying. The parents believe that, with practice, their baby will walk.

Failing from time to time—which you will do—doesn't mean you're a failure. It simply means you're not perfect and don't do everything right all of the time. Well, neither does anyone else! But all the while, your heavenly Father is cheering you on, telling you to keep practicing, believing that you will succeed.

Be patient with yourself. As you change your thinking, your words will change...and so will your life.

PRAYER FOR TODAY: *God, grant me patience with myself, and help me celebrate the growth in my life as I learn to align my thoughts and words with Your Word. Amen.*

DAY 298: WHERE THE MIND GOES

For who has known the mind of the Lord and who has understood His thoughts, or who has [ever] been His counselor?
ROMANS 11:34

One of my favorite phrases is "Where the mind goes, the man follows," because your thoughts shape your life.

If you think you are going to have a bad day, you can actually sabotage your day with a negative attitude. However, when you meditate on God's Word, which says that His mercies are new every morning and tells you to rejoice and be glad in this day, you'll step into the day with a positive mindset.

Here is another example: If you think you're going to be defeated, your attitude will likely reflect that and lead to defeat. But if you choose to focus on God's promises, you'll have a faith-filled, expectant, and victorious outlook.

Yesterday, you may have let your mind focus on the negative—what you can't do, how badly you've messed up, all the things that could go wrong—but you don't have to repeat yesterday today. You can submit your mind to the Word of God. You can choose the thoughts you are going to dwell on.

With the help of the Holy Spirit, you can change your thoughts today and have a better, more positive, more fulfilling life.

PRAYER FOR TODAY: *God, I need Your help to change my thoughts from negative to positive, my attitude from defeated to victorious, and my life from mediocre to miraculous. Show me steps I can take today to start making these changes. Amen.*

DAY 299

DON'T DREAD

Yes, though I walk through the [deep, sunless] valley of the shadow of death, I will fear or dread no evil, for You are with me; Your rod [to protect] and Your staff [to guide], they comfort me.

PSALM 23:4

God never intends for us to be miserable or to have a horrible day. Even when things aren't going as we'd like, He wants us to expect good things and stay full of hope, regardless of our circumstances. Two simple words will help you to do just that: *Don't dread*.

What is dread? Dread is simply expecting an unpleasant experience—the opposite of hope.

People often dread going to work on Monday mornings. They dread mowing the lawn and doing the dishes. They dread family gatherings at the holidays, monthly bills, and having tough conversations. But dread can rob our joy and ruin our days before we've ever even faced our circumstances.

The Lord wants us to be able to have success and joy in every area of our lives, and conquering dread is a major part of that. Our choice to have positive, hopeful attitudes can literally make all the difference.

No matter what life brings your way, God has a plan to make it better—a plan filled with hope and good things. Get in agreement with Him. Approach each day with a positive attitude and choose to not dread.

PRAYER FOR TODAY: *God, help me focus on the positive and expect good things to happen today. Let me know if I start to dread something so I can change and expect good things. Amen.*

DAY 300

THE FUTURE IS BRIGHTER THAN THE PAST

For behold, I create new heavens and a new earth. And the former things shall not be remembered or come into mind.

ISAIAH 65:17

There comes a time in each of our lives when we must make some critical decisions if we want to move forward with God. One of those key decisions is letting go of the past and daring to believe God has a great future in store for you. God wants us to enjoy each day that we have right now, and we cannot do that if we are living in the past.

There are all kinds of reasons why people will not let go of the past. Some may believe their past was so wonderful that nothing else could ever live up to those "glory days." Others may no longer be able to do the things they once did, and they don't feel they have value in the present. Another person may be stuck because of a heartbreak or loss that they have not been able to move past.

The truth is, we have a choice. We can either dwell on what life was like before, or we can decide to look ahead in faith, trusting that God is doing something new and that the days ahead can be even better than those behind us.

PRAYER FOR TODAY: *God, give me the strength to let go of my past. Help me focus on the bright future You have planned for me, so that I may believe the best is yet to come. Amen.*

DAY 301: HOW TO HAVE PEACE, PART 1

May grace (God's unmerited favor) and spiritual peace [which means peace with God and harmony, unity, and undisturbedness] be yours from God our Father and from the Lord Jesus Christ.
EPHESIANS 1:2

Paul prayed for the Ephesians to have "spiritual peace," which is an attitude of the heart and a gift from God that is available to everyone. If you're feeling anxious and irritable instead of peaceful and kind, here are some tips to help you regain your peace:

- Take a deep breath and receive God's peace (John 14:27). When things get hectic, take some time to talk to God and receive His peace and refreshment.
- Read the Word (Proverbs 4:20–22). God's Word is alive and full of power—and it has the ability to revive and refresh you when you get weary and worn out.
- Listen to praise and worship music (Psalm 100:2). Worship is the quickest way to change your attitude, because you invite His joy and presence into your life.
- Go to bed early (Psalm 127:2). Sometimes, the simplest, most practical things make the greatest difference. A good night's sleep will help you wake up with a better attitude.

The Bible tells us that Jesus leaves us with His peace so that our hearts won't be troubled. It is a peace that surpasses understanding, meaning that you can have God's peace regardless of your circumstances.

PRAYER FOR TODAY: *God, thank You for giving me Your peace so that no matter what I'm facing, I can maintain a good attitude. Help me receive and walk in that peace today and every day. Amen.*

DAY 302: HOW TO HAVE PEACE, PART 2

Continually pursue peace with everyone, and the sanctification without which no one will [ever] see the Lord.

HEBREWS 12:14 AMP

This passage tells us to "continually pursue peace." God's peace isn't something we receive once and then never need to maintain. We must actively and continually pursue it. Here are some tips on pursuing peace:

- Spend time with an encouraging friend (Galatians 6:2). When life gets hectic, we sometimes forget to do the things that help us relax—like spending time with someone we enjoy.
- Enjoy a delicious, nutritious meal (3 John 1:2). Taking a little time to eat something that's nutritious can impact your attitude in a positive way.
- Write down your worries...then throw them away. As it says in 1 Peter 5:7 (NIV), "Cast all your anxiety on him because he cares for you."
- Make a list of things you're thankful for (1 Thessalonians 5:18). Cultivating a thankful heart can bring joy and shift our perspectives.
- Go outside (Psalm 19:1). Fresh air has a way of refreshing us mentally and physically.
- Be playful and laugh. Remember that God wants you to enjoy your life (John 10:10).

PRAYER FOR TODAY: *God, thank You for wanting me to enjoy my life and for giving me Your peace. Help me constantly pursue peace in my attitude and my relationships. Amen.*

DAY 303

WORDS IN WINTER

It was you who set all the boundaries of the earth; you made both summer and winter.

PSALM 74:17 NIV

Winter is a dormant season. Trees become bare, and most of the grass, plants, and flowers die off. In much the same way, you and I go through spiritually dormant seasons. These are the seasons when God seems silent—when our dreams and visions for the future seem lifeless—and we must believe by faith, not by sight. And while we may not *see* or *feel* anything exciting, it doesn't mean nothing is happening.

A lot of inner work must take place before we're ready for the future God has for us. Just as winter prepares plants and trees for warmer weather, a spiritually dormant season is a time of preparation—when our inner character is developed and strengthened for what's to come.

In a "winter" season, we must discipline our mouths to speak what God says rather than what we see or feel. We must call forth the things He has promised us and the dreams He has planted within us rather than discourage ourselves with words of defeat. We prove our spiritual maturity by the words that we speak as we prepare for God's blessings yet to come.

PRAYER FOR TODAY: *God, thank You for this season of preparation as You ready me for the place You have for me. Help me speak words of life, especially when it feels like nothing is happening. My trust is in You. In Jesus' name, amen.*

DAY 304: JOY COMES FROM WITHIN

Create in me a clean heart, O God, and renew a right, persevering, and steadfast spirit within me.

PSALM 51:10

If you are in a bad mood, it could be that you have a case of the "ifs." Many people mistakenly believe that if only they had something different—whether it's more money, a bigger house, a different job, or a change in family circumstances—they would finally be happy and fulfilled.

We find ourselves saying things like "If I didn't have to work..." "If we had more money..." "If I had a bigger house..." "If the kids were grown..." "If I were married..." Or even "If I was married to someone else..."

Stop thinking that you could be happy if your circumstances were different, and start being happy right now because God loves you and has already blessed you in many ways.

Our bad moods often come from something *within* us, not from something around us. So, take responsibility for your own joy and stop blaming the lack of it on anything or anyone else. The people who are happy are the ones who decide to be happy, because good moods also come from within.

PRAYER FOR TODAY: *God, create in me a clean heart, a happy heart, a joyful and persevering heart that overflows as a good mood regardless of my circumstances. I am so grateful for all of the blessings You have given me. Amen.*

DAY 305: THE TRUTH ABOUT YOUR MOODS

He who walks and lives uprightly and blamelessly, who works rightness and justice and speaks and thinks the truth in his heart.
PSALM 15:2

The daily ups and downs of our moods can be a real struggle in our quest to enjoy life. If we allow our moods to dictate our day—deciding whether it will be good or bad, productive or lazy, joyful or grumpy—we'll never become who we were meant to be. Rather than riding an emotional roller coaster, we need to become stable, solid, steadfast, persevering, and determined people.

One way we can do that is by focusing on what is true. The *fact* is, your moods will go up and down, your circumstances won't always be pleasant, and you won't always understand the "why" behind it all. But *truth* is greater than facts, and it can ultimately change them.

The *truth* is, God loves you. The *truth* is, God has a good plan for your life. The *truth* is, God will never leave you nor forsake you. The *truth* is, even if you don't know the answer, God does.

Keep focusing on the truth (which never changes) instead of on your feelings (which can change from moment to moment), and you will become the stable, solid person God wants you to be.

PRAYER FOR TODAY: *God, thank You for showing me the difference between truth and facts. Your Word is truth. Help me think, speak, and live according to what is true rather than what I feel. Amen.*

DAY 306: THE PROVERBS 31 WOMAN

She looks well to how things go in her household, and the bread of idleness (gossip, discontent, and self-pity) she will not eat.
PROVERBS 31:27

The Proverbs 31 woman is a responsible woman. She remains attentive to the needs of her household, she refuses to be idle, and she doesn't waste her time gossiping or wallowing in self-pity. She is content. She appreciates life and celebrates it fully each day.

The apostle Paul gave this exhortation to some members in the church in Thessalonica: "Indeed, we hear that some among you are disorderly [that they are passing their lives in idleness, neglectful of duty], being busy with other people's affairs instead of their own and doing no work" (2 Thessalonians 3:11). In other words, they were neglecting their own work to gossip about others and meddle in other people's affairs.

Idleness, wasted time, self-pity, gossip, and discontentment are thieves of the great life Jesus died to give you. Instead of wondering what other people are doing, our thoughts should be on what God wants us to do. Instead of talking about what other people are doing, our words should be praising God for all that He has done. When your thoughts, words, and attitudes line up with God's will, you will begin to experience true contentment (Philippians 4:11–12).

PRAYER FOR TODAY: *God, help me be like the Proverbs 31 woman. I am tired of wasting time wondering about things that are none of my business. Thank You for providing everything I need to fully enjoy the life You've given me. Amen.*

DAY 307
WHAT ATTITUDE WILL YOU TAKE?

Teaching them to observe everything that I have commanded you, and behold, I am with you all the days (perpetually, uniformly, and on every occasion), to the [very] close and consummation of the age. Amen (so let it be).

MATTHEW 28:20

When good things happen to us, praise comes naturally. It's easy to lift our hands and our voices when God answers our prayers and delivers us from problems. But what about when things go wrong? What do we do when we're sick, lose a job, or face criticism from others?

The negative response is to take the attitude of Job's wife, who was so overwhelmed by the loss of their children and possessions that she told her husband: "Renounce God and die!" (Job 2:9). But Job answered with great wisdom: "You speak as one of the impious and foolish women would speak. What? Shall we accept [only] good at the hand of God and shall we not accept [also] misfortune and what is of a bad nature?" (v. 10). Job understood that living righteously doesn't guarantee a life free from challenges.

The positive response is to praise God despite what's going on in our lives. It may take effort, but if we can turn our eyes away from our immediate problems, we can find something that is good. We also can rejoice because God has faithfully taken us through the turmoil of the past, and we can trust that He'll do the same again.

PRAYER FOR TODAY: *God, thank You for Your Word, which promises that You are with me always and on every occasion. Help me praise You in both good and challenging times. May my attitude reflect trust in You. Amen.*

DAY 308

WHEN YOUR LIFE NEEDS A TURNAROUND

Before I was afflicted I went astray, but now Your word do I keep [hearing, receiving, loving, and obeying it].

PSALM 119:67

Sometimes we grasp the important lessons in our lives only when we fall flat on our face. God wants us to follow Him, and He knows that some of us will have to go through some storms or even hit rock bottom before we make that decision. Sometimes that's why He allows us to go through trials and challenges in our lives—to remind us that we need to stop living for ourselves and start trusting and relying on Him. There are many reasons for difficult times, but they often put us in a place where we cannot help ourselves and must depend on God.

Take John Newton, for example. In the 1700s, he was active in the slave trade, living for his own gain. However, it was during a literal storm at sea that marked a turning point in his journey toward faith in God. He encountered Christ and committed his life to Him. As a Christian, he repented of how he had treated enslaved people and worked with politicians to abolish the slave trade in Britain. He also penned the famous hymn "Amazing Grace."

Whenever we face trials of any kind, we should approach them with this attitude: What can I learn from this? How is God using this situation to draw me closer to Him and to better understand His grace?

PRAYER FOR TODAY: *God, help me see that You always have my best interest in mind, even when it means allowing me to face challenges. Give me a teachable attitude so that I can learn from You and grow in my faith. Amen.*

DAY 309: SECURE IN CHRIST

But let every person carefully scrutinize and examine and test his own conduct and his own work. He can then have the personal satisfaction and joy of doing something commendable [in itself alone] without [resorting to] boastful comparison with his neighbor.
GALATIANS 6:4

The apostle Paul knew the importance of living a life of joy. In his letter to the Galatians, he told them not to be conceited, competitive, envious, irritating to one another, or jealous of one another (Galatians 5:26). Instead, if they wanted to have joy, they should focus on what they knew God was calling them to do and on doing it to the best of their ability.

Once you know who you are in Christ, you are set free from the stress of comparison and competition. You know you have worth and value apart from your works and accomplishments. Therefore, you can do your best to glorify God rather than just trying to be better than someone else. What a glorious, wonderful freedom to be secure in Christ and not have to be controlled by strife, envy, or jealousy.

You are free to be who God created you to be, and you can enjoy the freedom of seeing yourself the way Christ does. He loves you just as you are—and He doesn't make mistakes!

PRAYER FOR TODAY: *God, I don't want to live in jealousy or comparison anymore. Help me find my security in You and live for Your approval alone. May I focus on glorifying You and stop measuring myself against others. Amen.*

DAY 310 — EXAMINE THE FRUIT

Therefore, you will fully know them by their fruits.

MATTHEW 7:20

We can easily deceive ourselves into thinking we are something we are not if we don't take the time to examine the fruit of our lives. David asked God to examine him, and Paul told the Corinthians to examine, test, and evaluate themselves to see whether they were holding to the faith and showing the proper fruit of it (Psalm 26:2; 2 Corinthians 13:5). If we want to know if we are being faithful in our thoughts, words, moods, and attitudes, we too should test and examine our ways and ask God to prune off any bad fruit. If we find we have failed in some area, we should repent. But don't waste your time feeling guilty. God only shows us our failures so we can gladly receive His correction, not so we can feel guilty. Being genuine is crucial. We shouldn't quote Scripture one minute and then be rude to others the next. We shouldn't read the Word and then immediately fall into worry.

We want God to prune off the bad fruit so that the entire tree doesn't become diseased. Perhaps you are still struggling in your thought life or some other area. If you're not sure where you still need to grow, ask God to reveal it to you so that you can repent and begin to bear good fruit in that area.

Our lives should bear the fruit of what we claim to be: loving, patient, kind, generous, and faithful.

PRAYER FOR TODAY: *God, I only want to bear good and positive fruit in my life. Please help me diligently examine myself, trusting You to prune what needs to be removed. Amen.*

DAY 311

WHAT TO DO WITH INSECURITY

Do not judge and criticize and condemn others, so that you may not be judged and criticized and condemned yourselves.

MATTHEW 7:1

Sometimes when we feel insecure, rejected, or inferior to others, we struggle to simply admit we feel left out, ignored, or somehow less than the people around us. Instead of acknowledging these feelings, we respond by becoming critical or judgmental in our thoughts and words. But this is not the way God wants us to behave or to treat people.

We should choose to focus on God's love for us and remember that He accepts us unconditionally (Ephesians 1:4–6). He calls us "the apple of His eye" (Deuteronomy 32:10 NKJV) and says that our picture is engraved on the palm of His hand (Isaiah 49:16). The more secure we are in His love, the less we will feel critical or negative toward others. The greater our understanding of God's love for us, which we could never deserve, the more we realize that God loves everyone the same. Because He loves people, we can choose—with His help—to love them, too, without judgment.

Next time you're tempted to criticize or judge someone, resist the urge. Instead, choose to think and speak blessings over them, and show love.

PRAYER FOR TODAY: *God, when I feel rejected or inferior to others, help me not to judge or criticize them. Let me find rest in Your love so I can love and bless everyone around me. Amen.*

DAY 312: A FRESH START

For I will be merciful and gracious toward their sins and I will remember their deeds of unrighteousness no more.

HEBREWS 8:12

God's Word is full of stories about people who were given a fresh start:

- A woman known only as "Rahab the harlot" was rescued and became part of the bloodline of Jesus Christ (Joshua 2; 6:17–25).
- Peter, who denied Jesus out of fear, was forgiven and later preached at Pentecost, sharing the gospel with thousands (Luke 22:54–62; Acts 2:14–42).
- The apostle Paul (formerly Saul), a Pharisee who persecuted the early Christians, was transformed by God and went on to write much of the New Testament (Acts 8:1–3; 9).

God loves new beginnings, and He has one for you, too! Spend time in His Word, and let the Holy Spirit guide you to the fresh start He has planned.

Stop remembering what God has forgotten. Yes, you can learn from your mistakes, but that isn't who you are anymore. You are a new creation in Christ (2 Corinthians 5:17). The old has gone; the new has come. Believe it, speak it, and live it!

PRAYER FOR TODAY: *God, thank You for giving me a brand-new start. Help me not to dwell on my past mistakes—they are forgiven and forgotten. Keep my mind focused on You, Your goodness, and the wonderful plan You have for my life. Amen.*

DAY 313: DON'T CURSE WHAT GOD HAS BLESSED

And Balaam said to Balak, Indeed I have come to you, but do I now have any power at all to say anything? The word that God puts in my mouth, that shall I speak.

NUMBERS 22:38

Numbers 22 tells the story of Balak, king of Moab, who feared the Israelites because they were many in number, and it was well known that God was on their side. In desperation, King Balak sought out Balaam, who had direct access to God, and asked him to curse the Israelites so that the Moabites could defeat them.

Balaam responded, "I can't say whatever I please. I must speak only what God puts in my mouth" (v. 38 NIV).

King Balak offered sacrifices to the Lord and waited to hear what God would tell Balaam to say. And Balaam responded with these words: "How can I curse those whom God has not cursed?...I have received a command to bless; he has blessed, and I cannot change it...May those who bless [the Israelites] be blessed and those who curse [the Israelites] be cursed!" (Numbers 23:8, 20; 24:9 NIV).

King Balak was furious, demanding Balaam remain silent rather than bless the Israelites. But Balaam answered, "Did I not say to you, All the Lord speaks, that I must do?" (Numbers 23:26).

Just like Balaam, we should align our words with what God says. Our words have the power to bless and the power to curse, and we should not curse with our mouths what God has blessed.

PRAYER FOR TODAY: *God, help me speak only what You put in my mouth to say. May my lips always honor You, and when I fall short, correct me with Your grace. In Jesus' name, amen.*

DAY 314
WITH POWER COMES RESPONSIBILITY

Nothing in all creation is hidden from God's sight. Everything is uncovered and laid bare before the eyes of him to whom we must give account.

HEBREWS 4:13 NIV

Words have both the power to create and the power to destroy (Proverbs 18:21). Any time we have power, we also have responsibility.

When Solomon replaced his father, David, as king, he prayed for "an understanding mind and a hearing heart to judge [God's] people" (1 Kings 3:9). As king, he had power over all the people, but the weight of that responsibility inspired him to ask God for wisdom in how to lead them.

Since God has given us power in our words, He expects us to be accountable for how we use them. Like Solomon, we can pray for wisdom—we can pray to be wise with our words.

In Matthew 12:36, Jesus says that on the day of judgment we will each give an account for the words that we speak. We'll be held responsible for words of doubt, unbelief, complaining, grumbling, unforgiveness, and fear—words that empower the enemy. But we'll also give an account for our confessions of faith, encouragement, forgiveness, and hope—words that align with God's purpose and bring life.

Take responsibility for your words, and choose to speak wisely.

PRAYER FOR TODAY: *God, grant me wisdom in how I use my words. You know every word that I speak, and I am accountable to You, so help me choose words that glorify and honor You. In Jesus' name, amen.*

DAY 315
GOD SEES YOUR HEART; THE DEVIL HEARS YOUR WORDS

Because if you acknowledge and confess with your lips that Jesus is Lord and in your heart believe (adhere to, trust in, and rely on the truth) that God raised Him from the dead, you will be saved.
ROMANS 10:9

We see in Romans 10:9 the importance of both confessing *with your lips* and believing *in your heart* in the process of salvation. What we believe in our hearts justifies us and makes us right with God. When we believe Christ died for us and was raised from the dead, we receive Him as Savior. Our confession with our mouths affirms our faith publicly and aligns us with the truth of God's Word.

While God sees our hearts, both people and the enemy hear our words. Therefore, when battling the enemy, it is not enough to think right thoughts and believe in God in our hearts. We need to believe right, think right, *and* speak our confession aloud.

Our confession boldly declares a change of allegiance. Before we were saved, we were serving the enemy. So, when we receive salvation, we must confidently confess so that we stand firm and declare that we serve a new master: Jesus Christ.

PRAYER FOR TODAY: *God, thank You for opening my eyes today to the truth that the devil can't see my heart. Help me remember to speak my faith and belief in You out loud so he knows I am a child of God. Amen.*

DAY 316: SPEAK ACCORDINGLY

As it is written, I have made you the father of many nations. [He was appointed our father] in the sight of God in Whom he believed, Who gives life to the dead and speaks of the nonexistent things that [He has foretold and promised] as if they [already] existed.

ROMANS 4:17

Romans 4:17 is a very powerful scripture. It says that God speaks of things that don't exist as though they do. For example, God called Abram "Abraham," meaning "father of a multitude," long before Abraham had even one child. He knew His plan for Abraham and spoke about him accordingly.

Because our goal is to become more and more like the One who created us, we can do the same as He does. We can see with "eyes of faith" and speak of things that don't exist yet as if they do. We have the power to do this when we believe what God says more strongly than what we see or feel.

Calling things that are not as though they are can work against us, however, if we are not careful. For example, if someone around you gets sick, avoid saying, "I'll be next; I always get whatever bug is going around." You don't want to bring that into your life! Instead, declare, "I am healthy. My immune system is strong. A cheerful heart is good medicine."

When we declare God's Word out of our mouths, with hearts full of faith, those faith-filled words go forth to help establish God's plan in our lives.

PRAYER FOR TODAY: *God, thank You for setting the example of how to see with eyes of faith and speak accordingly. Help me speak Your promises over my life so I can partner with You in establishing Your plans for me. Amen.*

DAY 317: UNANSWERED PRAYERS

For everyone who continues to feed on milk is obviously inexperienced and unskilled in the doctrine of righteousness (of conformity to the divine will in purpose, thought, and action), for he is a mere infant [not able to talk yet]!

HEBREWS 5:13

When we first begin to walk with God, we do not have the wisdom and experience we need to say and pray for the right things all the time. When we are in this stage of spiritual growth, we should be glad God shows us mercy and does not give us everything we ask for!

In this stage, as "mere infants" in Christ, we tend to say a lot of things that are based in our will, not in God's will, simply because we cannot yet tell the difference. We start with "baby talk," and then our vocabulary grows, and eventually we will grow into learning to speak God's way.

Proverbs 3:7 teaches us not to be wise in our own eyes. In other words, we should not think we know best. God is the only one who really knows what is best for us and when the perfect timing is.

As you study God's Word and learn how to apply His principles in your life, Hebrews 5:14 says that "by practice" you will learn to distinguish what is morally good for you and what isn't. We can learn a lot from our mistakes if we are willing to.

PRAYER FOR TODAY: *God, please withhold from me anything that is not aligned with Your perfect will and timing. Grant me the wisdom and discernment to trust in Your plan as I follow You. Amen.*

DAY 318: ARE YOU EASILY ANNOYED?

But the former preach Christ out of a party spirit, insincerely [out of no pure motive, but thinking to annoy me], supposing they are making my bondage more bitter and my chains more galling.
PHILIPPIANS 1:17

In Philippians 1:17, Paul says that he knows some people aren't preaching from pure hearts. Their motives, in fact, may be to "annoy" Paul while he is stuck in prison, rather than to glorify God.

In this life, you will have many opportunities to be annoyed, whether someone is intentionally trying to bother you or not. But it is your choice whether or not you let yourself be annoyed.

When you give in to those emotions, your feelings can actually grow into bitterness and take root, so it is better to resist them from the start.

Paul responded by saying that whether they preached with false motives or in truth, he was going to rejoice because the gospel was advancing.

Your outlook is more important than your circumstances. You can choose to keep a positive attitude regardless of what you are going through. Paul was able to keep a joyful attitude in difficult circumstances because his mind was fixed on what was excellent and praiseworthy, and God was his source of strength (Philippians 4:8–13).

PRAYER FOR TODAY: *God, thank You for giving me the strength to be content regardless of my circumstances. Help me today to let go of frustration and choose joy as I place my trust fully in You. Amen.*

DAY 319 — THE JOY OF THE LORD

Nehemiah said, "Go and enjoy choice food and sweet drinks, and send some to those who have nothing prepared. This day is holy to our Lord. Do not grieve, for the joy of the Lord is your strength."
NEHEMIAH 8:10 NIV

I define *joy* as "anything from extreme hilarity to calm delight, a feeling of pleasure." We all enjoy extreme hilarity from time to time, but what we want in everyday life is that calm delight—that steadfast sense of peace, pleasure, and well-being we can only find through a personal relationship with God.

Happiness is based on what happens, but joy is a fruit of the Holy Spirit, who dwells in us as believers in Jesus Christ (Galatians 5:22). That is why, even in the midst of difficulties or sadness, the joy of the Lord is available to you. His joy is your strength, regardless of your circumstances, allowing you to remain calm and at peace in every situation, because He is always there, working on your behalf, and desiring your greatest and highest good in all things.

Paul wrote in 2 Corinthians that the people in Macedonia had "an abundance of joy" despite going through severe trials (v. 8:2). In Philippians 4:7, he wrote about God's peace, "which surpasses all understanding" (ESV), filling our hearts and our minds when we entrust everything to Him. That same calm delight—the joy of the Lord—is available to all who believe.

PRAYER FOR TODAY: *God, give me the strength today to have peace regardless of my circumstances. Fill my heart with joy, to calmly delight in You, all the days of my life. Amen.*

DAY 320

PRAY FOR OTHERS

Therefore confess your sins to each other and pray for each other so that you may be healed. The prayer of a righteous person is powerful and effective.

JAMES 5:16 NIV

The more we think about ourselves and our problems, the more likely we are to be depressed, anxious, and worried. Intercession, or praying for others, can actually decrease anxiety and worry simply because you have your mind on someone else and their needs rather than on yourself and what you are going through.

At any given time, we all know several people who are facing problems and could use our prayers. Be intentional in praying for God to comfort them, strengthen them, and meet their specific needs. Ask God to give them patience, perseverance, and the wisdom to discern His will for their lives.

The Bible says that we reap what we sow (Galatians 6:7–9). When we sow prayers for others, God will touch the hearts of many people to pray for us. So, while you are praying for God to meet another person's need, someone else will be praying for God to answer yours. Not only will you be less anxious because your mind is off yourself, but you will be participating in God's plan to love and care for one another, and your needs will be met.

Your prayers are more powerful than you realize, and other people's prayers for you are more important than you may ever know.

PRAYER FOR TODAY: *God, put people on my heart every day who need my prayers. Help me to shift my focus away from myself, to believe that my prayers are powerful and effective, and to use that power to bring strength and healing to others. In Jesus' name, amen.*

DAY 321: WASTED TIME VS. TIME WELL SPENT

Come to Me, all you who labor and are heavy-laden and overburdened, and I will cause you to rest. [I will ease and relieve and refresh your souls.]

MATTHEW 11:28

Sometimes we waste time on frivolous or foolish things that bear no lasting fruit. Often, though, we waste time feeling sorry for ourselves, being consumed by anger or depression, allowing fear to control us, or getting trapped in anxiety and worry. Anxiety is rooted in fear, and because we are afraid, we try to take care of situations ourselves. This causes us to worry and reason as we try to come up with solutions to problems that we cannot solve without God's help.

It is God's will for us to be at peace and for our souls to be at rest. God's peace and rest are available to us when we cast our burdens on Him (Psalm 55:22; 1 Peter 5:7). Though the enemy may tempt us to pick those burdens back up, God wants us to leave them with Him, trusting fully in His care, so that we can enter His perfect rest.

In times of trouble, seeking God's guidance in prayer and meditating on specific scriptures like Matthew 11:28–29 will bring comfort and help you leave your worries in His care. Any time spent trusting God is time well spent!

PRAYER FOR TODAY: *God, I am struggling today with burdens that are too heavy for me to carry. Thank You for reminding me through Your Word that You will bear them for me. Help me to release them into Your hands and to leave them there. Amen.*

DAY 322
WHAT IS DRAINING YOU?

As he thinks in his heart so is he.

PROVERBS 23:7

The mind and body are deeply connected, which means all of our thoughts—whether good or bad—have a direct impact on our physical well-being. Positive, hopeful thoughts energize our souls and physical bodies, whereas negative, hopeless thoughts drain our energy.

If you have been exceptionally tired lately, ask yourself, *What have I been thinking about?* Have you been worried about many things rather than casting your cares on the Lord? Are you harboring a grudge against someone instead of quickly forgiving? Perhaps someone said something that you can't stop overanalyzing, or you're replaying a conversation, worrying about how you might have been misunderstood. Maybe you've gone to bed dreading going to work and have carried that negativity into your morning. These thoughts could be a major factor in your exhaustion.

Of course, physical tiredness is not always a result of wrong thinking. We can certainly have a sickness or disease that leads to fatigue. But science and medical technology verify that the mind and body have a close connection, so it is important to ask ourselves if our thoughts are draining us.

PRAYER FOR TODAY: *God, fill my mind with positive, life-giving thoughts today so that I have all the energy I need to carry out Your will. Show me if I have been negative about anything so I can shift my words and thoughts to align with Your truth. In Jesus' name, amen.*

DAY 323: THE SPIRIT OF GOD LIVES IN YOU

Little children, you are of God [you belong to Him] and have [already] defeated and overcome them [the agents of the antichrist], because He Who lives in you is greater (mightier) than he who is in the world.

1 JOHN 4:4

The scripture above is saying that what is *in* you—Jesus—is more important than anything that happens *to* you!

We don't have to settle for a bad day. That is how we can rise above our challenging circumstances. But our thoughts and words must line up with the truth of God's Word for us to experience His joy, strength, and peace. Declare things like:

- I have received the power of the Holy Spirit, and He can do miraculous things through me. I have authority and power over the enemy (Mark 16:17–18; Luke 10:17–19).
- My life is rooted in my faith in Christ, and I overflow with thanksgiving for all He has done for me (Colossians 2:7).
- Christ lives in me, and I live by faith in Him and His love for me (Galatians 2:20).

If you've accepted Jesus Christ as your Savior, you have the Spirit of God within you. And that means His peace, joy, strength, and patience are all yours in Christ.

PRAYER FOR TODAY: *God, thank You for being my unshakable hope. Help me live by faith, believing that You are in me and that You are greater than anything that can come against me. Amen.*

DAY 324: TAKE YOUR MIND BACK

You are of your father the devil, and your will is to do your father's desires. He was a murderer from the beginning, and does not stand in the truth, because there is no truth in him. When he lies, he speaks out of his own character, for he is a liar and the father of lies.

JOHN 8:44 ESV

As you begin to reclaim your mind and your thoughts from the enemy, he will not want to give up the hold he has had on you. You will have to do battle with his lies and confusion.

Your first step is to declare out loud that you will not allow any outside force to do your thinking—no man and no spirit. Your power is in the name of Jesus, the blood of Jesus, and the Word of God.

Next, ask God for discernment to recognize the lies of the devil. As you identify a lie, defend yourself by speaking God's truth out loud. Use Scripture to resist the enemy, standing firm in faith and refusing to let him use your mind as a battlefield.

Finally, don't give up. As you battle, it may feel like things are getting worse at first, because demonic powers will fight to maintain their hold. But as you call upon God's grace and stand firm in the name of Jesus, the Holy Spirit will empower you to fully overcome every evil influence (2 Timothy 1:7). Stay persistent, knowing victory is yours in Christ.

PRAYER FOR TODAY: *God, I ask for Your strength to reclaim my mind and my life from the enemy's lies. Help me recognize the truth that comes from You and to reject the deceit the enemy uses to harm me. Thank You for Your power, wisdom, and love. Amen.*

DAY 325: THE PROBLEM WITH PRIDE

Take My yoke upon you and learn of Me, for I am gentle (meek) and humble (lowly) in heart, and you will find rest (relief and ease and refreshment and recreation and blessed quiet) for your souls.
MATTHEW 11:29

In Proverbs 6:16–19, God lists seven things He hates—and one of those things is pride, which the Amplified Bible, Classic Edition defines as "the spirit that makes one overestimate himself and underestimate others" (v. 17). Since God hates pride, we must be diligent in preventing it from taking root in our minds and in our lives.

The antidote to pride is humility, which is defined as "freedom from pride" and "a modest estimation of your own worth." It doesn't mean you think lowly of yourself; it means you are very careful not to think more highly of yourself than you ought to.

Unlike a prideful person, a humble person is quick to forgive and slow to take offense, and trusts God to right any wrongs. A humble person doesn't brag but always gives God the glory. And a humble person is patient, joyfully waiting on God, and obedient in whatever instructions He gives.

God has chosen to work through us to accomplish His purposes here on earth. Everything we are, every talent we possess, and every good thing that we do is because of Him, our Creator. How humbling!

PRAYER FOR TODAY: *God, help me maintain the right attitude about myself. When I am tempted to be independent, draw me closer to You. When I am tempted to boast, remind me to give thanks instead. In Jesus' name, amen.*

DAY 326: PREPARE YOUR MIND

Therefore gird up the loins of your mind, be sober, and rest your hope fully upon the grace that is to be brought to you at the revelation of Jesus Christ.

1 PETER 1:13 NKJV

What does it mean to "gird up the loins of your mind"? *Gird* means to prepare yourself for something difficult or challenging, so Peter is telling us to prepare our minds for action. There is work to be done, and he wants us to be able to think thoughts that agree with the mind of God so that we can advance in that work with the power that is available to us in Christ Jesus.

When we rid our minds of negative thinking that doesn't line up with God's Word and then fill our minds with truth, we can run our race and have the victory He wants us to have. This mental preparation enables us to follow God's plan for our lives with purpose and strength.

Every day, you will need to renew your mind with the truth about what God says—about His love for you, His plan for you, and how He wants you to live and behave—in order to experience the fullness of the new life we can all have in Christ. It's a life filled with joy, peace, and the ability to become all that God has created us to be.

PRAYER FOR TODAY: *God, thank You for giving me Your Word as a guide for how to think, speak, live, and behave. Thank You for loving me and for having a good plan for my life. Align my thoughts with Yours so that I am prepared for all that You have in store for me. Amen.*

DAY 327
PURE IN HEART

Blessed (happy, enviably fortunate, and spiritually prosperous—possessing the happiness produced by the experience of God's favor and especially conditioned by the revelation of His grace, regardless of their outward conditions) are the pure in heart, for they shall see God!

MATTHEW 5:8

One of the biggest revelations I've received from God is that my real life is the life that's *in me*, not what happens *to me*. Life is not your circumstances, the kind of house you live in, the kind of job you have, or how much money you have. You can have the best of these things and still be miserable.

On the other hand, it's amazing how happy and peaceful you can be in the middle of the most unpleasant circumstances, including the turmoil that's going on in the world today, if you keep your heart in the right condition.

Matthew 5:8 says, "Blessed are the pure in heart, for they will see God" (NIV). The Amplified Bible, Classic Edition defines blessed as "happy, enviably fortunate, and spiritually prosperous...regardless of their outward conditions." While God may want to bless you financially, with a promotion at work, or other "outward conditions," to be truly blessed in God is to be able to have joy on the inside—in your heart and in your mind—regardless of whether you have plenty or are in want (Philippians 4:12).

PRAYER FOR TODAY: *God, I am asking You to bless me today with every spiritual blessing so that I can be content in any and every situation. Remind me that my real life is what is happening on the inside of me while I trust You with my circumstances. Amen.*

DAY 328: WHAT IT MEANS TO THINK RIGHT

For to set the mind on the flesh is death, but to set the mind on the Spirit is life and peace.

ROMANS 8:6 ESV

Our thoughts are forerunners for everything that we do. Right thinking can enable you, and wrong thinking can disable you. It's amazing what you can do if you believe you can. It's equally surprising what you won't do if you think you can't.

Right thinking means to think the way that God thinks. This is possible when we renew our minds with God's Word (Romans 12:2). When you spend time purposely studying what the Bible says about you, your thoughts will begin to line up with God's thoughts and plans for your life.

For example, God's Word says you are "ready for anything and equal to anything through Him Who infuses inner strength into me" (Philippians 4:13). Whenever you are tempted to think *I can't*, remember that God's Word says you can do "all things in Christ Who empowers me" (Philippians 4:13). He will give you the grace to do anything He wants you to do.

God's Word also says that as believers we are "more than conquerors through him who loved us" (Romans 8:37 NIV). You can decide ahead of time to have a "more than a conqueror" attitude so that when trials come you will be confident that you are up to anything.

Right thinking—having a mind like Christ—is the key to experiencing the amazing life God has planned for you.

PRAYER FOR TODAY: *God, thank You for giving me the freedom to think on purpose and to choose right thinking. Help me keep my mind set on Your Spirit and what Your Word says about me so that I can face each day with a "more than a conqueror" attitude. Amen.*

DAY 329

NOT BY MIGHT, NOR BY POWER

Then he said to me, "This is the word of the Lord to Zerubbabel: Not by might, nor by power, but by my Spirit, says the Lord of hosts."

ZECHARIAH 4:6 ESV

Many of us enter into a relationship with God by faith but then try to maintain that relationship by our own methods. We believed Him for our salvation but then try to make that salvation work on our own. But God didn't call us to be achievers, living by our own human efforts. He has called us to be believers—resting in His grace and following the leading of the Holy Spirit into an abundant, productive, victorious life. We are saved by faith, and we should live our lives the same way.

The truth is, we need a continuous flow of the Holy Spirit in our lives to transform us to be more like Him in our thoughts, words, and actions. We can't do it on our own strength or in our own power. Only when we ask God for His help and depend on His Spirit to lead us will we begin to see real, lasting changes in our lives.

Philippians 1:6 says that "he who began a good work in you will bring it to completion" (ESV). God started the process, and you can trust Him to finish it.

PRAYER FOR TODAY: *God, when I start to worry that I am not doing enough and not changing quickly enough, or when I still struggle in my thoughts and words, give me the grace to trust in You and the leading of the Holy Spirit. I cannot change on my own; thank You for being there from start to finish. Amen.*

DAY 330: GOD'S WORD IS POWERFUL

And we also [especially] thank God continually for this, that when you received the message of God [which you heard] from us, you welcomed it not as the word of [mere] men, but as it truly is, the Word of God, which is effectually at work in you who believe [exercising its superhuman power in those who adhere to and trust in and rely on it].

1 THESSALONIANS 2:13

In Philippians 3:1, the apostle Paul wrote that he didn't mind writing the same things over and over again to the people, because he knew what he was saying was beneficial to them. We cannot hear these truths about God's Word enough. God's Word is powerful. God's Word is true. God's Word is "effectually at work in you who believe" (1 Thessalonians 2:13). That means it is effective and successful and powerful beyond our human measure.

Hebrews 4:12 (NIV) calls the Word "alive and active" because it has the power to transform your mind and emotions and make you free. The Bible was written for you; therefore, you can take each thing you read personally. Speak what you read out loud—speak to your circumstances, declare what God says about you, receive His promises—and watch God move in your life.

God's Word will renew your mind, so love the Word, live the Word, speak the Word, and meditate on the Word. When we meditate on His Word—when we speak out what He says about us—we are releasing our faith and cooperating with Him to see His good plans come to pass in our lives.

PRAYER FOR TODAY: *God, thank You for the gift of Your Word. I ask You to ignite in me a deep love for Your Word. May I meditate on it, live by it, and allow its power to be at work within me. Amen.*

DAY 331

LEARN THE SECRET

I know what it is to be in need, and I know what it is to have plenty. I have learned the secret of being content in any and every situation, whether well fed or hungry, whether living in plenty or in want.
PHILIPPIANS 4:12 NIV

Paul says in Philippians 4:12 that he has learned the secret of being content regardless of his circumstances. When you choose to become a believer, that secret becomes available to you too. Suddenly, you can enjoy life no matter what you are going through—you can even enjoy your life when you're going through things that are hard, painful, or unjust.

The secret is this: Trust God completely. When you trust God completely, you will know that He is with you, working on your behalf, and He will carry you through to the other side of your situation. You will know that what you are going through is just a season, and this too shall pass.

When you truly trust God, your words will change and line up with what He says instead of how you feel. No longer will you say: "I hate this situation." "I hate my job." "I hate how I look." "I hate my life." Instead, your words will be filled with life and faith: "I don't like this situation, but I trust God to work good out of it." "I am thankful that I have a job to go to." "I am fearfully and wonderfully made." "I enjoy my life!"

PRAYER FOR TODAY: *God, thank You for revealing truth to me. Help me fully enjoy my life and cherish every moment as a precious gift from You. Lord, I trust You; help me trust You completely. Amen.*

DAY 332
WHAT YOUR POSTURE SAYS ABOUT YOU

Be joyful in hope, patient in affliction, faithful in prayer.
ROMANS 12:12 NIV

Attitudes begin in our hearts and are fed by our thoughts, but they show in our words and through our postures and body language. Posture refers to how you physically hold yourself when you are sitting or standing, but it can also describe your mental approach or attitude toward a situation.

For example, if I have an impatient attitude while waiting at the doctor's office, I might shift in my seat like I can't get comfortable. I might sigh loudly or mutter under my breath about how long it is taking. I might look at my watch every few minutes, rest my chin on my hand, or roll my eyes. I might even get up and walk around, as if that will make the doctor hurry up!

However, if I have a patient attitude, I will have a smile on my face. I will be relaxed in my seat, and others will see me as approachable. I will look for people to encourage, and I will be an active listener when someone speaks to me. I might even be humming a worship song under my breath as I think about how grateful I am that God created people to be doctors to care for our physical health and that He is the Great Physician who still performs miracles today.

Our attitudes are our choice, and they affect not only us but also the people around us who see our posture toward others and our circumstances.

PRAYER FOR TODAY: *God, I realize I can't hide a bad attitude. It shows up not only in my words but also in my body language. I understand that this is a heart issue, so I'm asking You to cultivate a spirit of gratitude in me for all that You have done. In Jesus' name, amen.*

DAY 333: THIS IS NOT TOO DIFFICULT

For this commandment which I am commanding you today is not too difficult for you, nor is it out of reach.

DEUTERONOMY 30:11 AMP

We are anointed for hard things. The power of the anointing comes from the Holy Spirit and enables us to do whatever God asks us to do. He would not ask you to do something that He would not then give you the power and the ability to accomplish, which is why today's passage says, "This...which I am commanding you...is not too difficult for you."

Philippians 2:13 (AMP) says,

> For it is [not your strength, but it is] God who is effectively at work in you, both to will and to work [that is, strengthening, energizing, and creating in you the longing and the ability to fulfill your purpose] for His good pleasure.

God not only gives you the power and the ability to accomplish His plan for your life, but He also gives you the energy, the desire, the longing, and the will to do it. When God calls you to something, you will have a heart for it, a passion for it. You will think about it and talk about it and be willing to sacrifice for it, and that gives God pleasure in return.

Remember: *This* is not too difficult. Have a determined attitude and press through to victory!

PRAYER FOR TODAY: *God, help me trust Your Word when it says "this" is not too hard. Give me the strength, the passion, the energy, and everything I need to live in victory. In Jesus' name, amen.*

DAY 334: SELF-FULFILLING POWER

For as [surely as] the earth brings forth its shoots, and as a garden causes what is sown in it to spring forth, so [surely] the Lord God will cause rightness and justice and praise to spring forth before all the nations [through the self-fulfilling power of His word].

ISAIAH 61:11

When a farmer plants a seed in the ground, that seed contains the power to produce a plant. The Word of God functions the same way. When we plant the Word in our hearts and water it with our faith—by thinking and speaking in agreement with what it says—we will see amazing results. Both the seed and the Word of God have self-fulfilling power.

"Faith is the substance of things hoped for, the evidence of things not seen" (Hebrews 11:1 NKJV). A tomato seed does not look like a tomato, yet the farmer trusts that by planting the seed, a tomato plant will grow. In the same way, some aspects of our lives may look hopeless, yet God's Word tells us that we can have hope—that we can confidently expect something good to happen—because God has a good plan for our lives.

There is no circumstance that is able to keep God from doing what He promises to do. Think and speak according to God's Word, and "rightness and justice and praise" will spring forth.

PRAYER FOR TODAY: *God, thank You for the measure of faith You have given me. Thank You that Your Word does not return void. Guide me to study Your Word deeply so that my thoughts and words align with its power. In Jesus' name, amen.*

DAY 335
WHEN INFORMATION BECOMES REVELATION

And He said to them, Be careful what you are hearing. The measure [of thought and study] you give [to the truth you hear] will be the measure [of virtue and knowledge] that comes back to you—and more [besides] will be given to you who hear.

MARK 4:24

Have you ever read something in the Word of God but had a hard time believing it? It might be because the words were only information to you. To *know* that the Word of God is truth, the information must become revelation to you.

Revelation is that moment when everything clicks and you suddenly have a deeper understanding of the truth of what the Word says. Revelation doesn't typically come from hearing something once. You will have to put in some effort. Meditate on it, study it, read it often, and pray for revelation.

Mark 4:24 says that the measure of thought that you give to the Word is the measure that it will be given back to you. So, if you want revelation, you can't just listen to a message on Sunday and get everything that God wants you to get out of it. You will have to go home, dive deeper into scripture, and study everything you can find on that topic. You must allow the truth to roll over in your mind repeatedly—until it becomes a personal revelation.

When revelation comes, you will know with every cell of your being that the Word of God is true, and it is true for you.

PRAYER FOR TODAY: *God, I sense Your conviction today that there are areas of Your Word that are information to me, not revelation. Show me the difference. Help me see what areas I need to give my mind to so that I may gain a revelation of Your truth. In Jesus' name, amen.*

DAY 336: GUARD YOUR HEART

Keep and guard your heart with all vigilance and above all that you guard, for out of it flow the springs of life.

PROVERBS 4:23

Today's scripture exhorts us to guard our hearts "with all vigilance." Practically, that means we need to examine our attitudes and our thoughts on a regular basis and adjust as needed.

Many people are deceived into believing they cannot help what they think, but the truth is, we can choose our thoughts. We need to think about what we have been thinking about. When we do that, it doesn't take very long to discover the root cause of a bad attitude.

Satan will always try to fill our minds with wrong thinking, but we do not have to receive everything he tries to give us. I would not take a spoonful of poison just because someone offered it to me, and neither would you. If we are smart enough not to swallow poison, we should also be smart enough not to allow Satan to poison our minds, attitudes, and, ultimately, our lives.

Guard your heart vigilantly. Fill your mind with thoughts that are good, honorable, and true (Philippians 4:8), and watch your heart attitude change.

PRAYER FOR TODAY: *God, help me think about what I have been thinking about. Close my mind to wrong thinking and the lies of the enemy. Teach me to think right thoughts that line up with Your plan for me. Amen.*

DAY 337
WHO ARE YOU SPENDING TIME WITH?

Iron sharpens iron; so a man sharpens the countenance of his friend [to show rage or worthy purpose].

PROVERBS 27:17

You are influenced by those you spend time with and what you open your heart to. For example, if you surround yourself with positive, spiritually mature people, they will help you grow spiritually in your thoughts and your attitudes. However, if you regularly spend time with negative people—people who are greedy, jealous, critical, or judgmental—you become more vulnerable and are likely to pick up those negative attitudes.

When Job was being tested, his friends were initially supportive. They sat with him in his grief to comfort and console him. However, they later judged him and tried to make him feel condemned for sins they assumed he committed that upset God. His own wife encouraged him to "curse God and die" (Job 2:9 NIV). Job had to guard his heart against their influence to cling to his faith in the most difficult season of life.

We aren't supposed to cut ourselves off from everybody who isn't a positive influence, and there will be people you need to reach so you can lead them to Christ. But you must make sure you are affecting those people instead of letting them infect you.

PRAYER FOR TODAY: *God, help me glorify You with my friendships. Bring spiritually mature people into my life to be a positive influence on me, and show me those whom I can influence in a positive way so that we are all coming up higher. In Jesus' name, amen.*

DAY 338: RID YOUR LIFE OF STRIFE

Let him turn away from wickedness and shun it, and let him do right. Let him search for peace (harmony; undisturbedness from fears, agitating passions, and moral conflicts) and seek it eagerly. [Do not merely desire peaceful relations with God, with your fellowmen, and with yourself, but pursue, go after them!]

1 PETER 3:11

Today's scripture tells us that it is God's will for us to live in peace and harmony with one another, but it's not enough to just want peaceful relationships. We must actively "search for peace," "seek it eagerly," and "pursue" peaceful relationships.

Having peace with others doesn't mean we won't ever disagree, but we must do it respectfully and avoid strife. The dictionary defines *strife* as "bickering, arguing, a heated disagreement, or an angry undercurrent."

Sometimes your "wants" can cause strife, whether it's for a promotion, a material thing, or even a ministry. And so can your "if onlys": "If only I had this…" "If only I had that…" "If only I had what she has…" Dissatisfaction often leads to trouble. Think about how easy it is to be resentful and stir up strife when you don't get what you want. You can get critical of others, but it's not other people or circumstances that make you unsatisfied. It is a lack of trust that God will provide what is best for you.

If you truly trust God, if you believe He loves you and has a good plan for your life, and if you believe that His timing is always right, there is no need to envy or be jealous of a single person.

PRAYER FOR TODAY: *God, teach me to trust You, Your timing, and Your will for my life. I desire peace in my relationships, and I know that starts with having peace with You. I am eager to seek and embrace peace in every aspect of my life. Amen.*

DAY 339: WHO YOU ARE IN CHRIST

For He made Him who knew no sin to be sin for us, that we might become the righteousness of God in Him.

2 CORINTHIANS 5:21 NKJV

One of the ways the enemy tries to deceive God's people is by trying to convince us that we must do everything right in order to be accepted and have a relationship with God. He tries to lure us into thinking that the good things we do will make us right in God's eyes. As a result, when we're doing "good" things, we are in a good mood and feel like we're alright with God. But when we think we've failed, our mood drops, and we can feel like God is angry with us.

This is why it's so important to know the difference between our "who" and our "do." Our identity, worth, and value—our "who"—depends entirely on what Jesus did for us, not on the good things we do.

When we enter a relationship with Him, Jesus offers us everything that He is, including His righteousness. We can feel right about ourselves, not because we do everything right, but because we have been made right by our faith in Jesus (2 Corinthians 5:21). Our emotional stability improves when we understand that God loves us unconditionally and that we have right standing with Him.

PRAYER FOR TODAY: *God, thank You for sending Your Son to die for me so that I could have right standing with You. There is nothing I could ever do to earn it. I don't deserve it. And yet, out of Your love for me, You did it anyway. Remind me who I am in You. Amen.*

DAY 340: THE LORD OUR STRENGTH

So I am well pleased with weaknesses, with insults, with distresses, with persecutions, and with difficulties, for the sake of Christ; for when I am weak [in human strength], then I am strong [truly able, truly powerful, truly drawing from God's strength].

2 CORINTHIANS 12:10 AMP

Fear is one of Satan's favorite deceptions, and he uses it to keep us from moving forward and becoming all that God created us to be. Fear shows up in our lives through doubt, insecurity, worry, and anxiety. Most of the things we fear never happen.

This is why we need to watch out for thoughts that begin with *I can't* or *I'm not*. The enemy stays busy telling us about our weaknesses—everything we are *not* and what we *can't* do. But we don't have to listen to him. If we know God's Word, we can find out everything we *are* in Him.

The apostle Paul learned this lesson well. He said that when he was trusting in God's strength instead of in his own abilities, he was "truly able" and "truly powerful."

If we're not careful, we can allow our weaknesses to prevent us from stepping out into God's plan for our lives. However, the Lord wants us to trust Him with our weaknesses and receive His strength in those areas. He wants us to focus our thoughts on how much we *can* do and then lean on His ability to do the rest.

PRAYER FOR TODAY: *God, help me fill my mind with* I can *and* I am *thoughts. Thank You for being the strength to my weakness and the ability to my inability. I want everything You have for me in this life. In Jesus' name and power, amen.*

DAY 341: LISTEN TO WISDOM

When you walk, they will guide you; when you sleep, they will watch over you; when you awake, they will speak to you.

PROVERBS 6:22 NIV

Proverbs is a book of wisdom. When you study it, you will start to hear wisdom whisper to you throughout your day. As today's verse says, wisdom "will speak to you."

For example, you might wake up and think, *Do I feel like reading my Bible now, or should I run my errands first?* Wisdom will no doubt speak to you and say, *Don't put off until later what will benefit you now. Spend time in the Word, and your day will be prosperous.*

Another example is something that often happens to me. I will hear part of a conversation and immediately start imagining all the possible scenarios. Then wisdom will whisper to my mind and my heart: *You don't need to try to reason this out. Trust God for discernment and guidance.*

When we get involved in situations that don't concern us, we can quickly lose our peace and our focus. By staying out of those situations, we keep our minds at rest and can focus on our priorities instead of being distracted by other things.

The more you pay attention to wisdom, and listen for it to fill your mind and heart, the more you will enjoy your life.

PRAYER FOR TODAY: *God, help me hear wisdom and to follow it. Keep my mind at peace and at rest. Thank You for making Your wisdom available to me in my everyday life. Amen.*

DAY 342: SET YOUR MIND ON JOY

And set your minds and keep them set on what is above (the higher things), not on the things that are on the earth.

COLOSSIANS 3:2

My husband, Dave, can set his mind and keep it set better than almost anyone else I have ever met. If he decides to do or not to do something, he sticks to his decision.

When I think about how miserable I was to live with in the early days of our marriage, I wonder: *How could he have lived with me? How could he have stayed with me…and been happy about it?!* And Dave says, "I wanted you to be happy, but I set my mind that even if you weren't, I was going to be happy anyway."

Too often we let other people's moods determine our own, but we can decide that we are going to enjoy our lives no matter what anyone else does.

Dave is a very active person, but one year he got a blood clot in his leg that required him to rest for a month. I asked him if it was driving him crazy to have to just sit there and he said, "No. I don't like it, but I've decided that if this is what I have to do, then I am going to enjoy my life while I sit here."

While Dave may be better at this than most people, the power to set our minds and keep them set is available to all of us. You can enjoy your life no matter what you are going through if you set your mind and keep it set.

PRAYER FOR TODAY: *God, help me to set my mind and to keep it set on things above. Help me remain stable in my moods and attitudes and not be influenced by the ups and downs of those around me. In Jesus' name, amen.*

DAY 343
FIVE THINGS TO SAY ON PURPOSE

[The Servant of God says] The Lord God has given Me the tongue of a disciple and of one who is taught, that I should know how to speak a word in season to him who is weary. He wakens Me morning by morning, He wakens My ear to hear as a disciple [as one who is taught].

ISAIAH 50:4

Our words can do serious damage to our relationships, careers, and the world around us. But with the help of the Holy Spirit, they can also bring great good. Here are a few tips to help you tame your tongue and shape your life:

1. Use your words to bless. Avoid speaking negatively about yourself or others. Instead, speak blessings over everything. In other words, declare what God says.
2. Be thankful and say so. Thank God for everything, especially if you are waiting on a breakthrough, and show gratitude to those around you.
3. Encourage, edify, and build others up. Ask the Holy Spirit to show you who you can encourage. Ask for specific words that will build a person up.
4. Tell the truth. Don't compromise your integrity. There is no such thing as a little white lie. Commit to the truth, even when it requires sacrifice.
5. Speak the Word of God out loud, faithfully. Nothing will help you fight the enemy like speaking God's Word.

PRAYER FOR TODAY: *God, help me honor You with my words today—to bless, to thank, to encourage, to tell the truth, and to speak Your Word faithfully. In Jesus' name, amen.*

DAY 344
BLESSED ARE THE PEACEMAKERS AND MAINTAINERS

Blessed (enjoying enviable happiness, spiritually prosperous—with life-joy and satisfaction in God's favor and salvation, regardless of their outward conditions) are the makers and maintainers of peace, for they shall be called the sons of God!

MATTHEW 5:9

If we value peace and desire to walk in it, we need to be willing to adapt ourselves to other people and situations (Romans 12:16). There are, of course, times when we should stand firm on our convictions and refuse to compromise, but there are also times when keeping the peace is more important. Peace and power go together, and anyone desiring to have power in their life must also have peace.

Peace is what makes life enjoyable. In fact, truly enjoying life is impossible without it. We often give up our peace for things that are not worthy of the sacrifice—things like winning a useless argument or remaining angry when we feel we have been mistreated.

Jesus said that we are to be "makers and maintainers of peace." This means that we must take the initiative in making peace rather than waiting for someone else to do it. It means that sometimes we will have to remain quiet rather than defend ourselves or our positions. Being peacemakers is how we can be blessed in this life, which Matthew 5:9 says is possible regardless of outward circumstances. Peace is a choice and an attitude of the heart.

PRAYER FOR TODAY: *God, help me make and maintain peace with the thoughts that I think, the words that I speak, and the attitudes that I express. Show me when to let others win for the sake of peace. Amen.*

DAY 345
WHO TO TALK TO IN YOUR TIME OF NEED

However, I am telling you nothing but the truth when I say it is profitable (good, expedient, advantageous) for you that I go away. Because if I do not go away, the Comforter (Counselor, Helper, Advocate, Intercessor, Strengthener, Standby) will not come to you [into close fellowship with you]; but if I go away, I will send Him to you [to be in close fellowship with you].

JOHN 16:7

Often when we are hurting, we look to other people to help us feel better, only to discover they don't have what we need. In fact, if you aren't talking to the right people, they could make you feel worse. And if you aren't saying the right things—if you are complaining instead of being thankful—you can make yourself feel worse!

The Bible says that God is "the God of all comfort" (2 Corinthians 1:3 NIV). The Holy Spirit, who dwells on the inside of us, knows us better than anyone else, and when life is painful, He has the ability to bring strength and healing right where we hurt. Yes, the Lord will often use others to bring us comfort, but running to God first opens the door for Him to help us in the best way possible.

The truth is, the Holy Spirit is concerned about everything that concerns you—whether it's a "serious" matter, like a relationship issue, or something as simple as what to wear in the morning. The more we acknowledge the Holy Spirit and ask for help, the more we'll discover His presence and ability in everything we do. Whatever situation you're facing, you can take comfort knowing that God Himself is on your side and is always ready to listen.

PRAYER FOR TODAY: *God, thank You for being a good listener. Guard my mouth against complaining to others, and help me turn to You first when I have a need. In Jesus' name, amen.*

DAY 346
WHAT TO SAY WHEN YOU DON'T KNOW HOW TO PRAY

So too the [Holy] Spirit comes to our aid and bears us up in our weakness; for we do not know what prayer to offer nor how to offer it worthily as we ought, but the Spirit Himself goes to meet our supplication and pleads in our behalf with unspeakable yearnings and groanings too deep for utterance.

ROMANS 8:26

We know that one of the most meaningful ways to use our words are to pray and to praise. But what about those times when we don't know what or how to pray?

In Luke 11:1, Jesus' disciples said, "Lord, teach us to pray." Jesus had just been praying, so you can imagine that the disciples heard the power of His prayer. The things He prayed for were not "things" of this earth but things of spiritual importance. They wanted to know how to pray and what to pray for. So, Jesus gave them the words of the Lord's Prayer: "Our Father Who is in heaven, hallowed be Your name..." (v. 2).

If the disciples who walked daily with Jesus struggled with what and how to pray, then it is no wonder that we do, too!

God knew that, and it is one of the reasons that He sent us the Holy Spirit—to be our intercessor. Romans 8:26 says He comes to our aid and helps us to pray that perfect prayer when we don't know what or how to pray. It also says He prays to God for us when the cries of our hearts cannot be put into words.

PRAYER FOR TODAY: *God, thank You for the gift of the Holy Spirit, who prays on my behalf and speaks to my heart the things that I should pray for. Help me listen for wisdom as You teach me to pray. Amen.*

DAY 347: GOD IS QUICK TO HELP US

Be pleased to save me, Lord; come quickly, Lord, to help me.
PSALM 40:13 NIV

Have you ever struggled with despair, depression, or discouragement, and you didn't know how to get out of those dark moods? When we don't know what to do, God is always available to help us.

David, who wrote many psalms, struggled with depressed moods. He openly prayed to God when he felt weary, abandoned, and alone. But the Psalms also show us how David trusted God to lift him out of the pit of despair and deliver him from the destruction his enemies had planned for him (Psalm 40:2). Even when David's moods were connected to his own sins, he believed that when he asked for forgiveness, God would be quick to forgive and still be willing to bless him.

Satan wants to destroy your body, mind, emotions, relationships, finances, joy, peace, and everything else God wants you to enjoy. But the good news is that Jesus has already provided all we need for healing and help in every area of our lives—including our moods and attitudes. Asking God for help to overcome the enemy's attacks is a right and a privilege that Jesus purchased with His blood, and it's available to all of us.

PRAYER FOR TODAY: *God, You know what I am going through. Remind me in my times of need to call on You first. I know You will be quick to help me. Amen.*

DAY 348

HOW TO CHANGE

For the word of God is alive and active. Sharper than any double-edged sword, it penetrates even to dividing soul and spirit, joints and marrow; it judges the thoughts and attitudes of the heart.
HEBREWS 4:12 NIV

God's Word is alive and active and has the power to change us. Instead of struggling to try to change ourselves, we should study what God's Word says about our weaknesses and trust that God will give us the grace and strength to do His will.

For example, if your mood can swing from trusting and calm to anxious and worried in an instant, then study everything the Bible says about anxiety and worry: "Can any one of you by worrying add a single hour to your life?" (Matthew 6:27 NIV). "But make up your mind not to worry" (Luke 21:14 NIV). "Do not be anxious about anything, but in every situation, by prayer and petition, with thanksgiving, present your requests to God" (Philippians 4:6 NIV).

The same is true if you are struggling with wrong thoughts: Study what the Word of God says about taking wrong thoughts captive. If you are struggling with speaking positive words that line up with what God says, then study what the Scriptures say about the power of the tongue.

The more time you spend studying what the Word of God says about the area of your life you want to improve, the more you will be changed into His image.

PRAYER FOR TODAY: *God, thank You for Your grace and patience as I make progress little by little. Show me which areas of my life need change, and point me in the direction of Your Word so that I can improve in these areas. In Jesus' name, amen.*

DAY 349: WORDS THAT ARE TRUE

All the words of my mouth are righteous (upright and in right standing with God); there is nothing contrary to truth or crooked in them.
PROVERBS 8:8

Proverbs 8 describes what should be our confession, our testimony, and our reputation. Our reputation involves not only what we say about ourselves, but also what others say about us.

"Listen, for I have trustworthy things to say; I open my lips to speak what is right. My mouth speaks what is true, for my lips detest wickedness. All the words of my mouth are just; none of them is crooked or perverse. To the discerning all of them are right; they are upright to those who have found knowledge" (Proverbs 8:6–9 NIV). In these verses, we see that we should speak right words that please God. We should speak honest and trustworthy things. We should speak clearly and plainly so people can understand.

Unfortunately, many people talk in circles, saying lots of words but leaving the listener confused about what has been said. We need to learn how to engage in clear, straightforward, honest, and truthful communication that brings others into the knowledge of Jesus Christ.

James 3:10 tells us that we should not let both blessings and curses come from our mouths. As children of God, we need to be excellent in our speech and speak words that are righteous and true.

PRAYER FOR TODAY: *God, help me think before I speak so that my words are true, honest, clear, and honoring to You. Use my mouth as an instrument to instruct, encourage, and communicate things that are worthy and true. In Jesus' name, amen.*

DAY 350: A WELL-BALANCED LIFE

I know that there is nothing better for people than to be happy and to do good while they live.

ECCLESIASTES 3:12 NIV

Maybe you have heard it said that if the devil can't make you bad, he'll make you busy. It is true that even good things aren't good for us when they are out of balance.

For example, selflessness can be addictive. It feels so good to do things for others, and it makes us feel important, but when the only thing that gives your life meaning is doing things for others, you have forgotten that your life has worth simply because you are a child of God. Because you are one of God's dearly beloved children, He wants you to take care of yourself and your needs, too.

When you don't, you are likely to end up with a bitter attitude. You may start to feel resentment. Martyrs (those who sacrifice their own needs for the needs of others) often feel taken advantage of rather than blessed to serve, and they can get ill to the point of exhaustion. Once the body breaks down and life is no longer joyful, it becomes increasingly hard to serve anyone.

God wants us to live sacrificially and be involved in doing good works, but we must not ignore our own basic needs in the process. Ecclesiastes 3 says that there is a time and a season for everything. God's best for us is a well-balanced life.

PRAYER FOR TODAY: *God, it is easy for me to swing between extremes: either totally selfish or completely selfless. Help me instead to live a well-balanced life so that I maintain good health and have the energy to serve You and others. Amen.*

DAY 351
START YOUR DAY WITH A GOOD ATTITUDE

But first and most importantly seek (aim at, strive after) His kingdom and His righteousness [His way of doing and being right—the attitude and character of God], and all these things will be given to you also.

MATTHEW 6:33 AMP

I like to get up early to spend time alone with God. I have a clearer mind in the morning than I do in the evening, and I need God's help in every area of my life, including my attitude, before I go out in the world and do all the things I need to do.

Sometimes I just tell God how much I love Him and thank Him for all the things He's done for me. I also love to study the Word and journal about what it's speaking to me. I've found that writing scriptures, speaking them out loud, and praying them is an effective way to get God's Word rooted in my heart.

There are other times when I don't say anything, and I simply wait on God. He wants to speak to our hearts, and we can hear His still, small voice when we are quiet and still in His presence.

God holds the answer to every problem in this life. That's why it's important for each of us to make time with God our top priority and seek Him diligently. Spending time with God keeps our faith strong, increases our peace and joy, and helps us feel satisfied regardless of our circumstances.

PRAYER FOR TODAY: *God, help me build my day around You, rather than trying to fit You into my busy schedule. I want to make You my first priority; redirect me when I start living out of order. In Jesus' name, amen.*

DAY 352: FIRMLY PLANTED

For he shall be like a tree planted by the waters that spreads out its roots by the river; and it shall not see and fear when heat comes; but its leaf shall be green. It shall not be anxious and full of care in the year of drought, nor shall it cease yielding fruit.

JEREMIAH 17:8

In the past I experienced a lot of ups and downs, or what we call mood swings. This kind of behavior was hard on me as well as everyone around me. When I was experiencing so many ups and downs, I was also physically tired as a result. It takes a lot of energy to go through so many kinds of emotional changes. I noticed that as God helped me learn to manage my emotions, I also had more energy to enjoy my life and serve Him.

Jeremiah 17:8 and Psalm 1:3 both instruct us to be like trees firmly planted. First Peter 5:8–9 teaches us to be well-balanced and self-controlled. Philippians 1:28 tells us to be constantly fearless when Satan comes against us. Psalm 94:13 says God wants to give us power to stay calm in adversity. All these scriptures refer to our ability to be stable, and we know that God doesn't tell us to be anything that He has not given us the strength and power to be.

Jesus is referred to as "the Rock" because He's the same Jesus all the time—always faithful, loyal, and true to His Word. The Bible says that Jesus left us His peace (John 14:27), so we too can be stable and peaceful.

PRAYER FOR TODAY: *God, this emotional roller coaster is exhausting. Grant me stability in my moods and attitudes so that others can rely on me and I can have the energy I need to follow Your will. Amen.*

DAY 353: KEEP A CLEAR CONSCIENCE

Whoever conceals their sins does not prosper, but the one who confesses and renounces them finds mercy.

PROVERBS 28:13 NIV

If you want to have peace with God and succeed in this life, then you will need to have a clear conscience, not a guilty one. A guilty conscience means you know in your mind and in your heart that you have done something that God would not approve of and have not yet asked forgiveness for it. But there is no point in trying to conceal it from Him, because God sees everything.

He sees your going in and your coming out. He sees the secret thoughts of your heart. And He is ready and willing to forgive anything you present to Him. You never have to worry that He might not forgive you. When you ask with a sincere and repentant heart, He will always respond: "My child, your sins are forgiven. Now, go and sin no more" (John 8:11, paraphrase).

Each day, one of the first things I do is ask God to forgive any sins I have committed in word, thought, or deed, and then I receive His forgiveness. I do this because I want to begin each day at peace with God. I want my mind to be clear and free from anything that hinders me from doing well and succeeding at what He calls me to do.

PRAYER FOR TODAY: *God, thank You for Your unending mercy. Help me to not hide in guilt and shame but to come quickly to You when I do something wrong. In Jesus' mighty name, amen.*

DAY 354: DO NOT COMPROMISE

He chose to be mistreated along with the people of God rather than to enjoy the fleeting pleasures of sin.
HEBREWS 11:25 NIV

When it comes to the thoughts you think and the words you give your attention to, you cannot compromise. *To compromise* in this sense means to do a little less than what we know to be right.

For example, maybe your friends are going to see a comedian and invite you to come, but the comedian has a reputation for crude humor and offensive language. You might think, *This one time won't matter* or *I can block out anything ungodly* or *I'll still get up early for church in the morning*, but if you are honest about what is in your heart, you know you don't have peace about going.

The "little bit" of compromise often deceives us. We think a little bit can't possibly matter much, but it does. The enemy is looking for any opening, no matter how small, to influence your thoughts—because he knows that if he can shape your thinking, he can lead you away from God's truth. That is why you have to set your mind and keep it set, casting down every wrong thought and imagination and bringing them captive to the obedience of Christ—every single time (2 Corinthians 10:5–6).

The author of Hebrews tells us that the pleasures of sin are fleeting—they don't last. If you want *all* that God wants you to have, then you will have to fully surrender *all* of yourself—including your mind—to Him in total obedience.

PRAYER FOR TODAY: *God, help me to stand firm in my convictions, to shut my mind to things that aren't Your best for me, and to not give in to temptation. Thank You for giving me the strength to choose what's right. Amen.*

DAY 355: PRIDE SAYS I CAN DO IT BETTER

For the sins of their mouths, for the words of their lips, let them be caught in their pride. For the curses and lies they utter.
PSALM 59:12 NIV

Whenever we say something negative about someone else or judge them critically, it is because of a spirit of pride. We think *I would never do that*, or *I would make a better choice*, or *I know the answer*, or *I could do that faster*, and those thoughts become negative words.

If you want to know if you have a spirit of pride, listen to the words you speak. Do you regularly criticize the way others do things because you wouldn't do it that way or you think you can do it better? When something goes wrong, do you look for someone or something else to blame rather than taking responsibility? How often do you hear yourself say, "What is taking so long?" or "Why are we going so slow?"

The good news is, you can change your words, and when you change your words, you can change your attitude. Begin to speak positive, encouraging words as you look for the good in people. Accept that God makes each person unique and that others have strengths that you don't have. Be open to new ways of doing things rather than assuming your way is the only way. Not only will others be encouraged, but you will have more joy in your life.

PRAYER FOR TODAY: *God, help me to use my words to encourage others, not to discourage them. Help me have a healthy view of myself—as valuable and dearly loved, just like everyone else. In Jesus' name, amen.*

DAY 356

THE DEVIL'S STRATEGY

Put on the full armor of God [for His precepts are like the splendid armor of a heavily-armed soldier], so that you may be able to [successfully] stand up against all the schemes and the strategies and the deceits of the devil.

EPHESIANS 6:11 AMP

Matthew 15:11 says that what goes into your mouth (the food that you eat) isn't as important as what comes out of your mouth (the words that you speak). In other words, the words that we speak have the potential to pollute our lives—even worse than food poisoning—and the enemy loves to use our words against us to keep us from God's best.

For example, if the enemy can keep us distracted, thinking and talking about everybody else, we will be more focused on what others are doing instead of giving our thoughts to what God wants to accomplish in and through us. The enemy will try to poison our words with gossip, criticism, and judgment about other people to divert our attention away from the areas that we ourselves need to grow in. If the enemy can get us to talk critically after church about the pastor or what someone was wearing, he can turn our attention away from receiving the wisdom of the Word that was taught.

Paul tells us in Ephesians that the enemy schemes and strategizes and deceives us in unsuspecting ways, and that's why it is so important that we put on the full armor of God, which includes the Word of God and saying what God says.

PRAYER FOR TODAY: *God, protect me from the enemy's schemes; he is a deceiver and a liar. Guide me to use my words to speak truth, to declare honorable things, and to fulfill Your plan for my life. Amen.*

DAY 357: WISE WORDS BRING HEALING

Pleasant words are as a honeycomb, sweet to the mind and healing to the body.

PROVERBS 16:24

According to the wisdom found in the book of Proverbs, our words can bring a sweet calmness to our minds as well as healing to our bodies. Many sick people make the mistake of speaking negatively and voicing fear regarding their illness, but we can declare that Christ is our Healer and that He is working in us every day. Proverbs 17:22 says that "a cheerful heart is good medicine" (NIV), so speaking happy and positive words can be healing and helpful to those who are ill.

Proverbs 12:18 says, "the tongue of the wise brings healing" (NIV). Healing, in this sense, can be considered in different ways. Our words can bring healing to broken relationships. They can comfort and bring healing to those who have wounded souls and who have been hurt mentally, emotionally, and spiritually. And they can also bring physical healing through prayer to those whose bodies are sick.

Proverbs is a book of contrasts—contrasting those who are wise and who follow God's will with those who are foolish and disobedient. Clearly, we can see from these verses that choosing positive, gracious, and cheerful words is wise and brings healing.

PRAYER FOR TODAY: *God, help me be wise with my words, because life and death are in the power of the tongue. Thank You for giving my words the power to heal. Help me choose my words wisely. Amen.*

DAY 358: BE LIGHTHEARTED

Anxiety in a man's heart weighs it down, but an encouraging word makes it glad.

PROVERBS 12:25

The King James Version of today's scripture says, "Heaviness in the heart of man maketh it stoop: but a good word maketh it glad." When you are burdened, you can feel the weight of your stress pressing down on you. But as you release your worry, your body, mind, and spirit will lift.

We do not have to live with troubled, anxious, heavy hearts, or with a spirit of heaviness on us. In John 14:1, Jesus told His disciples, "Do not let your hearts be troubled (distressed, agitated)." Isaiah 61 says that God wants to lift the heaviness off of people, to give them "beauty instead of ashes, the oil of joy instead of mourning, the garment [expressive] of praise instead of a heavy, burdened, and failing spirit" (v. 3).

Proverbs 12:25 says that "an encouraging word" can help relieve a person's anxiety. Don't add to someone else's burdens with your own negativity. Speaking words of kindness is a way of blessing and giving to other people. Praying with and listening to others will comfort and encourage them. You may also discover a tangible need that you can meet to lighten their load. God wants to use us to relieve one another's burdens, and you can see someone's entire mood lift with the words that you speak.

PRAYER FOR TODAY: *God, put people in my path today for me to encourage. Give me eyes to see and a heart that is open to blessing others. Help me speak the right word at the right time that will help someone else have a great day. In Jesus' name, amen.*

DAY 359
WHY IS IT TAKING SO LONG

And let them also be tried and investigated and proved first; then, if they turn out to be above reproach, let them serve [as deacons].
1 TIMOTHY 3:10

I clearly recall the day when God said to me, "Joyce, however many people I let you help, that is how many people you can hurt." We need to be mature in our minds, mouths, moods, and attitudes so that we are helping the people we have influence over, not hurting them.

Life and death are in the power of the tongue; therefore, we need to get control over our mouths and the words that we speak so that we are inspiring people and not using our words to shame and condemn, to tear down, or to ruin relationships.

God will bring you to trials in your life to test what is in you and to mature those areas that need growth. Nothing reveals your true attitude like a difficult circumstance! God wants you to be able to walk through those trials with a positive, hope-filled attitude that is an example of true faith to other believers.

You can trust that God wants to use you for His glory and that He has a good plan for your life—because His Word says so! But if it seems to be taking longer than you want it to, it could be that you have areas to mature in first so that you can help people that God gives you influence over and not hurt them through your immaturity.

PRAYER FOR TODAY: *God, thank You for the good plan You have for my life. Don't give me anything that I am not mature enough to handle, but strengthen me so that at the right time I can enter fully into the destiny that You planned for me from the beginning of time. Amen.*

DAY 360
WHAT TO THINK ABOUT IN THE SILENCE

And now you will be silent and not able to speak until the day this happens, because you did not believe my words, which will come true at their appointed time.

LUKE 1:20 NIV

The book of Luke opens with a priest named Zechariah who had been chosen for the once-in-a-lifetime duty of burning incense in the Holy of Holies. Inside the temple, Zechariah had an encounter with an angel, who told him that God had heard his prayers and that his wife—despite being "advanced in years" (Luke 1:18)—would conceive and give birth to a son.

Zechariah's response was one of unbelief: "How can I be sure of this?" (v. 18 NIV). And God responded to Zechariah's unbelief by taking away his ability to speak for the next nine months.

As he watched Elizabeth grow round with pregnancy, I can only imagine what went through Zechariah's mind. I imagine he prayed for God to forgive him his doubts. I imagine he reflected on all the ways God had blessed them in the past. He may have recalled the Old Testament story of Abraham and Sarah giving birth to Isaac in their elderly years. And I am certain that he praised God for the miracle of a son of his own, because when his tongue was loosed, the Bible says, "he began to speak, praising God" (v. 64 NIV).

If your words aren't right—if they are filled with doubt and unbelief and negativity—try being quiet for a while. Fill your mind with positive thoughts and the Word of God, so that when you speak again, your words will be filled with praise.

PRAYER FOR TODAY: *God, help me respond to Your miracles with words of praise. Help me keep my mind focused on You and Your miracle-working power. Amen.*

DAY 361: BE DECISIVE

[For being as he is] a man of two minds (hesitating, dubious, irresolute), [he is] unstable and unreliable and uncertain about everything [he thinks, feels, decides].

JAMES 1:8

Indecision is a miserable state to be in and certainly is not a fruit of a life lived confidently in Christ. The apostle James said the double-minded man is unstable in all his ways.

Being indecisive because you're afraid you'll make the wrong decisions will get you nowhere. How much time do you think we waste when we can't make up our minds?

With God's help, you can start making decisions without second-guessing yourself or worrying about the choices you make. In your quiet time with God, ask Him for wisdom and confidence so you can move forward boldly. Don't be double-minded or wishy-washy; doubting your decisions after you make them will steal the enjoyment from everything you do.

If you do make the wrong decision, it's not the end of the world. Pray for God's redirection, and He will help you get back on the right path. But trust that God will give you the wisdom and the power to make right decisions the first time. He will honor your desire to walk in His ways by speaking the right choice to your heart.

PRAYER FOR TODAY: *God, please help me to be confident in You, to make decisions boldly, and to not second-guess myself or live in the constant fear of making a mistake. Thank You for Your wisdom. Amen.*

DAY 362
AVOIDING EXTREMES

Be well balanced (temperate, sober of mind), be vigilant and cautious at all times; for that enemy of yours, the devil, roams around like a lion roaring [in fierce hunger], seeking someone to seize upon and devour.
1 PETER 5:8

In order for a scale to be "balanced," the weight on each side has to be equal. So, when Peter tells us to be "well balanced," he is warning us against extremes in all areas of life, including our thoughts and our attitudes. He is telling us that the enemy will do whatever he can to get us out of balance, because an unbalanced life gives him a foothold.

We should maintain balance between work and rest, giving and receiving, saving and spending, socializing and solitude; even our diets need to be balanced.

Maintaining balance in our minds, mouths, moods, and attitudes is equally important. For instance, dwelling on positive things is important, but refusing to face and deal with the problems in our lives is out of balance. We can talk too much, but some people are so quiet that being with them is uncomfortable. We should be in a good mood, but we shouldn't pretend that nothing ever hurts us.

I often say that being extreme is the devil's playground. If he can't get us to do nothing, then he will try to keep us too busy. If he can't get us not to spend any money on worthwhile causes, then he will urge us to spend too much money on ourselves. Try to avoid extremes, and you will avoid opening a door for the devil in your life.

PRAYER FOR TODAY: *God, show me the areas in my life where I am out of balance. Give me wisdom to make adjustments where they are needed. Not my will, but Yours be done. Amen.*

DAY 363: HOPE CAN BE REKINDLED

Hope deferred makes the heart sick, but when the desire is fulfilled, it is a tree of life.

PROVERBS 13:12

"Hope deferred" is what we might call disappointment. We all get disappointed when things do not work out the way we want them to—when a plan fails, a goal isn't reached, or the thing we are praying for doesn't materialize. But when we experience disappointment, we have a choice to make. Will we let disappointment lead to discouragement, depression, and hopelessness? Or will we be "prisoners of hope" (Zechariah 9:12), refusing to give up hope and pressing on joyfully?

Hope is a positive attitude, and our attitudes belong to us. No one can make us have a bad attitude if we don't want one. When our thoughts and emotions could easily go up and down with our circumstances, hope is our stability, anchoring us to the promises of God (Hebrews 6:19).

When we cling to hope, the Holy Spirit inside of us will give us new vision, new direction, and new goals to help us overcome our disappointment. Hope deferred does make the heart sick, but hope can be rekindled. Believe in God's promises, be hopeful that the future looks bright, and expect something good to happen to you today.

PRAYER FOR TODAY: *God, please take the disappointment that I feel and replace it with Your hope. I want to trust You, even in this. Give me a new vision to rekindle the hope within me. In Jesus' name, amen.*

DAY 364 — COMPLETE HEALING

I will greatly rejoice in the Lord, my soul shall be joyful in my God; for He has clothed me with the garments of salvation, He has covered me with the robe of righteousness, as a bridegroom decks himself with ornaments, and as a bride adorns herself with her jewels.

ISAIAH 61:10 NKJV

This world is filled with people burdened by hurt and pain. Many are dealing with the emotional pain of abuse or past hurts—pain that prevents them from enjoying the good life God has planned.

Isaiah 61:1–3 says the Lord came to heal the brokenhearted. He wants to give us joy instead of mourning, beauty for ashes, praise instead of despair, and hope.

No matter what you've been through, I want you to know that God can restore your life and help you to fully recover from the emotional pain of abuse. I can say this with certainty because I have been there myself. In fact, He has taken what the enemy meant for harm and worked it out for my good (Genesis 50:20). God's Word has set me free and has restored my soul.

Through a personal relationship with Jesus, you can receive complete healing in your soul—your mind, will, and emotions. God can restore your life and heal you as if the hurt never happened. Trade your pain for God's promise. He makes everything beautiful in its time (Ecclesiastes 3:11).

PRAYER FOR TODAY: *Lord Jesus, thank You for giving Your life for me and forgiving me of my sins so I can have a personal relationship with You. I am sincerely sorry for the mistakes I've made, and I know I need You to help me live right. Take me just as I am and work in my mind, mouth, moods, and attitudes to make me the person You want me to be. In Your name I pray, amen.*

DAY 365
THE POWER OF HOPE

Since we have such [glorious] hope (such joyful and confident expectation), we speak very freely and openly and fearlessly.
2 CORINTHIANS 3:12

Hope is a central theme in the Bible. It is the key to going through hard times and never giving up. Jesus says in John 16:33, "In the world you have tribulation and distress and suffering, but be courageous [be confident, be undaunted, be filled with joy]; I have overcome the world" (AMP).

God doesn't promise we will never have pain, but He does assure us that during trouble and suffering, we can remain stable in His peace and have confidence that life can be good again. This truth gives us every reason to have a hopeful attitude for the future, no matter how deep our hurt goes or what our issues or circumstances may be.

Hope in Christ is powerful because it's a confident belief and expectation that something good is going to happen. It strengthens your faith in God's love for you and His goodness. You know that in the worst kind of tragedy, the worst kind of pain, Jesus can redeem and heal your hurt and brokenness, and something good will happen again.

PRAYER FOR TODAY: *God, thank You for the reminder that trouble will come, but when it does, I can cling to hope. Help me keep my mind on the truth: I am loved, valuable, needed, wanted, and chosen by You. In Jesus' name, amen.*

SOURCE NOTES

Unless otherwise noted, Scripture quotations are taken from the Amplified® Bible, Copyright © 1954, 1958, 1962, 1964, 1965, 1987 by The Lockman Foundation. Used by permission. www.Lockman.org.

Scripture quotations marked NIV are taken from the Holy Bible, New International Version®, NIV®. Copyright ©1973, 1978, 1984, 2011 by Biblica, Inc.™ Used by permission of Zondervan. All rights reserved worldwide. www.zondervan.com The "NIV" and "New International Version" are trademarks registered in the United States Patent and Trademark Office by Biblica, Inc.™

Scripture quotations marked CEV are from the Contemporary English Version Copyright © 1991, 1992, 1995 by American Bible Society. Used by Permission.

Scripture quotations marked ESV are taken from The Holy Bible, English Standard Version. ESV® Text Edition: 2016. Copyright © 2001 by Crossway Bibles, a publishing ministry of Good News Publishers.

Scripture quotations marked MSG are taken from THE MESSAGE, copyright © 1993, 1994, 1995, 1996, 2000, 2001, 2002 by Eugene H. Peterson. Used by permission of NavPress. All rights reserved. Represented by Tyndale House Publishers, Inc.

Scripture quotations marked NKJV are taken from the New King James Version®. Copyright © 1982 by Thomas Nelson. Used by permission. All rights reserved.

Scripture quotations marked NLT are taken from the Holy Bible, New Living Translation, copyright ©1996, 2004, 2007, 2013, 2015 by Tyndale House Foundation. Used by permission of Tyndale House Publishers, Inc., Carol Stream, Illinois 60188. All rights reserved.

Scripture quotations marked AMP are from the Amplified® Bible. Copyright © 2015 by The Lockman Foundation. Used by permission. www.lockman.org

All Scripture marked with the designation GW is taken from GOD'S WORD®. © 1995, 2003, 2013, 2014, 2019, 2020 by God's Word to the Nations Mission Society. Used by permission.

Scripture quotations marked KJV are taken from the King James Version of the Bible.

Scripture quotations marked TPT are from The Passion Translation®. Copyright © 2017, 2018, 2020 by Passion & Fire Ministries, Inc. Used by permission. All rights reserved. ThePassionTranslation.com.

Scripture quotations marked ICB are taken from The Holy Bible, International Children's Bible® Copyright© 1986, 1988, 1999, 2015 by Thomas Nelson. Used by permission.

Do you have a real relationship with Jesus?

God loves you! He created you to be a special, unique, one-of-a-kind individual, and He has a specific purpose and plan for your life. And through a personal relationship with your Creator—God—you can discover a way of life that will truly satisfy your soul.

No matter who you are, what you've done, or where you are in your life right now, God's love and grace are greater than your sin—your mistakes. Jesus willingly gave His life so you can receive forgiveness from God and have new life in Him. He's just waiting for you to invite Him to be your Savior and Lord.

If you are ready to commit your life to Jesus and follow Him, all you have to do is ask Him to forgive your sins and give you a fresh start in the life you are meant to live. Begin by praying this prayer...

> *Lord Jesus, thank You for giving Your life for me and forgiving me of my sins so I can have a personal relationship with You. I am sincerely sorry for the mistakes I've made, and I know I need You to help me live right.*
>
> *Your Word says in Romans 10:9, "If you declare with your mouth, 'Jesus is Lord,' and believe in your heart that God raised him from the dead, you will be saved" (NIV). I believe You are the Son of God and confess You as my Savior and Lord. Take me just as I am, and work in my heart, making me the person You want me to be. I want to live for You, Jesus, and I am so grateful that You are giving me a fresh start in my new life with You today.*
>
> *I love You, Jesus!*

It's so amazing to know that God loves us so much! He wants to have a deep, intimate relationship with us that grows every day as we spend time with Him in prayer and Bible study. And we want to encourage you in your new life in Christ.

Please visit joycemeyer.org/KnowJesus to request Joyce's book *A New Way of Living*, which is our gift to you. We also have other free resources online to help you make progress in pursuing everything God has for you.

Congratulations on your fresh start in your life in Christ! We hope to hear from you soon.

ABOUT THE AUTHOR

Joyce Meyer is one of the world's leading practical Bible teachers and a *New York Times* bestselling author. Joyce's books have helped millions of people find hope and restoration through Jesus Christ. Joyce's program, *Enjoying Everyday Life*, is broadcast to millions worldwide in 113 languages.

Through Joyce Meyer Ministries, Joyce teaches internationally on a number of topics with a particular focus on how the Word of God applies to our everyday lives. Her candid communication style allows her to share openly and practically about her experiences so others can apply what she has learned to their lives.

Joyce has authored more than 150 books, which have been translated into more than 164 combined languages and over 42.5 million of her books have been distributed worldwide. Bestsellers include *Power Thoughts*; *The Confident Woman*; *Look Great, Feel Great*; *Starting Your Day Right*; *Ending Your Day Right*; *Approval Addiction*; *How to Hear from God*; *Beauty for Ashes*; and *Battlefield of the Mind*.

Joyce's passion to help people who are hurting is foundational to the vision of Hand of Hope, the missions arm of Joyce Meyer Ministries. Each year Hand of Hope provides millions of meals for the hungry and malnourished, installs freshwater wells in poor and remote areas, provides critical relief after natural disasters, and offers free medical and dental care to thousands through their hospitals and clinics worldwide. Through Project GRL, women and children are rescued from human trafficking and provided safe places to receive an education, nutritious meals, and the love of God.

JOYCE MEYER MINISTRIES

U.S. & FOREIGN OFFICE
ADDRESSES

Joyce Meyer Ministries
P.O. Box 655
Fenton, MO 63026
USA
(636) 349-0303

Joyce Meyer Ministries—Canada
P.O. Box 7700
Vancouver, BC V6B 4E2
Canada
(800) 868-1002

Joyce Meyer Ministries—Australia
Locked Bag 77
Mansfield Delivery Centre
Queensland 4122
Australia
(07) 3349 1200

Joyce Meyer Ministries—England
P.O. Box 8267
Reading RG6 9TX
United Kingdom
01753 831102

Joyce Meyer Ministries—South Africa
Unit EB06, East Block
Tannery Park, 23 Belmont Road
Rondebosch, Cape Town
South Africa 7700
(27) 21-701-1056

Joyce Meyer Ministries—Francophonie
BP 53, 77832 Ozoir la Ferriere
France
+33 610 288 944

Joyce Meyer Ministries—Germany
Bachstr 1
22083 Hamburg
Germany
+49 (0)40 / 88 88 4 11 11

Joyce Meyer Ministries—Netherlands
P.O. Box 55, 7000 AB
Doetinchem
The Netherlands
+31 657 555 9789

Joyce Meyer Ministries—Russia
P.O. Box 789
Moscow 101000
Russia
+7 (985) 233-56-30

OTHER BOOKS BY JOYCE MEYER

100 Inspirational Quotes
100 Ways to Simplify Your Life
21 Ways to Finding Peace and Happiness
The Answer to Anxiety
Any Minute
Approval Addiction
The Approval Fix
*Authentically, Uniquely You**
The Battle Belongs to the Lord
*Battlefield of the Mind**
Battlefield of the Mind Bible
Battlefield of the Mind for Kids
Battlefield of the Mind for Teens
Battlefield of the Mind Devotional
Battlefield of the Mind New Testament
*Be Anxious for Nothing**
Be Joyful
Beauty for Ashes
Beginning Your Day God's Way
Being the Person God Made You to Be
*Blessed in the Mess**
Change Your Words, Change Your Life
Colossians: A Biblical Study
The Confident Mom
The Confident Woman
The Confident Woman Devotional
The Courage to Change
*Do It Afraid**
Do Yourself a Favor... Forgive
Eat the Cookie... Buy the Shoes

Eight Ways to Keep the Devil under Your Feet
Ending Your Day Right
Enjoying Where You Are on the Way to Where You Are Going
Ephesians: A Biblical Study
The Everyday Life Bible
The Everyday Life Psalms and Proverbs
Filled with the Spirit
Finding God's Will for Your Life
Galatians: A Biblical Study
Good Health, Good Life
Habits of a Godly Woman
Healing the Soul of a Woman*
Healing the Soul of a Woman Devotional
Healing the Wounds of Rejection
Hearing from God Each Morning
How to Age without Getting Old
How to Hear from God*
How to Succeed at Being Yourself
How to Talk with God
I Dare You
If Not for the Grace of God*
In Pursuit of Peace
In Search of Wisdom
James: A Biblical Study
The Joy of an Uncluttered Life
The Joy of Believing Prayer
The Keys to a Happy and Healthy Marriage
Knowing God Intimately
A Leader in the Making
Life in the Word
Living beyond Your Feelings
Living Courageously
Look Great, Feel Great

Love Out Loud
The Love Revolution
Loving People Who Are Hard to Love
Making Good Habits, Breaking Bad Habits
Making Marriage Work (previously published as *Help Me—I'm Married!*)
Managing Your Emotions
*Me and My Big Mouth!**
*The Mind Connection**
Mornings with God
My Time with God
Never Give Up!
Never Lose Heart
New Day, New You
Overcoming Every Problem
Overload
The Pathway to Success
The Penny
Perfect Love (previously published as *God Is Not Mad at You*)*
Philippians: A Biblical Study
The Power of Being Positive
The Power of Being Thankful
The Power of Determination
The Power of Forgiveness
The Power of Simple Prayer
Power Thoughts
Power Thoughts Devotional
Powerful Thinking
Quiet Times with God Devotional
Reduce Me to Love
The Secret Power of Speaking God's Word
The Secrets of Spiritual Power
The Secret to True Happiness

Seven Things That Steal Your Joy
Start Your New Life Today
Starting Your Day Right
Straight Talk
Teenagers Are People Too!
Trusting God Day by Day
Uniquely You
What About Me?*
The Word, the Name, the Blood
Woman to Woman
You Can Begin Again
Your Battles Belong to the Lord*

JOYCE MEYER SPANISH TITLES

Amar a la gente que es muy difícil de amar (Loving People Who Are Hard to Love)
Auténtica y única (Authentically, Uniquely You)
Belleza en lugar de cenizas (Beauty for Ashes)
Benedicion en el desorden (Blessed in the Mess)
Buena salud, buena vida (Good Health, Good Life)
Cambia tus palabras, cambia tu vida (Change Your Words, Change Your Life)
El campo de batalla de la mente (Battlefield of the Mind)
Cómo envejecer sin avejentarse (How to Age without Getting Old)
Como formar buenos habitos y romper malos habitos (Making Good Habits, Breaking Bad Habits)
La conexión de la mente (The Mind Connection)
Dios no está enojado contigo (God Is Not Mad at You)
La dosis de aprobación (The Approval Fix)
Efesios: Comentario biblico (Ephesians: Biblical Commentary)
Empezando tu día bien (Starting Your Day Right)

Hágalo con miedo (Do It Afraid)
Hazte un favor a ti mismo... perdona (Do Yourself a Favor... Forgive)
Madre segura de sí misma (The Confident Mom)
Momentos de quietud con Dios (Quiet Times with God Devotional)
Mujer segura de sí misma (The Confident Woman)
No se afane por nada (Be Anxious for Nothing)
Pensamientos de poder (Power Thoughts)
Sanidad para el alma de una mujer (Healing the Soul of a Woman)
Sanidad para el alma de una mujer, devocionario (Healing the Soul of a Woman Devotional)
Santiago: Comentario bíblico (James: Biblical Commentary)
Sobrecarga (Overload)*
Sus batallas son del Señor (Your Battles Belong to the Lord)
Termina bien tu día (Ending Your Day Right)
Tienes que atreverte (I Dare You)
Usted puede comenzar de nuevo (You Can Begin Again)
Viva amando su vida (Living a Life You Love)
Viva valientemente (Living Courageously)
Vive por encima de tus sentimientos (Living beyond Your Feelings)
Y que hay de mi (What About Me?)

* Study Guide available for this title

BOOKS BY DAVE MEYER

Life Lines